The Reception of
Myth in English
Romanticism

The Reception of
Myth in English
Romanticism

Anthony John Harding

University of Missouri Press

COLUMBIA AND LONDON

Library of Congress Cataloging-in-Publication Data

Harding, Anthony John.
    The reception of myth in English romanticism / Anthony John
  Harding.
       p.   cm.
    Includes bibliographical references (p.   ) and index.
    ISBN 0-8262-1007-4 (alk. paper)
    1. English literature—19th century—History and criticism.
  2. Archetype (Psychology) in literature.   3. Romanticism—Great
  Britain.   4. Mythology in literature.   5. Myth in literature.   I. Title.
  PR468.A72H37   1995
  820.9'145—dc20   95-10287
                                                     CIP

Text Design: Elizabeth K. Fett
Jacket Design: Kristie Lee
Typesetter: BOOKCOMP
Printer and binder: Thomson-Shore, Inc.
Typefaces: Elante and Novarese Book

The University of Missouri Press gratefully acknowledges
the support of the University of Saskatchewan.

For Patty

Contents

Abbreviations

Note: For primary texts not included here, see Selected Works Cited.

BL   S. T. Coleridge. *Biographia Literaria.* Ed. James Engell and W. Jackson Bate. *Collected Works,* Bollingen Series 75, vol. 7. 2 vols. London and Princeton: Routledge and Kegan Paul and Princeton University Press, 1983.

CL   S. T. Coleridge. *Collected Letters.* Ed. Earl Leslie Griggs. 6 vols. Oxford: Clarendon Press, 1956–1971.

CN   S. T. Coleridge. *Notebooks.* Ed. Kathleen Coburn. Bollingen Series 50. New York: Bollingen Foundation/Pantheon Books; Princeton: Princeton University Press, 1957–.

CPW   S. T. Coleridge. *Complete Poetical Works.* Ed. Ernest Hartley Coleridge. 2 vols. Oxford: Clarendon Press, 1912.

CW   S. T. Coleridge. *Complete Works.* Ed. W. G. T. Shedd, 7 vols. New York: Harper and Brothers, 1853–1858.

Friend S. T. Coleridge. *The Friend.* Ed. Barbara E. Rooke. *Collected Works,* Bollingen Series 75, vol. 4. 2 vols. London and Princeton: Routledge and Kegan Paul and Princeton University Press, 1969.

KP   John Keats, *Poems.* Ed. Jack Stillinger. Cambridge: The Belknap Press of Harvard University Press, 1978.

Lects 1795 S. T. Coleridge. *Lectures 1795 on Politics and Religion.* Ed. Lewis Patton and Peter Mann. *Collected Works,* Bollingen Series 75, vol. 1. London and Princeton: Routledge and Kegan Paul and Princeton University Press, 1971.

Lects 1808–1819 S. T. Coleridge. *Lectures 1808–1819 on Literature.* Ed. R. A. Foakes. *Collected Works,* Bollingen Series 75, vol.

5. 2 vols. London and Princeton: Routledge and Kegan Paul and Princeton University Press, 1987.

LS   S. T. Coleridge. *Lay Sermons.* Ed. R. J. White. *Collected Works,* Bollingen Series 75, vol. 6. London and Princeton: Routledge and Kegan Paul and Princeton University Press, 1972.

P Lects S. T. Coleridge. *Philosophical Lectures.* Ed. Kathleen Coburn. London: Routledge and Kegan Paul, 1949.

SCW   Percy Bysshe Shelley. *Complete Works.* Ed. Roger Ingpen and Walter E. Peck. 10 vols. London and New York: The Julian Editions, 1926–1930.

SP&P   Percy Bysshe Shelley. *Poetry and Prose.* Ed. Donald Reiman and Sharon B. Powers. New York: Norton, 1977.

Watchman S. T. Coleridge. *The Watchman.* Ed. Lewis Patton. *Collected Works,* Bollingen Series 75, vol. 2. London and Princeton: Routledge and Kegan Paul and Princeton University Press, 1970.

WHG   William Wordsworth. *Home at Grasmere: Part First, Book First, of* The Recluse. Ed. Beth Darlington. Ithaca: Cornell University Press, 1977.

WPrelude William Wordsworth. *The Prelude: or, Growth of a Poet's Mind.* Ed. E. de Selincourt, 2d ed., rev. Helen Darbishire. Oxford: Clarendon Press, 1959.

WPrel 1799 William Wordsworth. *The Prelude, 1798–1799.* Ed. Stephen Parrish. Ithaca: Cornell University Press, 1977.

WPW   William Wordsworth. *Poetical Works.* Ed. Ernest de Selincourt and Helen Darbishire, 2d ed. 5 vols. Oxford: Clarendon Press, 1952–1972.

Acknowledgments

A book that has been more than ten years in the making accumulates debts far too numerous and complex to acknowledge fully. To students in the Romantics classes I have taught at the University of Saskatchewan I am greatly and constantly indebted, both for contributing many particular insights and for stimulating me to think in new ways about the literature of this period. To the University of Manchester, for (in a sense) starting the series of inquiries that led to this book, and to Cambridge University, for bringing me into touch with the resources, people, and challenges I needed at the time, a debt hardly less great. To many, many individual colleagues and friends I am grateful for their encouragement and advice along the way, and that indefinable quality I can only call taking an interest: among many others, Lionel Adey, Bob Barth, John Beer, Fred Burwick, Stuart Curran, Toby Foshay, Tim Fulford, Marilyn Gaull, Susan Gingell, Richard Gravil, Keith Hanley, Athelyn Haydon, Graham Haydon, Dorte Heurlin, Terence Hoagwood, Helen Irwin, Heather Jackson, Robin Jackson, Don Jewison, Steffen Kjeldgaard-Pedersen, Ken Johnston, Keith Johnstone, Lionel Knights, Greg Kucich, Peter Larkin, Molly Lefebure, Lisa Low, Richard Matlak, Tom McFarland, James McKusick, Anne Mellor, David Miall, Peter Millard, Craig Miller, Judith Miller, Raimonda Modiano, Carol Morrell, Lucy Newlyn, Eric Nye, Mary Anne Perkins, Stuart Peterfreund, the late H. W. (Pip) Piper, Heinrich Plett, Renate Plett, Tilottama Rajan, the late William Ruddick, Camille Slights, William Slights, Claudia Strasky, Anya Taylor, Ronald Tetreault, Claud Thompson, Nicola Trott, Lisa Vargo, Anca Vlasopolos, Jeanie Watson, Mary Wedd, Kathleen Wheeler, Diana Wilson, Douglas Wilson, Milton Wilson, Joseph

Anthony Wittreich Jr., Pamela Woof, Robert Woof, and Jonathan Wordsworth.

I am grateful to Professor Don Baronowski, McGill University, for tracing the source of a quotation from John Jortin. For their enthusiasm for Dorothy Wordsworth, and criticism that helped me to see her relationship to Wordsworth in a new light, I am indebted to Janice Acoose, Catherine Gutwin, Jolly Mazimhaka, and Maryna Romanets. I am grateful to Felicia Daunt for bringing to my attention a passage from Coleridge's *Literary Remains*; to Cindy Clarke for pointing out the relevance of the passage in John Keats's *Letters* stating that poetry should "appear almost a Remembrance"; and to Corinne Tanchak for alerting me to Milton Wilson's discussion of "Song of Apollo" and "Song of Pan."

Raimonda Modiano, of the University of Washington, read an early draft of the Introduction and made a number of helpful criticisms. Conversations with Terence Allan Hoagwood, of Texas A & M University, supplied me with some valuable leads in developing the argument of Chapters 1 and 6. Toby Foshay, of the University of Victoria, gave a constructive critique of an earlier version of Chapter 4. Chapter 9 benefited from many discussions with Tim Fulford, of Jesus College, Cambridge. I am grateful to Anne-Marie Buchmann-Gerber and Heinz Gerber for assistance in translating some passages from German. Martin Dawding prepared the index, with exemplary thoroughness.

The staffs of the British Library, London; the Bodleian Library, Oxford; and the University of Saskatchewan Library have been reliable, helpful, and courteous; studies like the present one could not exist without the dedication shown by them and by other professional librarians. I would also like to thank Mr. Clair Willcox, Ms. Sara Fefer, and Ms. Jane Lago, of the University of Missouri Press, for their professional efficiency, promptness in answering my queries, and support of the project. Ms. Barbara O'Neil Phillips has been an unusually alert and meticulous copy editor.

My wife, Patricia Williams, has been encouraging from the beginning, showing almost heroic patience with me and with this project through many anxious times.

Earlier versions of some chapters of this book have appeared as journal articles, and I am grateful to the editors of the journals in question, first for making these essays available to their readers and second for permitting me to reuse material that originally appeared there: to the editors of *Nineteenth-Century Contexts* for permission to reuse for Chapters 3 and 9 material first published in their journal in 1988 and 1989; to the editor of *The Wordsworth Circle* for permission to reuse material first published there in 1991; to Duke University Press, holders of copyright for *Modern Language Quarterly*, for permission to reuse material published there in 1983; and to the editor of *Keats-Shelley Journal* for permission to reuse material published there in 1986.

Extracts from the following works are reprinted by permission of Oxford University Press:

S. T. Coleridge, *Collected Letters,* ed. Earl Leslie Griggs. 6 vols. (Oxford: Clarendon Press, 1956–1971).

S. T. Coleridge, *Complete Poetical Works,* ed. Ernest Hartley Coleridge. 2 vols. (Oxford: Clarendon Press, 1912).

William Wordsworth, *Poetical Works,* ed. Ernest de Selincourt and Helen Darbishire, 2d ed. 5 vols. (Oxford: Clarendon Press, 1952–1972).

William Wordsworth, *The Prelude: or, Growth of a Poet's Mind,* ed. E. de Selincourt, 2d ed., rev. Helen Darbishire (Oxford: Clarendon Press, 1959).

Extracts from the following works are reprinted by permission of Princeton University Press.

S. T. Coleridge, *Notebooks,* ed. Kathleen Coburn. Bollingen Series 50. New York: Bollingen Foundation / Pantheon Books; (Princeton: Princeton University Press, 1957–).

S. T. Coleridge, *Lectures 1795 on Politics and Religion,* ed. Lewis Patton and Peter Mann. *Collected Works,* Bollingen Series 75, vol. 1. (London and Princeton: Routledge and Kegan Paul and Princeton University Press, 1971).

S. T. Coleridge, *The Watchman,* ed. Lewis Patton. *Collected Works,* Bollingen Series 75, vol. 2. (London and Princeton: Routledge and Kegan Paul and Princeton University Press, 1970).

S. T. Coleridge, *The Friend,* ed. Barbara E. Rooke. *Collected Works,* Bollingen Series 75, vol. 4. 2 vols. (London and Princeton: Routledge and Kegan Paul and Princeton University Press, 1969).

S. T. Coleridge, *Lay Sermons,* ed. by R. J. White. *Collected Works,*
Bollingen Series 75, vol. 6. (London and Princeton: Routledge
and Kegan Paul and Princeton University Press, 1972).

S. T. Coleridge, *Biographia Literaria,* ed. James Engell and
W. Jackson Bate. *Collected Works,* Bollingen Series 75, vol. 7.
2 vols. (London and Princeton: Routledge and Kegan Paul and
Princeton University Press, 1983).

S. T. Coleridge, *Aids to Reflection,* ed. John Beer. *Collected Works,*
Bollingen Series 75, vol. 9. (London and Princeton: Routledge
and Kegan Paul and Princeton University Press, 1993).

S. T. Coleridge, *On the Constitution of the Church and State,*
ed. John Colmer. *Collected Works,* Bollingen Series 75, vol.
10. (London and Princeton: Routledge and Kegan Paul and
Princeton University Press, 1976).

S. T. Coleridge, *Marginalia,* ed. George Whalley and H. J. Jackson.
Collected Works, Bollingen Series 75, vol. 12. 3 vols so far.
(London and Princeton: Routledge and Kegan Paul and
Princeton University Press, 1980–   ).

Extracts from the "reading texts" contained in the following works
are reprinted (with respect to the United States and Canada) by permission of Cornell University Press and (with respect to the United
Kingdom, Ireland, and the British Commonwealth except Canada)
by permission of Harvester Wheatsheaf:

William Wordsworth, *The Borderers,* ed. Robert Osborn (Ithaca:
Cornell University Press, 1982).

William Wordsworth, *Home at Grasmere: Part First, Book First, of*
The Recluse, ed. Beth Darlington (Ithaca: Cornell University
Press, 1977).

William Wordsworth, *The Prelude, 1798–1799,* ed. Stephen Parrish
(Ithaca: Cornell University Press, 1977).

Quotations from T. S. Eliot, *Collected Poems: 1909–1962* (London: Faber and Faber, 1963) are reprinted by permission of Faber and
Faber, London, with respect to all countries in which the present
work is published except the United States, and by permission of
Harcourt Brace Inc. with respect to the United States.

The Reception of Myth in English Romanticism

Myth has always already passed over into the process of reception, and it remains in that process no matter what violence is applied in order to break its bonds and to establish its final form. If it is present to us only in the forms of its reception, there is no privilege of certain versions as more original or more final.

—Hans Blumenberg, Work on Myth

Introduction

Until recently, "myth criticism" as commonly practiced by those who teach and study English literature has effectively ignored one central fact about its supposed subject: that the very term "myth" designates something that has slipped from our grasp, and can be studied only as a reconstruction or reinterpretation of what someone else might at one time have believed. As a result, it seems that, having flourished briefly in the 1940s and 1950s, "myth criticism" has been largely moribund since about 1970. One particular *kind* of myth criticism, the kind that took Frazer and the Cambridge school as its starting point, has fallen into disfavor, and an entire area of critical study, the literary *uses* of myth, has virtually ceased to exist. One sign of this is the neglect of myth in recent general works on literary theory, and even in guides and introductions to Romanticism. In one recent introductory work on contemporary literary theory, there is no chapter on myth criticism, because in the opinion of the author myth critics have not contributed significantly to the most important recent advances in literary theory. The word "myth" does not appear in the index to the *The Cambridge Companion to British Romanticism,* though one chapter contains a useful if brief treatment of mythography.[1]

1. See Raman Selden, *A Reader's Guide to Contemporary Literary Theory* (Lexington: University Press of Kentucky, 1985), 5; Timothy Webb, "Romantic Hellenism," 165–67. A survey of contemporary literary theory more advanced than Selden's that also omits myth criticism is D. W. Fokkema and Elrud Kunne-Ibsch, *Theories of Literature in the Twentieth Century* (New York: St. Martin's Press, 1978).

If it is true that today's students are discouraged from considering the literary uses of myth as a fertile subject, the reason cannot be that the best critical minds have weighed the evidence and decided that such study is pointless. In fact, leading critics of Romanticism, at any rate, do frequently refer to particular myth traditions, and it would be hard to imagine any treatment of Romanticism that entirely ignored mythology. What these critics do not do, however, is write "myth criticism." This is not simply because myth criticism has become intellectually disreputable; rather, too many myth critics have forgotten the point made by, among others, Jean-Pierre Vernant: that the very existence of a myth depends on its being transposed or translated. That is, its existence for those whose allegiance is not to a cult but to *logos*, to rational thought, discourse, and analysis.[2] The mistake is to assume that something called "the Demeter myth" or "the Adonis myth" can be used as a key to unlock or "explain" a literary work, when all that is available to us is not some "original myth" but the transformations and reinterpretations of something whose origins are ultimately indefinable. It is the process of transformation and reinterpretation that repays study, not the "original myth," which, inevitably, we can only "know" as a reconstruction; and the scholar's reconstruction is at least as distant from origins as the poet's. This point is made by Hans Blumenberg: "The myth that is varied and transformed by its receptions, in the forms in which it is related to (and has the power of being related to) history, deserves to be made a subject of study if only because such a study also takes in the historical situations and needs that were affected by the myth and were disposed to 'work' on it."[3]

Blumenberg identifies the problem that literary scholarship—as opposed to, for instance, anthropology, comparative religion, psychotherapy, and other disciplines for which "myth" can be a key term—is equipped to deal with: the "receptions" of myth, and the associated "historical situations and needs" that provide not only the context but the very form in which "the myth" becomes an object of knowledge. As Blumenberg makes clear, myth is related to history and has the power of being related to history only *in* certain forms that themselves exist in a problematic relationship to a hypothetical "origin." (One of Blumenberg's chapter titles cleverly condenses this

---

2. Jean-Pierre Vernant, *Myth and Society in Ancient Greece*, 204.
3. Hans Blumenberg, *Work on Myth*, 174.

point—"The Reception of the Sources Produces the Sources of the Reception.") This is the point that has been obscured by the tendency of myth critics to focus on the so-called archetypes, either Jung's or Frye's.

It is not simply that the emphasis on "archetypes" draws the scholar's attention away from other, arguably more vital concerns— namely, the historical conditions in which a work was produced. That point has been made often enough by critics of both Jung and Frye. It is that the very process of imagining or constructing an archetype obscures *both* the historically determined nature of the sources from which that archetype is constructed *and* the historical situation of the critic who is doing the constructing. At worst, as Bernhard Ostendorf charged, literature is rescued from the dogmatism of theology and philosophy only to be reconstructed according to the dogmas of anthropology and psychology—the anthropology and psychology, that is, of a certain era, the era of Frazer and Freud.[4] There is too easy a segue from the concept of archetype as hermeneutic tool to the system or pattern of archetypes as a preexisting or implicit structure within which a given literature is presumed to have its meaning: the "total mythological structure" that Frye imagines as having existed for each Romantic poet.[5] The limits of the usefulness

4. Ostendorf is one of Frye's strictest critics in this regard. He writes: "In place of the dogma and the determinism of philosophy and theology, from which he would like to detach literature, he now refers everywhere to the dogma of anthropology and depth psychology; his 'immanent in litera- ture' schemata are nothing more than the literary copy of culture, specific 'patterns of behavior' and archetypes which he assumes reside within the 'organism' of a mature literature. So without warning he moves into the dogmas of a pre-established mythology to which he relegates regressively all literature" (Aus dem Dogma und dem Determinismus der Philosophie und Theologie, von denen er die Literatur lösen möchte, begibt er sich nun allerdings in das Dogma der Anthropologie und Tiefenpsychologie; denn seine "literaturimmanenten" Schemata sind nichts als der literarische Abdruck der Kultur, bestimmte "patterns of behavior" und Archetypen, die er im "Organismus" einer verselbständigten Literatur vermutet. So gleitet er unversehens in die "Dogmen" einer prästabilierten Mythologie, auf die er jegliche Literatur regressiv verweist [*Der Mythos in der Neuen Welt: Eine Untersuchung zum amerikanischen Myth Criticism*, 140]).

5. Northrop Frye, A *Study of English Romanticism*, 4–5. I do not mean to accuse Frye himself of lacking sensitivity to cultural context in deploying his concept of mythological structure. Indeed, in reviewing Joseph Campbell's

of hypostatizing such a structure become obvious if one asks whether this structure existed in 1795, when Coleridge had written "The Eolian Harp" but not "Kubla Khan," and whether it still existed in 1816, when Shelley wrote "Mont Blanc."

There are some signs, however, that interest in the literary uses of myth is reviving, and even that closer attention is now being paid to the interrelations of history and myth. The danger is that the extent to which "myth" is already a historical construct, and always in process, will be ignored. In other words, we will anachronistically apply a modernist, archetypalist concept of myth as forming a "total mythological structure" to a period that had its own very different conceptions of myth. A recent essay by Stephen Behrendt, for instance, points out that the controls on the press that Pitt's government introduced during the Napoleonic War made the adoption of mythic analogues very attractive to poets such as Blake, as a way of commenting obliquely on current events without risking prosecution for sedition or treason. Yet Behrendt also appeals to a notion of timelessness:

> The realization that the archetypal patterns of human experience that underlie Western mythology are *in fact* timeless, that their periodic particularizations in certain worldly events, persons, or works of art are *in fact* merely manifestations in temporal form of eternal realities is at the heart of Blake's project in his historical prophecies, as it is in Shelley's.[6]

It is questionable whether Romantic writers (even Blake) saw archetypal patterns as timeless in quite this way. Shelley, for one, was certainly aware of the way that myths are constantly in the process of being reinterpreted as they reach a new audience. But even if we assume that Behrendt has correctly represented the Romantics' view

---

The Masks of God, Frye criticized Campbell for just such insensitivity (*Book Week,* March 22, 1964, 6, 19). One aim of *A Study of English Romanticism* is precisely to show how large historical forces changed these mythological structures in the Romantic period. What I am arguing for, however, is partly a greater historicizing of concepts of myth themselves, and partly an even greater skepticism about these overarching mythological structures than that shown by Frye.

6. Stephen Behrendt, "Introduction," in *History and Myth: Essays on English Romantic Literature,* 26 (emphasis added).

of myth, it is surely necessary for us to place this view historically—to be aware of it as a historically conditioned belief and not an inevitable or self-evident truth.

Another recent commentator expresses the hope that a "new myth criticism" will enable us to call up "the powers latent in the psyche." He shows how earlier writers struggled "to find an inner core of heroism . . . a shamanic voice . . . from which springs the continual renewal of language."[7] This attempt to align the goals of literary criticism with those of psychotherapy and the "dream-work" movement has its own interest and its own validity, but to the extent that Spivey's "new myth criticism" is predicated on a flight from history I think it is mistaken. Spivey is aware that the working of myth on the individual psyche itself has a history: he draws a parallel between the current sense of crisis in literary studies and the situation in the late nineteenth century to which Nietzsche responded and which marked the beginning of what we know as modernism. Unfortunately, however, Spivey sets history and myth in opposition, repeating and perpetuating the reaction of modernist writers in the 1920s—the flight from history. He thus proposes to initiate a "new" myth criticism that reproduces the confusions of the old. Describing the present era as resembling the late nineteenth century, "a time when only a series of new visions can push aside the heavy weight of historicism," Spivey continues: "In fact, it is the very nature of historicism, with its emphasis only on historical fact, that has made all myths seem superfluous" (181). The sentence is revealing. If historicist critics sometimes seem to want to crush human creativity and optimism by reminding us of a deadweight of mostly depressing "facts," it is surely an overreaction to push history aside entirely, in favor of someone's "new visions." The point is not to reject historical fact in favor of myth (or vice versa) but to understand the dialectic that exists between the two. In the early days of modern historicism, Coleridge wrote that history itself "in the rich purple of her Dawning" *was* mythology (CN, 4648). In divorcing history from mythology, we risk abandoning this perspective, which enabled Coleridge and Shelley—not to mention their contemporaries in the

7. Ted R. Spivey, *Beyond Modernism: Toward a New Myth Criticism,* 6–7.

field of mythography such as Dupuis, Faber, and Creuzer—to explore the rich relationship between them.

Both Spivey and Behrendt write as if the different archetypalisms of C. G. Jung and "early" Frye had never been challenged. Both ignore the subtle and useful revaluation of the concept of archetype contained in Eric Gould's *Mythical Intentions in Modern Literature*, which proposes that "the archetype is not essentialist but a function of the open-endedness of discourse." Gould recognizes that an archetypal pattern is never a self-subsistent, extralinguistic entity, or a "reality" to which we can confidently refer in explicating this or that expression of the archetype, but is *"transactional,"* operating within the normal conditions of semiosis, that is, "revealing its form only in language and interpretation."[8] (Jung, as Thomas Belmonte points out, "had neither a theory of information and feedback nor a theory of communications.")[9] Such attention to the linguistic and, therefore, metaphorical situation of myth, as opposed to its presumed psychotherapeutic or even religious authority, is a welcome step toward a truly critical myth criticism. Indeed, in theorizing the archetype Frye's own work never treats it as anything other than a function of what Gould calls "discourse"; the archetype, to Frye, is *theoretically* no more than a communicable unit of the strictly literary use of language. It is possible to challenge Frye's conception of the literary, of course, but for present purposes I am more concerned to call in question the sense, familiar to most readers of Frye, that the archetypal patterns he traces take on a life of their own. They become constitutive rather than regulative, and group themselves according to a vision of human reality that has less to do with the needs of "objective" literary analysis than with a particular moment of cultural crisis—the collapse of Christian metaphysics and the modernist attempt to salvage some elements of Christian sensibility by finding them reflected in allegedly "universal" myths.

We also need to recognize, however, that while it may be appropriate to draw on Frazer's hypothesis about primitive ritual, and his interpretation of myths in terms of such ritual, when studying T. S. Eliot, W. B. Yeats, or even William Golding, it would be a mistake

8. Eric Gould, *Mythical Intentions in Modern Literature*, 55, 63.
9. Thomas Belmonte, "The Trickster and the Sacred Clown: Revealing the Logic of the Unspeakable," 47.

to project such an understanding back to the 1790s or the years 1810–1820. The Romantics had their own debates about the origin, transmission, and significance of myth, and a truly historicist myth criticism must address the question of how the writers in a given period understood and received myth; what they understood "the mythic" to be. For their understanding of "the mythic" will certainly not be coterminous with ours.

The major problem with Northrop Frye's treatment of myth in the Romantic period from this point of view, then, is that Frye's own understanding of myth is part Blakean and part modernist, and yet he does not in practice consider and qualify it as such. Frye did not ignore the obvious truth that any concretization of a myth or of an "archetypal pattern" takes place at a particular juncture in historical time, and can be seen in relation to events and trends of that time. Yet when he posits, in *Fables of Identity*, that "total literary history moves from the primitive to the sophisticated" and proposes as a corollary the tempting possibility that literature can be analyzed as "a complication of a relatively restricted and simple group of formulas that can be studied in primitive culture," we need to be aware that a historical assertion is here being used to justify an appeal to a suprahistorical level of truth.[10] The term "formulas" clearly suggests a quasi-scientific order of statements, one that can be added to but not otherwise altered. The idea that literary history starts with "the primitive" and progresses (or descends, perhaps) to "the sophisticated" is not intrinsically suprahistorical—this statement about history has its own history. It has obvious affinities with Schiller's distinction between naïve and sentimental poetry; more generally, as W. K. Wimsatt points out, it continues the tendency of the eighteenth-century "age of sensibility" to "validate literature by an appeal to the authentic mind and heart of the primitive folk and of the closely related childish and naïve."[11]

Besides the logical dubiousness of bringing forward a certain historical principle (which may indeed be correct *as an assertion*

10. Northrop Frye, *Fables of Identity: Studies in Poetic Mythology*, 12.
11. W. K. Wimsatt, "Northrop Frye: Criticism as Myth," 106. Frye himself points out the connection with Schiller in *Anatomy of Criticism*, 35. See also Howard Felperin's criticisms of Frye in *Shakespearean Romance* (Princeton: Princeton University Press, 1972), 315.

about the assumptions underlying a certain kind of literary history)
as a basis for a suprahistorical set of "formulas," and the distortions
resulting from the excessive closeness of the method of analysis to
the literature being analyzed (that of the late eighteenth and early
nineteenth centuries), there is also the danger that the appeal to
the search for archetypes as "literary anthropology, concerned with
the way that literature is informed by pre-literary categories such
as ritual, myth and folk tale"[12] will tend to highlight "the primitive" (whatever we assume that to be) and underemphasize "the
sophisticated." That is, it encourages readers to associate literary
experience with the thrill of detecting the primitive, ritualistic, and
thus "authentic" element under the veneer of sophistication. What
tends to be underestimated in this approach is the "work" done
on the myth—the strategies, questionings, ironies, and framing devices with which the author has transmuted and modified the allegedly primitive story—precisely because it *is* "sophisticated." "The
primitive" is in any case a construction of our own age, bearing
only a tenuous and problematic relationship to prehistoric cultures,
as is now widely recognized. The Victorian and early-twentieth-
century image of "the primitive" constructed by Frazer and the
Cambridge school has been radically changed in light of more recent research, and it is not enough to claim (as Frye's defenders
sometimes do) that Frye's schemes have their own coherence and are
independent of the now outdated work on ancient cultures which
first suggested them. Even such an admirer of Frazer as Herbert
Weisinger conceded long ago that "the foundation upon which the
elaborate edifice of *The Golden Bough* is raised is the homogeneity
of the human mind," and that Frazer expressed the "myth and ritual
pattern of birth, death, and rebirth . . . *in terms of the language, the
orientation, and the needs of our own times"*—by which Weisinger
clearly meant the first half of the twentieth century.[13] Frye's model of

12. Frye, *Fables of Identity,* 12.
13. Herbert Weisinger, *The Agony and the Triumph: Papers on the Use
and Abuse of Myth,* 128, 122 (emphasis added). Weisinger cites criticisms
of Frazer by such respected anthropologists as Malinowski, Frankfort, and
Raglan, but he continues: "I am not interested in Frazer the anthropologist
but in Frazer the myth-maker, for it is as a myth-maker that he has succeeded
in capturing the creative imagination of our time" (130).

the "pre-literary" is significantly informed by Frazerian assumptions; and to the extent that this is true, the model cannot escape critique from the same perspectives that now locate Frazer in a certain late-nineteenth-century phase of anthropological work.

None of this means that the question of myth is simply irrelevant to literary analysis and criticism, or that it can be reduced to a few standard *topoi*. Wimsatt, for instance, is understandably impatient with readings of Wordsworth's "A Slumber Did My Spirit Seal" that see Lucy as a Korè/Persephone figure, dismissing this as "a mythopoeist's cliché" (95–96). The point is not to deny the Persephone connection entirely, however (especially since another of the Lucy poems clearly alludes to Persephone, as Milton represents her), but to look more carefully at the way the text relocates and "works on" the myth. The judgment that it is a mythopoeist's cliché (and the likelihood that Wordsworth would have thought of it as such) is for us part of the context we must take into consideration. Writers have different notions of the mythic, the supernatural, and what Jungians call "the numinous"; they also situate themselves vis-à-vis the mythic quite differently. Some (Spenser, Blake, Yeats) may invite the kind of totalizing critical strategy Frye proposes in *Anatomy of Criticism* and *Fables of Identity*; others (Wordsworth, Shelley, Browning, Melville) do not respond so well to it, their works being in some ingenerate way resistant to the imposition of a metaphysical dogma, whether that dogma is overt and aggressive or whether it is smuggled in through an understandable and reasonable urge toward system and clarity.

Readers of Frye's work are well aware that for Frye, the major literary manifestation of the "pre-literary"—what he calls "the central myth of literature"—is the quest-myth.[14] Frye has assembled an impressive body of evidence to establish the predominance of the quest-myth in (at least) Western literature, and to support the methodology of the *Anatomy*, in which Frye classifies the major genres of literature according to the hero's relationship to the gods. Behind this premise appears to run the implicit assumption that readers will initially be interested in what befalls the hero, and even that readers will to a greater or lesser extent "identify with" the hero, whether that hero is Odysseus, the Ancient Mariner, or David

14. Frye, *Fables of Identity*, 18.

Copperfield. Two obvious problems arise here. First, the shortcomings of this method of classification: there is every likelihood that some important literary works do *not* invite the reader to direct his or her attention and sympathies to a hero (or heroine). In several of Chaucer's *Canterbury Tales,* a hero can be found only with some difficulty—"The Pardoner's Tale," "The Miller's Tale," "The Wife of Bath's Tale," for instance. Is it right to regard these as diverging from some normative tradition? Second, and more important, such an approach would rule out, or relegate to a less vital level of debate, counterreadings that place the hero in an unfavorable light: Prospero as an imperialist plantation-owner; the Ancient Mariner as a caricature of eighteenth-century ideals of primitive man; Captain Ahab as a deluded megalomaniac. Texts may, indeed, overtly anticipate such readings. To "identify with" the hero of Shelley's "Alastor" is to read the text naïvely; to identify with Captain Ahab, even more so.

The association of myth with the primitive and therefore somehow more "authentic" world, particularly evident in the work of Frye from the *Anatomy* (1957) to *A Study of English Romanticism* (1968), has had the effect of privileging certain kinds of myth as well as certain kinds of readings. While Gould is right to say that "in literary myth studies the question of myth's reference and significance as history and moment is still unresolved," students of literature have become habituated to thinking of myth in Frye's terms, even though Frye himself (as his critics did not fail to point out) was not quite consistent in his definitions of "myth" or in his structuring of the archetypes. In the *Anatomy,* Frye briefly recognizes the "common sense" of the term "myth" as "a story about a god," but this definition hardly fits certain narratives that many critics, including Frye himself, would treat as mythic, and also raises the difficult question of what constitutes a "god." (North American First Nations stories about Nanabush, Raven, or Coyote are about a "god," if at all, in a sense very different from what Europeans mean by the term, and yet most Western anthropologists would likely treat these stories as "myths," though others might consider them "folktales.") In *A Study of English Romanticism,* Frye's emphasis is different: myths are there defined as "fictions and metaphors that identify aspects of human personality with the natural environment, such as stories about sun-gods or tree-gods."[15] This is perhaps more in accord with the way the term was understood in the late eighteenth century and for most of the nineteenth, but, for precisely that reason, it should be historicized. As Richard Chase points out, too, to bring distinctions such as "natural" and "supernatural" into a discussion of non-European myths is to preimpose on the material a philosophical distinction that the mythmaker might not have recognized.[16] Chase's own definition— *"a myth is a story, myth is narrative or poetic literature"*—has the merits of simplicity and of faithfulness to the derivation of the term from the Greek; but since *"narrative or poetic literature"* includes at its widest far too much—everything from Homer to *The Mysteries of Udolpho*—this book will confine itself to the sense in which myth is usually associated with mythography and mythology, that is, to traditionary myths, the origins of which are assumed to be nonliterary and no longer accessible or even comprehensible to the writer who adapts and transmits them. The writer who "works on" such myths will often assume that myth can be, in Philip Wheelwright's words, "taken as expressing, and therefore as implicitly symbolizing, certain deep-lying aspects of human and transhuman existence."[17]

A further qualification should be added. Myth criticism that is sensitive to the strategies by which texts use, interpret, ironize, or subvert myths, and to its own historical situation, must recognize that to focus on a certain element in a text as "mythic," or as incorporating references to "a myth," already involves some complex negotiations between what we *now* consider the mythic to be and what the text's author might have understood about the mythic. For example, Coleridge was familiar with the "mythological school" of biblical criticism, and the view that certain Old Testament narratives were myths would not have struck him as scandalous or disturbing (though he might disagree, and did disagree, with Eichhorn,

---

15. Gould, *Mythical Intentions*, 5; Frye, *Anatomy*, 33; Frye, *A Study of English Romanticism*, 4.

16. Richard Chase, "Notes on the Study of Myth," 70.

17. *The Princeton Encyclopedia of Poetry and Poetics*, s.v. "Myth." Wheelwright also comments on Chase's definition that it is legitimate to distinguish myth from other forms of literary narrative (such as, presumably, novels), since, in myth, we assume that "the original sources of such storytelling lie somehow below or beyond the conscious invention of individual poets."

Michaelis, and Paulus about how far the mythic element reached). The same notion would have been treated by earlier writers, such as, say, Addison, with far more caution if not with hostility. This is perhaps obvious; but in more subtle ways classical mythology is also subject to changes in status, and differences in the way it is "received," even by authors of the same historical period.

The well-known story told by Joseph Severn, of Keats sitting in front of the Elgin Marbles and gazing enraptured at them, illustrates in a purely anecdotal way the presence of classical mythology in English Romanticism, not, primarily, as an awesome, unapproachable, lifeless "tradition," what W. J. Bate called the "burden of the past," but as an alien yet seductive sublime, all the more fascinating for its familiarity. The conditions of this response, however, have to be taken into account. The viewer's awareness of his own historical situation does not cease the moment he enters the British Museum.[18] If to Keats's eager eyes the Elgin Marbles seemed to represent not relics of a forgotten culture but the opportunity to recapture the freshness of the early world, the sculptor's feel for the texture of human and animal flesh, this response owes as much to the needs created by Keats's historical situation, the conditioning of his perceptions by contemporary nostalgia for a more vigorously lived past, as it does to any qualities intrinsic to the Marbles themselves. And Keats's perceptions must have been conditioned in part by the high claims Romantic critics had already made for poetry and art. If poetry were to rise to the sort of achievement represented, for Keats, by the Elgin Marbles, it could be what Schlegel called for, "poetry . . . based on the harmony of the ideal and the real . . . a new revelation of nature." But in the same essay Schlegel introduced the notion of active intuitive thought: "All thinking is a divining, but man is only now beginning to realize his divining power."[19] For

18. This point is well made by A. W. Phinney, "Keats in the Museum: Between Aesthetics and History," 212. I am also indebted to Grant F. Scott, "Beautiful Ruins: The Elgin Marbles Sonnet in Its Historical and Generic Contexts." Scott shows how testimony by contemporary artists such as B. R. Haydon to the beauty and value of the Marbles overcame the earlier view of them as mere "deteriorated fragments," and suggests that such testimony must have seemed "both impressive and somewhat daunting" to Keats (130).
19. Friedrich Schlegel, "Talk on Mythology," 84, 92, 88.

the writer in circa 1800, neither "nature" nor the beauties of the ancient world could be received passively, as if they were an inert, self-sufficient deposit, a legacy whose significance was self-evident. The point is that the Elgin Marbles, like the myths retold by Homer or Ovid and again retold by later writers, demanded, stimulated, and rewarded reinterpretation, the hermeneutic effort. "Romanticism," writes Jerome C. Christensen, "first recognizes itself in its will to interpretation."[20] Christensen correctly implies that to interpret a text is to will to exercise some sort of power over it, to appropriate it, not to serve it in a neutral or self-effacing way. This view of the matter is just as true applied to Wordsworth and Coleridge as to Shelley and Keats. While Coleridge, for instance, is surprisingly ready to consider whether biblical narratives, such as the Cain and Abel story or the story of Noah and the Ark, might actually be myths, he draws a sharp distinction between those myths that awaken the "higher" human faculties (Reason and Conscience) and those that, in his view, only celebrate the passions of individuals or the powers of nature. Clearly, Coleridge's reinterpretations of myth serve an ideology that requires historicist analysis.

One can find occasional references to this or that mythological figure or mythic tradition in studies of Keats, Shelley, or Coleridge, and particularly in some major studies of mythopoesis in Blake's and Shelley's work, but there is no longer a context, no real sense of the English Romantics' understanding and treatment of myth "in the forms in which it is related to (and has the power of being related to) history" (Blumenberg's formulation). Douglas Bush's very useful and painstaking study, published in 1937, remains the only attempt to deal comprehensively with the Romantics' use of myth, though Bush's approach is more taxonomic than critical. Except for

20. Jerome C. Christensen, *Coleridge's Blessed Machine of Language*, 23. The idea that the hermeneutic enterprise is more aggressive than it normally pretends to be and is actually a form of appropriation is taken considerably further in Julie Ellison's fine discussion of the relationship between F. D. E. Schleiermacher and Friedrich Schlegel, and of the former's "interpretation" of *Lucinde*. In Schleiermacher's *Monologen*, for instance, Ellison finds that interpretation of the speech and texts of others is a key phase in the "process of self-creation" (*Delicate Subjects: Romanticism, Gender, and the Ethics of Understanding*, 60).

a few recent studies that focus on a particular myth tradition or kind of myth, a subject of enormous richness and importance for our understanding of English Romanticism has virtually slipped out of sight, or, if the subject is considered at all, it seems to be as a way out of history, merely repeating, as Spivey does, the Nietzschean and modernist moment.[21]

The way Keats's contemporaries viewed myth is important in another respect, too. This was the age when mythological syncretism first excited the imagination of the general reader, the age, in Lowes' humorous description, "when the tracking of uncanny correspondences between the patriarchs before the flood and Egyptian and Phoenician deities of none too blessed memory was an accredited diversion."[22] Further, mythographers such as Bryant, Dupuis, and Jones grappled with the problems of understanding ancient cultures; Volney staged a fictitious debate between apologists for the world's religions to show how absurd their conflicting claims were; Thomas Taylor translated the Neoplatonists; Sir William Jones translated the Laws of Menu and Persian poets such as Firdausi; and the brothers Champollion profited from the discovery of the Rosetta Stone to decipher Egyptian hieroglyphics. Keats was not a "scholar," but he was aware of what scholars do, he discussed theology and problems of biblical interpretation with his friend Bailey, and he knew that historians were working toward a new understanding of the complex relationships among the Egyptian, Greek, and Near Eastern mythologies. Coleridge and Shelley were both well read in the scholarly literature and themselves contributed essays of no little significance. Wordsworth's interests were the folk traditions of his own country, as mediated by Akenside, Collins, and other eighteenth-century poets; the Genesis myth as retold in *Paradise Lost*; and to a lesser but still significant extent the mythologies of

21. Among the best recent studies I would include Stuart Curran, "The Political Prometheus"; Linda M. Lewis, *The Promethean Politics of Milton, Blake, and Shelley*; and Paul Cantor, *Creature and Creator: Myth-making and English Romanticism*. Recent work on *Frankenstein*—itself a major version of the Prometheus myth—could also be cited here. See, for instance, Anne K. Mellor, "Promethean Politics," chap. 4 in *Mary Shelley: Her Life, Her Fiction, Her Monsters*.
22. John Livingston Lowes, *The Road to Xanadu*, 255.

Greece and Rome, but he was no more passively subservient to these traditions than Shelley or Keats. All the poets were critical readers, that is, they realized that a myth only exists and lives as it is transposed and translated. The only Romantic reader who believed *Paradise Lost* to be a literally true narrative was the Creature in *Frankenstein,* and his reading is there to provide the starting point for Mary Shelley's own subversive recasting of the Genesis 2 and 3 as a story of alienation and the abandonment of a creature by its God.

It is wrong, then, to see the Romantic attitude toward myth as a reversion to credulity, and a simple nostalgia for an irretrievable past, after the skepticism of the Enlightenment. The Romantics learned a great deal from their immediate predecessors, and if they did in some ways react against the Enlightenment critique of myth, it was not merely by occupying an opposite position but by taking up the Enlightenment's rationalist analysis into a higher synthesis, and by recognizing the sheer difficulty of understanding ancient civilizations, their distance from us. Joseph Addison in 1712 warned aspiring poets away from mythological subjects precisely because of their overfamiliarity:

> When we are at School it is necessary for us to be acquainted with the System of Pagan Theology, and may be allowed to enliven a Theme, or point an Epigram with an Heathen God; but when we would write a manly Panegyric, that should carry with it all the Colours of Truth, nothing can be more ridiculous than to have recourse to our *Jupiters* and *Junos.*[23]

For educated readers of the early nineteenth century, by contrast, the work of the historians, archaeologists, and mythological syncretists had made Jupiter, Juno, and the rest unfamiliar again. Some of the hints by ancient authors—for example, Herodotus observed in the *Historiæ* (2.52, 2.171) that the ancient Pelasgians learned from the Egyptians how to name the previously nameless gods they sacrificed to, and that Hellenes took over these names and titles from the Pelasgians, long before the time of Homer—were receiving renewed attention from syncretic mythographers, and the result was actually to increase the mystery and unsuspected depth of the familiar

23. Addison quoted by Don Cameron Allen, *Mysteriously Meant: The Rediscovery of Pagan Symbolism and Allegorical Interpretation in the Renaissance,* 308.

Greek and Roman deities. Zeus/Jupiter and Hera/Juno were not, after all, poetic clichés; their sources were quite likely in ancient religious systems still not fully understood. The mischievousness of a Bayle or a Voltaire, and their animus against religion, gave way to a new enthusiasm among mythographers for the subject they had opened up, comparative mythology. What fueled this enthusiasm was a certain ideological commitment and the desire to account for ancient mythology in terms of a Christian or liberal or radical view of human development. On all sides of the debate, interpretation meant appropriation.

Richard Payne Knight's *Account of the Remains of the Worship of Priapus* (1786) provides an interesting transitional example of the mythographers' strategic use of myth. From archaeological evidence—coins, steles, pottery fragments—and by an "archaeological" reading of the ancient texts, Knight reconstructs, to his own apparent satisfaction, an ancient theology, one based on the worship of the male and female powers of generation, and of which the surviving myth traditions of Greece and Asia are merely the remnants. He specifically warns against identifying the familiar stories with the true beliefs of the ancients: "As for the mythological tales now current in INDIA, they throw the same degree of light upon the subject [the theological system of ancient India] as OVID's Metamorphoses do on the ancient Theology of GREECE; that is, just enough to bewilder and perplex those who give up their attention to it."[24] Having thus defamiliarized mythology, Knight is free to offer his own brilliant light to guide us through the suddenly darkened pathways of the primitive: the idea of a "natural and philosophical system of religion" (24), celebrating the fertility of earth and the human race, and expressing itself in sacred orgiastic rites of the god and goddess. On the basis of this hypothesis, Knight explicates most of the familiar and potent symbols that survive from the ancient world—the woman and serpent, the world-egg, the crescent moon, the bull's horns, the erect phallus. He also proposes to trace the later philosophical reinterpretations of this religion. For instance, he finds in the Neoplatonists' use of fire imagery a relic of the Orphic cultic

24. Richard Payne Knight, *An Account of the Remains of the Worship of Priapus*, 96.

practice of symbolizing the male generative principle by fire and the sun:

> Though the Ammonian Platonics, the last professors of the ancient religion, endeavoured to conceive something beyond the reach of sense and perception, as the essence of their Supreme God; yet, when they wanted to illustrate and explain the modes of action of this metaphysical Abstraction, who was more subtile than Intelligence itself, they do it by images and comparisons of Light and Fire. (112–13)

The point is not simply that evidence of an ancient "natural and philosophical" religion is here being found in the mythic symbols themselves; but that much later philosophy and religion, particularly Christianity, are represented as having perpetuated the ancient symbols in the form of poetic glosses on dogma. Knight cleverly hints that—rather than Neoplatonic theism adopting Orphic imagery for its own more noble purposes—ancient priapic worship is actually using Neoplatonism as its protective coloration. But other mythographers (Bryant, for instance), working with the same materials, came to quite different conclusions, more favorable to established religion. The myth traditions themselves are really public property, even sometimes "clichés"; it is the interpretive, appropriative strategy that is much more significant. The fact that one "does mythology" is secondary; what really matters is *how* one does it.

This recognition is the key to Coleridge's and Shelley's uses of myth. We can grasp some of the change of emphasis between late Enlightenment and Romantic appropriations of myth by contrasting a statement of Rousseau's with one of Shelley's. Rousseau argued, in *Du contrat social,* that the benevolent legislators of ancient times, being unable to use reason to govern the people, and unwilling to use force, had recourse to divine authority and approval so that they could control the people without having to persuade them to obey the laws by rational means. Shelley, familiar with this view, nevertheless treats the gods differently when he says, repeating the argument of ancient thinkers such as Xenophanes, "Every man forms as it were his god from his own character" (SCW, 6 [1929]:16). Shelley's maxim suggests one way of understanding "the gods"— psychologically, as projections of human characteristics—that leaves open the possibility of using and developing the god figures creatively and poetically while remaining, with Rousseau, fully skeptical about their actual existence. This attitude differs a great deal from that of the late Enlightenment, and yet without the Enlightenment critique of religion, Shelley might not have reformulated the ancient skeptic's precept in quite this way.

To an extent not, I think, fully realized, Shelley and Coleridge were aware of questions of reception and interpretation as part of their general knowledge of ancient texts, and by a number of means—including irony—they imported this awareness into their own texts. (Romantic irony could be defined as the simultaneous awareness of many different interpretive possibilities.) Shelley, benefiting from the late Enlightenment historicist understanding of the production of biblical texts, argues in "On the Devil, and Devils" that the serpent in the Book of Genesis is not the Christians' Satan; that Christians have reinterpreted not only the Genesis story but also Isaiah's reference to a fallen Assyrian king as "Lucifer" (Isaiah 14:12), in light of their own Book of Revelation, thus identifying both figures with the one St. John calls *diabolus* ("accuser") and adding horns and hooves from Greek representations of Pan and his fauns. In the ancient world, Shelley points out, the serpent, far from being evil, was an "auspicious and favourable" creature, one who attended Æsculapius the healer and Apollo the god of medicine and music. To the Egyptians, the serpent symbolized eternity. "The Christians have turned this Serpent into their Devil, and accommodated the whole story to their new scheme of sin and propitiation, &c." (*SCW*, 7 [1930]:103–4). The realization that the sources of our knowledge of ancient mythology are themselves reinterpretations, and probably reinterpretations of reinterpretations, pervades Shelley's prose writings on myth just as it does Nietzsche's *Birth of Tragedy*. The idea that much of human culture consists in finding new uses for existing but no longer understood customs, institutions, and beliefs is a product of eighteenth- and early-nineteenth-century historicist study. In Frazer's *Golden Bough* this habit of thought is so taken for granted that it becomes the vehicle for numerous sly Voltairean jokes. Frazer records, for example, that in Prague the May tree would be broken up and young men and women would keep pieces of it behind their holy pictures of Mary, Jesus, and the saints.[25] This wittily emblematizes

25. James Frazer, *The Golden Bough*, 145. Joseph Priestley made a similar point in 1782: "In fact, the christian saints succeeded, in all respects, to

the powerful critique of Christianity which is the barely concealed subtext of *The Golden Bough.* Christian images of Mary and Jesus are there to hide from view the fragments of a primitive totemism and animism, thus giving a veneer of respectable orthodoxy to ancient superstition. Frazer's dry, academic wit is vastly different from the devastating irony Nietzsche employs as he subverts the serene, pure, Apollonian façade of Greek culture to reveal the brutal, will-driven, cultic ritual it conceals; but all the same the two accounts have much in common. Neither is "objective" (though Frazer's pretends to be); both use a selected datum about a culture to advance an original, controversial, and (as we know) influential interpretation of the human condition; both mean to shock, by showing that the trusted, the known, the pious, has the function of concealing the savage, the violent, the unthinkable.

It is important to realize that strategies of reinterpretation masquerading as objective reporting are not modern in origin, nor are they the sole preserve of the freethinker and the skeptic. Those who write from within religious faith have used similar strategies of displacement and demystification. In his reinterpretation of the Demeter myth, but without the historicist outlook or the subversive intention of a Frazer, Philo Judæus does exactly the same thing—that is, he demolishes the credibility of an ancient belief while appearing to approve and even reaffirm it in a new form:

> And the earth also, as it seems, is a mother, from which consideration it occurred to the early ages to call her Demetra, combining the names of mother . . . and earth. . . . For it is not the earth which imitates the woman, as Plato has said, but the woman who has imitated the earth which the race of poets has been accustomed with truth to call the mother of all things, and the fruit-bearer, and the giver of all things, since she is at the same time the cause of the generation and durability of all things, to the animals and plants. Rightly, therefore, did nature bestow on the earth as the eldest and most fertile of mothers, streams of rivers, and fountains like breasts, in order that the plants might be watered, and that all living things might have abundant supplies of drink.[26]

---

the honours which had been paid to the pagan deities" (*An History of the Corruptions of Christianity,* 1:363).

26. Philo Judæus, "On the Creation of the World," *Works,* 1:89.

Philo is able cleverly to feign agreement with the poets for imagining the earth to be a mother while he subtly retranslates their imaginings into theological terms. An existing, traditional belief is demystified as a poetic fancy and reinterpreted in a manner favorable to a new logos. It is not enough for the literary analyst to seize on this passage as evidence that Philo, too, was subject to the power of the earth-mother "archetype." The point is that he transparently places the earth-mother archetype in the service of a monotheistic theology to which it is fundamentally alien. This, and not the supposed antagonism between mythology and the "mundane, diurnal, empirical, realistic, rational and secular," is why the tendency to archetypalize is misleading and dangerous. A theory of archetypes misdirects attention from a text's logical strategies and ideological predisposition, from the subtle transactions, the purposeful misreadings and reinterpretations, that are in fact taking place.[27] At best, identifying an archetype is a precritical exercise in imaginative play, a way of codifying certain kinds of "reader response."

Philo, though he reinterprets, does not ironize or "deconstruct." What he does do—faithfully obeying and giving expression to the intellectual responsibilities placed on him by his Judaism—is demythologize.[28] That is, he accepts the Demeter myth as a "poetic"

27. Marilyn Butler takes issue with Mircea Eliade and Northrop Frye for "denigrat[ing] realistic or representational art and ideas about art." As a historical materialist, Butler not only opposes myth and mythopoesis to what she calls—with culpable carelessness—"the series of ideas conveyed by, say, mundane, diurnal, empirical, realistic, rational and secular," but she also places religion on the side of myth and (therefore) of the irrational ("Myth and Mythmaking in the Shelley Circle," 51–52). My point is simply that the divisions between "myth" and "realism," between "religion" and "rationality," are not nearly so clear-cut, and that long before Bultmann, monotheistic thinkers showed a distinct interest in "demythologizing."

28. Judaism from its inception has striven to oppose myth and to eliminate whatever mythic elements have from time to time intruded into its own traditions. See Leo Baeck, *The Essence of Judaism* (New York: Schocken, 1961), 88–89; Blumenberg, *Work on Myth*, 220–21, 229–30; and Emil Fackenheim, *The Jewish Return into History: Reflections in the Age of Auschwitz and a New Jerusalem*, 11–12. Judaism's hostility to cults based on myth and visible symbols of the divine has led some commentators to accuse Jewish religious tradition of being somehow "anti-life" and "anti-nature." For

attempt to express a certain view of the relation between woman and the earth, and he distills this "content" from the myth while making it abundantly clear that the myth itself has no separate authority. It is the act of interpretation that (in a sense) destroys the myth while at the same time preserving it—the sort of paradox Blumenberg delights in pointing out.

A mythic pantheon, it has been said, is like a language: it imposes a certain order on the world, it establishes patterns by which events and relationships can be interpreted.[29] Another way in which it resembles a language is that it is constantly liable to misunderstanding—or, rather, it constantly generates misreadings, and these misreadings are themselves the source of new myths. This process was well understood in the Romantic period. Friedrich Creuzer, giving as a principle that language itself, because essentially metaphorical, proves a fecund mother of gods and heroes ("Die Sprache selbst wird eine fruchtbare Mutter von Göttern und Helden"), points to the way that metaphors are prolific of new readings, which lead in turn to new stories.[30] He gives as an example the metaphorical image of Pelops' ivory shoulder, which Pindar tried to explain by inventing a new narrative. We should not, therefore, expect the various cultic figures we know as the Olympian pantheon to constitute a fixed system, a geometry; still less should literary criticism give priority to the Olympian—or any other—pantheon or mythological tradition in itself. Rather, its job is to show the interrelationship between the "myth" (in whatever form it happens to be available to the period under study) and the writer's own historical situation and artistic imperatives.

---

an effective response, see Tamar Frankiel, "New Age Mythology: A Jewish Response to Joseph Campbell," 23–24, 120.

29. Vernant, *Myth and Society*, 94.

30. [Georg] Friedrich Creuzer, *Symbolik und Mythologie der alten Völker*, 1:84. Creuzer continues: "Pictorial and symbolic as it [language] was, it must often have been perceived by another people and during a different era as a very strange manifestation, and the misunderstood element is then marked by an explanatory myth" (Bildlich und sinnbildlich, wie sie [die Sprache] war, musste sie unter einem andern Volke und in einiger Zeitferne oft ein sehr fremdartiges Ansehen erhalten, und das Missverstandene ward in einem erklärenden Mythus ausgeprägt, 1:84–85). The example of Pelops' shoulder follows.

Nietzsche suggests that in our thirst for knowledge we have destroyed myth.[31] It is possible to argue that we have merely found different uses for it, but the real answer is that knowledge must always cast out myths, because knowledge can be challenged and myths cannot, and because myths only seem to be liberating whereas knowledge in the long run really is liberating.

One contemporary critic, Judith Ochshorn, argues for a reevaluation of polytheism, on the grounds that it is not ethically inferior to monotheism, as has often been asserted, and in particular is more just to women.[32] Insofar as this argument is meant to correct an imbalance in our understanding of history, it is welcome. But this does not mean that Ochshorn's readers should take her book as a justification for replacing knowledge with myth, or with the nostalgia for myth in the form of "archetypes," or with the adulation of "mythopoesis," or with the resurrection of an ethic appropriate to a state of society wholly different from our own. The same argument has to be made against some of the more sentimental supporters of the environmental movement: returning to the worship of nature, or of "deified parts of nature," is to be willfully blind to history and to abdicate that very ethic of responsibility on which environmentalism, like all other truly progressive movements, is based. As Emil Fackenheim observes, "To live a secular existence is to be responsible for the world. And indeed, so great is the burden of this responsibility in our own time that many among both the 'religious' and the 'irreligious' are in full flight from the world into a variety of fancies."[33]

This book does not pretend to be a comprehensive survey of the literary uses of myth in English Romanticism. Time, circumstance, and the inadequacy of my own knowledge dictated a more modest aim. I focus on the four poets whose work seems central to my topic (and on certain works by each poet), more as a way of suggesting and demonstrating an approach than of mapping out all the territory, which is far too great an ambition for one book or even for one lifetime. The omission of Blake may seem indefensible to some

31. Friedrich Nietzsche, *The Birth of Tragedy*, 139–40.
32. See Judith Ochshorn, *The Female Experience and the Nature of the Divine*, 5–6 and passim.
33. Fackenheim, *The Jewish Return into History*, 13.

readers: that of Byron, or of the women poets of the period, indefensible to others. A thorough reconsideration of Blake's mythmaking *in the context of the mythography of his time* is overdue, I think, but it is matter for a future book, not this one. Blake, who was born in 1757, reached the age of majority soon after the American Revolution. His earliest works are therefore informed by a somewhat different sociopolitical culture, and a different episteme, from those of the later poets we call "Romantic," and he seems to me to have dealt with questions somewhat different from those faced by Wordsworth, Coleridge, Shelley, and Keats (born between 1770 and 1795), and to have lived the crucial first thirty-five years of his life in a different intellectual climate, which is at once his own and that of the Enlightenment. Because of the amount of good work already available, too, I have avoided extensive discussion of the versions of the Prometheus myth in the work of Mary Shelley and Percy Shelley, though *Prometheus Unbound* is discussed in my last chapter alongside Coleridge's "On the Prometheus of Æschylus." Byron appears to me to lack the sort of *sustained* interest in myth that would justify his being treated with my four poets. Nevertheless, several of Byron's poems and plays rework myth in startling and historically interesting ways, and merit the same kind of analysis here given to his more obviously myth-conscious contemporaries. His appropriation of the Genesis myth in *Cain*, for instance, is a major instance of Romantic work on myth. Myth is also a central element in the work of Mary Tighe, Felicia Hemans, and several other women poets of the period whose poetry is long overdue for revaluation. This, too, may be material for a future book.

The arrangement of this book is approximately chronological. The chapter on "The Rime of the Ancient Mariner" attempts to do two things: to investigate some of the contemporary mythographical sources available to Coleridge in the 1790s (and in which he is known to have been interested), and then to show how "The Rime of the Ancient Mariner" does not simply draw on the researches of various mythographers, but is a response to and rejection of mythography, as it was practiced by two distinct and opposed schools. Three chapters on Wordsworth follow, which try to question the common view that Wordsworth owes little or nothing to classical mythology and refers to it but rarely. Wordsworth's way is to appropriate myth subtly and silently, usually without actually using the *names* of gods, goddesses, or geographical terms such as Olympus, Lethe, or Helicon, and suppressing much of the context of the myth elements he adopts. This only makes his allusions that much more effective, more "modern," even though the modern reader, who is generally not as well schooled in the classics as Wordsworth's university-educated contemporaries were, may not register his allusions in the same way. His strategy of decontextualizing myth elements is shown first in his use of imaginative animism—folk traditions closely related to "myth," and partly mediated by his poetic predecessors—in the early drafts of *The Prelude*. The third chapter argues that Wordsworth's handling of Theocritan idyll in such poems as "Nutting," "Tintern Abbey," "To M.H.," and "Three Years She Grew" weakens the association between nature and the female that is characteristic of some classical myths. The poems are ostensibly anti-mythological in that they focus on personal experience rather than on any sort of traditionary narrative; I will show, however, that a subtler kind of mythmaking is at work in the way they project human traits and powers onto nature. A chapter on "Home at Grasmere" then tries to demonstrate the conflict in that poem between two different ways of resolving the poet's solitariness, two ways of putting the individual in relation to nature, which derive from and allude to two different myth traditions. Chapter 5 argues for a reading of Coleridge's "Christabel" as mythopoeic rather than "Gothic," and particularly as a poem that reinterprets the temptation myth in the second chapter of Genesis. Two chapters on Percy Shelley's poetry examine, first, the far-reaching critique of the language of myth that is to be found in "Queen Mab," "Hymn to Intellectual Beauty," and "Mont Blanc" (a critique based on the same Enlightenment commentaries against which Coleridge reacted, those of Volney, Dupuis, and d'Holbach); and second, the way a particular myth tradition—the contest of Apollo and Pan—is remolded and reinterpreted in Shelley's later poetry. Chapter 8 attempts to show the relation between Keats's tropes for the enabling of poetic utterance and his reinterpretation of goddess figures. Finally, I look at the ideological ramifications of Coleridge's 1825 lecture on the *Prometheus* of Æschylus, contrasting it with Shelley's earlier reinterpretation of the myth in *Prometheus Unbound*.

One

Coleridge among the Mythographers
"The Rime of the Ancient Mariner"

It is now widely accepted that "The Rime of the Ancient Mariner" can be approached as a poem about the making of myth. Studies of the many sources that contributed to the poem, from J. L. Lowes to H. W. Piper, John Beer, and more recent critics, have immeasurably enriched our sense of the matrix within which the poem took shape: a matrix composed of seventeenth- and eighteenth-century travelers' tales, theological and philosophical literature, the speculations of psychologists and natural philosophers, mythographers' accounts of ancient Near Eastern and Asian mythologies, folktales, and events in the personal lives of Coleridge and his circle, particularly the Wordsworths and the Lambs. Moreover, thanks to studies such as John Beer's *Coleridge's Poetic Intelligence*, we are much closer to understanding the field of intellectual force that pulled these disparate elements together.

However, questions about the intellectual currents that contributed to the genesis of that extraordinary poem are intricately bound up with another question that has not yet been fully addressed. This is the question of the relationship between the "mythic" content of the poem and the wider historical context from which the poem emerged. If "The Rime of the Ancient Mariner" was more than an inconsequential "reverie" (the term used as part of its title in the 1800, 1802, and 1805 editions of *Lyrical Ballads*) or, pejoratively, a fantasy, a pastiche imitating the "spirit of the elder poets," as the Advertisement to the 1798 edition has it—and all but a few critics

25

now purport to take the poem more seriously than these designa-
tions suggest—what *contemporary* preoccupations might have led
Coleridge to explore the nature of mythmaking? And how is the
modern critic to assess the "myth" element in the poem? Doesn't
the critic have a responsibility to show that the myth element is
not transhistorical, any more than other literary features such as the
ballad genre or the theme of crime and punishment?

Like some of the eighteenth-century mythographers, modern
myth critics have tended to obscure the context within which the
myths they treat of were interpreted, transformed, and transmitted. If we shift the focus slightly and examine not the correlation
between elements of ancient myth and literary myth, but the way
ancient myth is appropriated, we may at least end with a clearer
understanding of the *uses* of myth, in "The Rime of the Ancient
Mariner" and elsewhere. If what takes place in "The Rime of the
Ancient Mariner" is in some sense a romantic renewal of myth, the
very meaning of the myth element in the poem surely depends on
the way it is situated within a complex contemporary understanding
of myth.

I wish to establish here that "The Rime of the Ancient Mariner"
questions both the orthodox kind of comparative mythography, according to which pagan myths were "fallen" versions of pre-Noachic
revealed truth, and the work of mythographers sympathetic to the
French Revolution, who traced all religious beliefs, including those
of the ancient Hebrews, to a primitive religion of Nature, a *religion
universelle.*

In the 1780s and 1790s, mythography was far from being ideologically neutral territory. This fact emerges from even the briefest examination of the work of the French mythographers Dupuis and Volney,
the historian of ideas Condorcet, and the English opponents of
their school, Jacob Bryant, Thomas Maurice, and Sir William Jones.
While some English students of myth may have been motivated by
a disinterested love of truth, a great many embarked on the work
in order to defend Christian beliefs against the critique mounted
by the comparative mythography of the French Enlightenment.
The need for such work was proclaimed by the Bishop of Llandaff,
who in 1780, speaking to the clergy of the diocese of Ely, called on
scholars to translate "the chief oriental manuscripts" and to research
"the Manners, Arts and Literature of the Eastern nations," partly to

improve current knowledge but also and "in particular" because "it would . . . tend to remove many of the difficulties, which have been conceived against the authority of Moses, from the supposed high antiquity of the Eastern histories and their silence concerning a deluge."[1] The absence from "the Eastern histories" of narratives that would corroborate the Genesis account of the Flood was seen as an embarrassment to Christian orthodoxy.

Maurice, Bryant, and others like them were concerned to collect information about the belief systems of the ancients, but it is clear that they would have been especially interested in evidence that might settle "the difficulties, which have been conceived against the authority of Moses." Dupuis and his follower Volney, on the other hand, seized on parallels between the biblical account and the mythology of Gentile nations as evidence that Judaism and Christianity were merely versions of the *religion universelle*, and that in the earliest times the universe itself was, as one rhapsodic essay has it, "l'être animé par excellence."[2]

First I propose to look at the work of some late-eighteenth-century mythographers, especially of course those Coleridge is known to have read, and to relate their various approaches to myth to what can be learned about Coleridge's own concern with poetic inspiration, religious belief, and political progressivism. This investigation will prepare the ground for a discussion of "The Rime of the Ancient Mariner" in which I hope to show that, in the context of the *appropriation* of myth, its uses in Coleridge's time and in ours, the poem is disruptive of certain newly sanctioned creeds, especially biblical literalism and the emerging "nature religion" of the revolutionary

1. Quoted from *Asiatic Miscellany* 1 (Calcutta, 1785) by Fatma Moussa Mahmoud, *Sir William Jones and the Romantics*, 66–67. Cambridge is part of the diocese of Ely, and the bishop's audience would likely have included many Cambridge scholars.

2. *Essai sur la religion des anciens Grecs*, 1:36. Published anonymously; another edition (Lausanne, 1787) is identified as by Leclerc de Sept-Chênes, in A.-A. Barbier, *Dictionnaire des ouvrages anonymes*, 3d ed. (Paris, 1882), 2:245. (The *Essai* may have had a distinguished author: Leclerc de Sept-Chênes was a pseudonym used by Louis XVI when he was dauphin. See J.-M. Quérard, *Les supercheries littéraires dévoilées* [Paris, 1850], 3:9–10. I am grateful to Claudia Strasky, of the University of Zurich, for helping to trace the authorship of this work.)

period.[3] The poem is not correctly described either as an escape from political reality or as a statement of faith, Christian or otherwise. Rather, it is a superbly indeterminate text that enables and compels the reader to participate in the process of rethinking myth, of "work on myth," that has to underwrite any permanent, fully achieved ideological change.

For much of the eighteenth century, young English readers derived their knowledge of Greek and Roman mythology from Andrew Tooke's *Pantheon,* a translation from the work of the French Jesuit François Antoine Pomey. According to Pomey, the gross and absurd mythology of pagan peoples arose through such causes as the excessive admiration of an ignorant populace for great men, and the selfish desire of those men to achieve a spurious immortality in magnificent images of themselves. Clearly, Pomey was more concerned to instruct his audience morally than to offer a considered historical theory. He parades the better-known stories about the misdeeds of gods and goddesses as warnings against human folly and pride: so, for instance, the metamorphoses of Jupiter (whom Pomey represents as originally a king of Crete) demonstrate "how many several Beasts a Person resembles, who has once put off his Modesty," and the Graces are shown naked "because Kindnesses ought to be done in Sincerity and Candor, and without Disguise."[4]

3. Jerome J. McGann discusses the relationship between the poem and Coleridge's growing interest in biblical criticism ("The Ancient Mariner: The Meaning of the Meanings," *The Beauty of Inflections,* 135–72), arguing that "the mariner interprets his experiences by his own lights, and each subsequent mediator—the ballad transmitters, the author of the gloss, and Coleridge himself—all represent their specific cultural views. In such a situation we must read the poem with the fullest possible consciousness of its poetically organised 'historical layerings'" (170). I am indebted to McGann's essay, though here my interest is the poem's relation to contemporary mythography, rather than its reflection of a new Coleridgean understanding of "faith" (poetic or religious). Daniel P. Watkins seeks to locate the poem in its sociohistorical context, claiming indebtedness to McGann, but his essay, "History as Demon in Coleridge's *The Rime of the Ancient Mariner,*" seems to allegorize the poem as unwittingly reflecting the transition from a society based on community and unquestioned religious faith to an atomized society based on individualism.
    4. Andrew Tooke, ed. and trans., *The Pantheon, Representing the Fabulous Histories of the Heathen Gods and Most Illustrious Heroes in a Short,*

Such assumptions about the folly of paganism brought about challenges from the deists. Early in the eighteenth century, the syncretism of deists Matthew Tindal and John Toland undermined Christianity's claim to uniqueness. They demonstrated that there was a common core of "rational" religious belief in many ancient religions, and that Christianity was least rational and least credible when it diverged from this core. The orthodox argument that pagan myths were merely corruptions of Scripture—Bacchus, for example, being identified with Nimrod, or even with Moses[5]—was challenged by new chronologies according to which Egypt, India, and other nations with rich mythologies were actually older than the oldest Jewish records.

These challenges to Christian orthodoxy were anticlerical, rather than antireligious. The object was to show that human happiness was better served by following the "light of nature," the simple universal religion of the ancients, than by allegiance to an exclusive, narrow, and irrational creed. John Toland vehemently attacked priestcraft, associating it with druidism, human sacrifices, and obscure ritual. Matthew Tindal argued that "if God intended man to come to religious truth . . . surely there was but one religion which all men were to know and whose duty it was to embrace." Pierre Bayle poured scorn on the scholars who alleged that pagan gods were mere copies of biblical characters such as Noah, and also observed (in recounting the calumnies spread about Martin Luther) that Christians were not notably more moral than pagans.[6]

The attacks of the deists forced more orthodox scholars to reevaluate their treatment of pagan myth, and, as Albert J. Kuhn puts it, "to concede that myth might represent an analogy of natural religion to revelation, and that it was not simply a wholesale perversion of Scriptures" (1115–16). This was the beginning of Romantic com-

---

Plain and Familiar Method . . . for the Use of Schools (1713), 19, 144. First published in 1698, it went through many editions. For Coleridge's knowledge of it, see *CN*, 2737 and n, *CL*, 1:1042, and J. B. Beer, *Coleridge the Visionary*, 65–66.

5. Tooke, *Pantheon*, 81.

6. Tindal, *Christianity as Old as the Creation* (1732), quoted in Albert J. Kuhn, "English Deism and the Development of Romantic Mythological Syncretism," 1107; Pierre Bayle, *Dictionnaire historique et critique*, 1:130 (s.v. "Cham"), 3:222–24 (s.v. "Luther").

parative mythology, which though still in the service of orthodoxy took a more liberal attitude toward pagan myth. Late-eighteenth-century Christian mythographers—including Unitarian writers such as Joseph Priestley—mounted a defense against the skepticism of the deists by saying that where pagan myth resembled the biblical account, it was not a perversion of Scripture but an analogous account—lacking, however, the special authority of revelation. The ancient Egyptians, Chaldeans, Babylonians, Greeks, Persians, and other peoples preserved, in distorted form, the stories of the Fall and the Flood as recounted in the biblical narratives.[7] In the eager search for evidence that would corroborate the Genesis account, some English scholars let themselves be duped into using Sanskrit and other Asian-language manuscripts that were in fact forgeries. Even the great Sir William Jones was taken in by one such forgery, supposedly part of an ancient Sanskrit text describing Noah under the name of Satyvrata or Satyavarman, which had been concocted by a pundit who was very willing to feed his pupil's interest in any narrative that resembled the biblical account of the Deluge.[8]

The aim of a syncretist study such as Bryant's *New System* was not simply to present a historical account of ancient myth, but to counter the Enlightenment critique of religious belief, by showing that the Genesis account of history was confirmed, not undermined, by the traditions of other peoples. Where Voltaire had exploited similarities between Genesis and the myths of Gentile nations to suggest that perhaps the Genesis account was also a fiction, Bryant argued that if other nations had records of such an event as the Flood, it must actually have happened.

> By the Mosaic history we are assured, that the calamity was universal; that all flesh died, excepting eight persons, who were providentially preserved. That the world was afterwards renewed in one man: and that from his three sons all the nations upon earth were derived. It

7. For Priestley's views on the priority of monotheism to polytheistic systems, see *The Doctrines of Heathen Philosophy, compared with those of Revelation,* esp. 10: "This universal opinion of the great superiority of Jupiter had certainly a higher origin than Hesiod's Theogony gives him, and must have been the remains of a much purer system of theology, which taught the doctrine of *one God.*"

8. Mahmoud, *Sir William Jones and the Romantics,* 33.

has been my purpose throughout to establish these great truths: to bring evidence from every age, and from every nation, to which we can gain access, in support of the history, as it has been delivered by Moses.[9]

Bryant's emphasis on the Flood as the key event of ancient history was in line with the arguments of seventeenth-century orthodox Christian historians. Like them, Bryant believed that the apparently diverse myth traditions of the various peoples of the world could be explained by the migrations of Noah's three sons and their descendants. The nations that did not enjoy the benefit of continued divine revelation—that is, the descendants of Ham and Japheth—gradually forgot the revealed truth of the earlier age, the history of humankind from Adam to Noah, and instead constructed a false mythology that attempted to preserve the divine power of sacred history, but without the benefit of direct revelation, which was granted only to Abraham and his seed. Other nations after their dispersal suffered the "disease of language," which caused the corruption and loss of the original, Amonian language.[10]

> The ark according to the traditions of the Gentile world was prophetic; and was looked upon as a kind of temple, a place of residence of the Deity. In the compass of eight persons it comprehended all mankind: which eight persons were thought to be so highly favoured by heaven, that they were looked up to by their posterity with great reverence; and came at last to be reputed Deities. Hence in the ancient mythology of Egypt, there were precisely eight Gods: of these the Sun was the chief, and was said first to have reigned.[11]

Bryant explained all the religions of the Near East as essentially one cult, originating with the descendants of Ham, whose four sons, Cush, Egypt, Put, and Canaan, identified their father with the sun, the sun being a substitute for, or false image of, the One True God. "Amon," a frequent element in Near Eastern place names, was a corruption of Ham, Bryant claimed. Cush, or Chus, gave us Thoth,

---

9. Jacob Bryant, A *New System, or, an Analysis of Ancient Mythology,* 2:532.

10. See Burton Feldman and Robert D. Richardson, eds., *The Rise of Modern Mythology 1680–1860,* 242, and Beer, *Coleridge the Visionary,* 212–13.

11. Bryant, A *New System,* 2:233.

and the Greek *theos*, and so on. The most ancient and universal form of pagan worship, however, was sun worship:

> The worship of Ham, or the Sun, as it was the most ancient, so it was the most universal of any in the world. It was at first the prevailing religion of Greece; and was propagated over all the sea coast of Europe: from whence it extended itself into the inland provinces. It was established in Gaul and Britain; and was the original religion of this island, which the Druids in after time adopted. (1:284)

Bryant's amateurish etymologies and his uncritical reliance on the Bible as the sole authority on ancient history associate his work with the 1670s rather than the 1770s, "a late-blooming version of a dead era in mythic thought."[12] Yet, helped by wealthy patrons and the support of John Wesley, who wrote an abridgment of the *New System*, Bryant's version of pagan mythology had a considerable impact. Those who were anxious to reconcile the pagan myths with the biblical account were attracted to it. To William Blake, for instance, Bryant's system reaffirmed the essential unity of spiritual revelation.

Thomas Maurice is even more explicit than Bryant in avowing the purpose of his *History of Hindostan*, strongly hinting, too, that he had performed a service that merited official recognition:

> For having devoted so considerable a portion of the subsequent pages to the defence of the Mosaic history, if any apology be necessary, I have this to urge in my vindication, that, leaving out of the question the hostile attacks recently made on that history and its author by infidelity, and urged with such increased virulence and malignity at the present momentous crisis, the writings of that sublime and venerable legislator must necessarily claim a very large share of the attention of every historian of those ancient periods, the transactions of which form the principal subject of this volume. Subordinate and laborious as is the station which, for many years, it has been my lot to fill in the profession of which I am a member, disappointment and neglect have not yet shaken the zeal of my attachment to it; nor could I avoid feeling equally with my brethren in the higher orders of the establishment, sentiments of just indignation at the insults offered to that profession, and indeed to the whole Christian church, by the insinuations of M. Volney, and other professed infidels of the age, that the noble system of the national theology rests upon no better basis than an Egyptian Allegory, relative to the introduction of evil into the world; that the fabulous Crishna of

12. Feldman and Richardson, *Modern Mythology*, 241.

India should be represented, both in name, character, and the miracles imputed to him by a superstitious people, as the prototype of the Christian Messiah; that in a fanciful hypothesis relative to the celestial Virgo, and the sun rising in that sign, the immaculate conception should be ridiculed, the stupendous event of the resurrection scoffed at, and the Sun of righteousness be degraded to a level with his creatures.[13]

As Maurice's reference to "the present momentous crisis" makes abundantly clear, in the years following the French Revolution mythography was suddenly a matter of vital interest—almost of vital national importance. The old Enlightenment notion of a simple universal religion founded on the "light of nature" was reborn in the vision of the French ideologues, and became part of their hopes for a new world order in which national and religious prejudices would be cast aside and humankind would live by a few simple laws drawn from nature and the human constitution itself. The biblical revelation would become wholly redundant; and for this reason even politically radical Unitarians attacked Dupuis and Volney. Both Joseph Priestley, the "Patriot, and Saint, and Sage" of Coleridge's "Religious Musings" (CPW, 1:123), and John Prior Estlin, a Unitarian minister in Bristol who was a close friend of Coleridge in the 1790s, published books attacking Dupuis. The Unitarian position was that Christian doctrine needed to be purged of certain accretions foreign to the spirit of the primitive church, such as the identification of the man Jesus with the Logos, or Wisdom, which was originally just an attribute of the divine mind. Their aim was not to reject revelation but to purify it, to free it from its "corruptions." Priestley therefore defends the Mosaic law against the imputation that it could be derived from an Egyptian version of the Hindu scriptures (the Vedas and more particularly the Laws of Menu) and upholds the idea of an original, patriarchal, monotheistic religion, preserved in its purest, revealed form in the Pentateuch, and of which Hinduism and other polytheistic religions are decayed versions, following the "dispersion" of humankind after the Flood.[14] Estlin's essay The Nature and the Causes of Atheism (the epigraph comes from Coleridge's contribution to Southey's

13. Thomas Maurice, The History of Hindostan: Its Arts, and its Sciences, 1:xxi–xxii.

14. See Joseph Priestley, An History of the Corruptions of Christianity, 1:28; A Comparison of the Institutions of Moses with those of the Hindoos and

Joan of Arc, 1796) is basically a restatement of the old "argument from design." Appended to it is a long critique of Dupuis, focusing particularly on the inadequacy of Dupuis' theological reasoning:

> The belief of a CREATOR of the world, in opposition to the doctrine of the God-world, the God-sun, the God-nature, and the like, has prevailed, and does now prevail. By creation, I mean not to refer to the *matter* of which the world was composed, but to the *composition.* . . . This belief must have arisen either from the deductions of reason, or from revelation, or from both. If the *reasons* upon which it is built, be weak and inconclusive, let M. Dupuis or M. Volney shew that they are so. *They have not yet done it: They have not even entered on the subject.*[15]

Coleridge was at least as familiar as Estlin was with the controversial works of Dupuis and Volney. He wrote to John Thelwall on November 19, 1796: "I am just about to read Dupuis' 12 octavos, which I have got from London. I shall read only one Octavo a week— for I cannot *speak* French at all, & I read it slowly" (*CL*, 1:260). Beer suggests that it may have been Coleridge who introduced Estlin to Dupuis' work, commenting "Coleridge had a particular interest in those studies of [mythology] which were hostile to the Christian faith," and a notebook entry of 1821 or 1822 (if the dates in volume 4 of *CN* are correct) lists Dupuis and Bryant among the

---

Other Ancient Nations; with Remarks on Mr. Dupuis' Origin of all Religions, 3–4, 15. See also this passage in *Comparison:*

> The principal object of Mr. Dupuis's elaborate work, and no doubt that of all unbelievers in Christian countries, is the overthrow of Christianity; and it is only *this* that they wish to wound thro' the sides of judaism; thinking that if one part of the system of revelation be overturned, the other part will fall with it. And on this account Mr. Dupuis represents the connection of christianity with judaism, and the most exceptionable parts of the writings of Moses, as of the strongest kind. (340–41)

The barely concealed anti-Semitism of much Enlightenment mythography is its most repellent aspect, though often passed over in silence. Shelley is not free from such prejudice: *Queen Mab* takes over from d'Holbach and Volney the view that the Jews of antiquity were a "barbarian" and "uncultured" race. See *Queen Mab,* canto 2, lines 149, 159 (*SP&P*, 25).

15. John Prior Estlin, *The Nature and the Causes of Atheism . . . To which are added, Remarks on a Work, entitled Origine de tous les cultes, ou Religion universelle,* 44–45.

authorities whose work Coleridge had read. As for Volney, though in 1822 Coleridge strongly denied that Volney made any impression on him, he knew *Les Ruines* well enough to attack it in the 1795 lectures.[16] To understand the threat that Unitarians such as Priestley and Estlin saw in the writings of Volney and Dupuis, however, we must look at the works themselves: Volney's *Les Ruines* and Dupuis' *Origine de tous les cultes*.

Chapter 22 of *Les Ruines, ou méditation sur les révolutions des empires* is the chapter that most offended Maurice, since it linked the story of Jesus' birth and passion to the Egyptian astrological tradition of an infant—the sun—born to the Celestial Virgin at the winter solstice and who, at his maturity (the spring equinox), crushes the head of the evil serpent, that is, the winter season. Volney by no means singles out Christianity for such treatment. The narrative of the historians of religion, the main polemical core of Volney's work, accounts for the growth of *all* the religions of the world, from shamanism and fetishism to Zoroastrianism, Judaism, and Islam, by tracing their fundamental doctrines to the observation of natural phenomena:

> We find these Gods . . . who display such singular characters in every system, are only the physical agents of nature, the elements, the winds, the stars, and the meteors, which have been personified by the necessary mechanism of language and of the human understanding; that their lives, their manners, their actions, are only their mechanical operations and their connexions; and that all their pretended history is only the description of these phenomena, formed by the first naturalists who observed them, and misconceived by the vulgar who did not understand them, or by succeeding generations, who forgot them.[17]

16. Beer, *Coleridge the Visionary*, 213; *CN*, 4839, 4916; *Lects 1795*, 99, 183.

17. Comte de Volney, *Ruins; or meditations on the revolution of empires*, 2:65–66. The 1791 text is as follows: "L'on trouve que ces Dieux, par exemple, qui jouent des rôles si singuliers dans tous les systêmes, ne sont que les *puissances physiques* de la nature, les *élémens*, les *vents*, les *astres* et les *météores*, qui ont été *personnifiés* par le mécanisme nécessaire du langage et de l'entendement; que leur *vie*, leurs *moeurs*, leurs *actions* ne sont que le jeu de *leurs opérations* de *leurs rapports*; et que toute leur prétendue histoire n'est que la description de leurs phénomènes, tracée par les premiers physiciens qui les observèrent, et prise à contre-sens par le vulgaire

This explanation adapts and develops d'Holbach's hypothesis, that the earliest human societies "ascribed to the elements of nature—or to the hidden agents which governed them—a will, a purpose, needs and desires, resembling those of men."[18] In Egypt, according to Volney's enlightened historians, early humankind's instinctual attempts to propitiate Sun, Moon, and other heavenly bodies gave way to a more regular and elaborate system of religious ritual, based on the close association that inevitably developed between certain constellations and the seasons of the agricultural year. So, the constellation ascendant at a time of flood was the Water Carrier (Aquarius); the Bull represented the time when land must be plowed, and so on. By a natural linguistic economy, it came to be said that the Bull scatters abroad the seeds of fecundity, or that the Lamb (or Ram) delivers the heavens from winter's maleficent influence.[19]

In the interests of liberty and world peace, Volney's "Legislators" explain to the assembled peoples of the world that there is now one nation—France—that has rejected the misleading and mutually incompatible claims of all religions and realized that the laws of a just and free society can be found only by the study of Nature itself, understood in this Holbachian way:

> Abolishing our artificial and arbitrary institutions, and recurring to the origin of all right and of all reason, we have found that there existed in the very order of nature and in the physical constitution of man, eternal and immutable laws, which only waited his observance to render him happy. . . . Since human nature has but one constitution, let there exist in future but one law, that of nature.[20]

---

qui ne l'entendit pas, ou par les générations suivantes, qui l'oublièrent" (*Les Ruines, ou méditation sur les révolutions des empires*, 222–23). The argument that the earliest gods were personified abstractions from natural phenomena is not original with Volney. D'Holbach put forward such a theory twenty years before the revolution, and a commonplace of late Enlightenment thought was that the earliest peoples were impelled by ignorance and fear to invent supernatural beings to explain the natural calamities that afflicted them. See Paul Henri Thiry, baron d'Holbach, *Système de la nature, ou Des loix du monde physique et du monde moral*, 2:8–9. I am grateful to Terence Hoagwood for directing my attention to d'Holbach.

18. D'Holbach, *Système de la nature*, 2:14.

19. Volney, *Les Ruines*, 241–42.

20. Volney, *Ruins*, 1:174–75. The 1791 text reads: "Annullant ses institutions factices et arbitraires, et remontant à l'origine de tout droit et de toute

Volney thus gives a clear ideological impetus to d'Holbach's materialism and to the mythographical researches of Dupuis, on whose
work he also draws. (Though not published in its entirety until 1795,
Dupuis' work was partly available to Volney long before that, and is
cited in Volney's notes.) The basis of Volney's attack on the conflicting claims of the various systems of religious belief, in other words,
is a mythography founded on the Holbachian hypothesis that, in
the earliest ages of the world, human beings ascribed mysterious
powers to natural phenomena: "even the most abstract and fantas-
tical ideas have some physical model [in nature]" (les idées, même
les plus abstraites et les plus fantastiques, ont, dans la Nature, un
modèle physique).[21]

Charles Dupuis' *Origine de tous les cultes*, which Coleridge told
Thelwall he intended to read in 1796, is an outstanding example of
the late Enlightenment analysis of myth. Marshaling an impressive
array of sources, the reports of modern travelers as well as the works
of classical historians and the church fathers, Dupuis attempted to
prove that astronomy, particularly the formation of the zodiac, is
the key to all myth and religion. His hypothesis was a variant of
the "solar" theory of myth, but with added emphasis on the sun's
passage through the twelve zodiacal signs, which was taken as the
origin of such myths as the Twelve Labors of Hercules. Dupuis,
who pointedly called himself "Citizen Dupuis" on the title page,
was, like Volney, a member of the National Assembly and believed
that the French Revolution would inaugurate a new age in which
men and women could love and admire nature in itself, free from
the distorting and oppressive beliefs purveyed by priests and the
nonsense of poets. "For me," he writes, "Gods are the children of
men; and like Hesiod I hold that the earth produced the heavens."
Jesus Christ was simply another sun god, and Christianity a variant of the *religion universelle*, the term *"universelle"* here meaning not only "universal, ubiquitous" but also "cosmic" or "product

---

raison, elle [la nation—i.e., France] a vu qu'il existoit dans l'*ordre même de
l'univers*, et dans la constitution physique de l'homme, des lois éternelles et
immuables, et qui n'attendoient que ses regards pour le rendre heureux. . . .
Puisque le genre humain n'a qu'une même constitution, qu'il n'existe plus
pour lui qu'une même loi, celle de la *nature*." (*Les Ruines*, 152–53). Compare
d'Holbach, *Système de la nature*, 1:6–7.

21. Volney, *Ruins* 2:59; *Les Ruines*, 217.

of the universe." "The Gods being Nature herself, the history of the Gods is thus the same as the history of Nature, . . . the adventures of the Gods are, then, natural phenomena turned into allegories."[22]

The first volume of Dupuis' study establishes the major premise of the work: that all the religious systems of ancient times were based on natural phenomena. In sacrificing to the Nile, the Egyptians were honoring the Nile itself, not the river as emblem of a god; their "gods" were none other than air, sky, earth, sun, moon, night, and day. Like Phoenicia, Syria, and Arabia, Egypt directed its whole worship to Nature and its phenomena and agents. The Greeks took Phoenician gods and embellished them, but they remained basically the same: sun, stars, moon, and so on. Likewise the religion of the Hebrews, at the time of Abraham, was Sabism: they worshiped fire and the powers of nature.[23]

Summarizing the findings of his first treatise, Dupuis writes:

> The most simple, most natural, and earliest idea that must have entered the minds of men, when they began to think seriously about the causes of the things observed on earth, and of which they were themselves part, was to locate these causes in Nature itself and its most apparent agents, whose activity revealed itself to their sight. Having given the name "God" to the idea of an eternal cause that governed their lives, it was thus in Nature and its various aspects that they saw their Gods, and they can have seen no others, until the mind, through its own abstractions, created new ones, calling them invisible and mental Deities.[24]

22. Charles François Dupuis, *Origine de tous les cultes ou religion universelle,* 1:xix–xx: "Les Dieux étant la Nature elle-même, l'histoire des Dieux est donc celle de la Nature; . . . les aventures des Dieux seront donc les phénomènes de la Nature mis en allégories." All translations from Dupuis are my own. For another way of interpreting the link between astronomy and early religion, see marquis de Condorcet, *Esquisse d'un tableau historique des progrès de l'esprit humain,* 23, 39, 43. I have benefited from seeing the *Lizentiatsarbeit* by Claudia Strasky, of the University of Zurich, "Objects of Sense and Superstition in Coleridge" (1989), in which she points out that Dupuis' aim was "a rational synthesis . . . of all rites of worship into one" (42).
23. Dupuis, *Origine de tous les cultes,* 1:33–36, 13–14.
24. "L'idée la plus simple, la plus naturelle, et la première qui a dû se présenter aux hommes, lorsqu'ils ont commencé à raisonner sur les causes des effets produits ici-bas, et dont ils font partie, a été de les placer dans la Nature même et dans ses agens les plus apparens, dont l'activité se

"God" and "the gods," then, were for Dupuis mere abstractions from the historically prior faculty of seeing the universe as itself divine (in the sense of "eternal" and *causa causarum*); the emergence of mental Deities ("Dieux intellectuels") marked a fall from the pristine unity of nature and humankind into a duality of invisible gods, existing only in the minds of human beings, and empty nature.

Having in this way evoked a primitive condition of harmony between man and nature, Dupuis proceeds to explain all of ancient mythology as stories about the sun, stars, moon, and earth viewed as intelligences or deities *in their own right*. Of the Egyptians, for instance, Dupuis says (citing Iamblichus as his authority): "The Egyptians, making the sun their chief God, architect and governor of the world, explained not only the story of Osiris and Isis, but all their sacred stories in general, by the stars."[25] An example of his applying astrology to classical myth (based on Porphyry) is the interpretation of the praise of Hercules in the Orphic hymns as a paean to the sun, "father of all things," "destroyer of all things," "creator of Time," "who brings the morning and the night," and so on; the Twelve Labors are seen as an allegorization of the sun's journey through the signs of the zodiac. The Egyptians' divinity, Osiris, and the Persians' divinity, Mithras, are similarly interpreted (following Strabo, Suidas, and Hesychius) as the sun (2:205–6, 398, 3:405). With inexorable logic, and almost casually as if unwilling to give the matter more

---

manifestoit à leurs yeux. Ayant rendu l'idée de cause éternelle et supérieure à eux par le mot Dieu, c'est donc dans la Nature et ses parties qu'ils ont vu leurs Dieux, et ils n'en ont pas dû voir d'autres, jusqu'à ce que l'esprit, par ses abstractions, s'en fût créé de nouveaux, sous le nom de Dieux invisibles et intellectuels" (ibid., 1:288). The concept of "mental Deities" should be compared to d'Holbach's view that, having separated nature's "power of working" ("sa faculté d'agir") from physical nature itself, early metaphysicians created an "incomprehensible" being, the driving force ("moteur") of nature, whom they called God: this abstraction was a purely spiritual or nonmaterial being. "Enfin quand, à force de subtiliser, il est parvenu à croire que le principe qui meut son corps est un *esprit*, une substance immatérielle, il fait son Dieu spirituel ou immatériel" (*Système de la nature*, 2:37, 41).

25. Dupuis, *Origine de tous les cultes*, 1:25: "Les Egyptiens, faisant du soleil le grand Dieu, architecte et modérateur du monde, expliquoient non-seulement la fable d'Osiris et d'Isis, mais toutes leur fables sacrées généralement, par les astres." See also 2:398.

importance than it deserves, Dupuis places Jesus in this succession of Asian and Mediterranean sun deities:

> What Osiris was to the Egyptians, and Bacchus to the Greeks, Adonis was to the Phoenicians; and his cult was that of the Sun-God, Lord of the Sky, worshiped under different names by different peoples. The name "Adonis," given him by the Phoenicians, is synonymous with that of "Lord." Christians, in speaking of Christ, their Sun-God, call him *Lord.* The Jews, the Phoenicians' neighbors, also had their *Adonis.* Like Apollo, beautiful Adonis shone with splendor and the graces of youth. The goddess of beauty, Venus, made him her lover and bestowed all her favors on him; and when cruel Fate cut short the life of this unfortunate young man, Venus, inconsolable, moistened his bier with her tears. In the same way Isis wept for Osiris, and Cybele for Attis; Jewish women wept for *their Christ,* and the priests of Mithras their dead and risen god.[26]

Both Volney's work and Dupuis' were well known to Coleridge, if not at first hand then certainly through the writings of Joseph Priestley and of Priestley's pupil, John Prior Estlin. Coleridge parodied Volney's argument in one of the "Lectures on Revealed Religion," referring to him ironically as a "Learned Infidel" (*Lects 1795,* 99), but his later interest in reading Dupuis shows that he did not

---

26. Ibid., 3:471–72:

> Ce qu'Osiris étoit chez les Egyptiens, Bacchus chez les Grecs, Adonis l'étoit chez les Phéniciens; et son culte étoit celui du Dieu-Soleil, seigneur du Ciel, adoré sous différens noms chez les différens peuples. Le nom d'Adonis, que lui donnoient les Phéniciens, est synonime de celui de monseigneur. Les Chrétiens, en parlant de Christ ou de leur Dieu-Soleil, l'appeloient le *seigneur.* Les Juifs, voisins de la Phénicie, avoient aussi leur *Adonis.* Comme Apollon, le bel Adonis brilloit de l'éclat et des graces de la jeunesse. La déesse de la beauté, Vénus en avoit fait son amant et lui prodignoit toutes ses faveurs; et lorsque la Parque cruelle moissonna les jours de cet infortuné, Vénus inconsolable arrosoit son cerceuil de ses larmes. Ainsi Isis pleuroit Osiris, et Cybèle son cher Atys; les femmes Juives *leur seigneur Christ*; et les prêtres de Mithra leur dieu mort et ressuscité.

Like Shelley a generation later, Dupuis suggests here a link between Hebrew "Adonai" and Phoenician/Greek "Adonis." Joseph Priestley's *Doctrines of Heathen Philosophy* makes the same association. (I am grateful to Terence Hoagwood for alerting me to this text.)

view these works with quite the abhorrence expressed by Thomas Maurice. He would have agreed with Dupuis' anticlericalism, but not his Holbachian materialism, his dismissal of all spiritual religion as a mere "chimera" (a term used also by Volney).[27] The "facts of mind" recorded by Dupuis, the fecundity of the human imagination revealed in the construction of these proliferating gods of nature, undoubtedly fascinated Coleridge. Even a Christian, especially one inclined toward an anti-Establishment, "Unitarian" faith, could respond to the sheer imaginative richness of Dupuis' account, much as a century later some Christians became excited by the dying and resurrected gods thronging the pages of James Frazer's *Golden Bough*. Dupuis even has something of Frazer's pitying contempt toward the irrationality of human behavior, as well as an enthusiasm for the wonders of nature that Frazer studiously avoids. Indeed, the underlying theme of Dupuis' work is that if "advanced" nations could only learn to love and admire nature with the simplicity and earnestness of the first ancients, we would eliminate superstition and suffering, along with the dark religions that give rise to them. Nature in this sense is the nature that the revolutionists praised, the nature that (in Condorcet's view) virtually guaranteed human progress. In the 1790s, this was a compelling vision, and poems such as "Religious Musings" and "The Destiny of Nations" make clear that Coleridge felt drawn to it, if only to the extent of wishing to offer an alternative, more Christian version.

One question that Volney, Dupuis, and the other Enlightenment mythographers raised most effectively was that of primitive belief. Just how would the earliest humans have reacted to their physical environment? Did they believe themselves mystically united to one great Universal Being, Dupuis' "L'Univers-Dieu"? Did they systematically interpret natural phenomena and the movements of heavenly bodies as signals from a realm of immortal beings, or were the super-

27. See Dupuis, *Origine de tous les cultes*, 1:288. For Coleridge's anticlericalism, see the contemptuous reference to priests in "A Moral and Political Lecture" (*Lects 1795*, 9), and a footnote to "Religious Musings": "PRIEST, a name, after which any other term of abhorrence would appear an anticlimax" (*CPW*, 1:117). D'Holbach frequently applies the word "chimère" to the gods, God, or any supernatural beings such as angels or devils; see, for example, *Système de la nature*, 1:2, 9, 2:16.

natural meanings mere falsifying accretions to what began as purely physical observations, as Condorcet suggested?[28] Did they have a concept of the infinite and the ungrounded? At what point did the concept of the immortal soul develop? These are the questions that Friedrich Creuzer was to raise in the early 1800s, with a good deal more subtlety than Dupuis,[29] but they are also implicit in Coleridge's inquiries during the 1790s into myth and early religious belief.

It is also clear that Coleridge's interest was not limited to mythographical works. The travel narratives to which Lowes traced the origin of so much that is vivid in "Kubla Khan" and "The Rime of the Ancient Mariner" also fed Coleridge's curiosity about the

28. Condorcet, like Dupuis, links the emergence of the first priestly castes to the abuse of astronomy, suggesting that early observation of the skies led the sages to name the constellations, then to record their observations in the form of stories around these names. Finally, these stories usurped their function and became the basis of superstitious religious practices:

> [Les prêtres] imposaient des noms à ces groupes d'étoiles. . . . Mais leur langage, leurs monuments, en exprimant pour eux ces opinions métaphysiques, ces vérités naturelles, offraient aux yeux du peuple le système de la plus extravagante mythologie, devenaient pour lui le fondement des croyances les plus absurdes, des cultes les plus insensés, des pratiques les plus honteuses ou les plus barbares.
> Telle est l'origine de presque toutes les religions connues. (*Esquisse,* 43)

29. Creuzer argues that men in ancient times faced the contradiction between the ideal world and the world of the senses, and that this conflict is the origin of the symbolic:

> The soul, entrapped by this contradiction and perceiving the entrapment, first sees itself transposed into a state of longing. . . . Considering the soul in this way as hovering between the world of ideas and the realm of the senses, so that it strives to join the two and to attain the finite within the infinite, how could it be otherwise than that the goal which it has aspired to and achieved while carrying the signs of its origins now reveals its double nature within its own existence? And in so doing let us clearly recognize that double origin, the essential characteristics, and equally, the elements of the symbol.
> (Die Seele, befangen in diesem Widerspruche, und ihn wahrnehmend, siehet sich mithin vorerst in den Zustand einer Sehnsucht versetzt. . . . Da mithin die Seele, so betrachtet, zwischen der Ideenwelt

mechanisms of belief and mythmaking. The leap from Dupuis, Condorcet, and Bryant to the narratives of European travelers in the New World is not so great as may first be thought. As the case of William Blake demonstrates, an intriguing and potentially fruitful relationship exists between the idea that pagan myth may contain relics of a prelapsarian revelation, and the idea that in a trance or moment of inspiration human beings may have a vision of a higher order of things, of the infinite or ungrounded. This link helps explain Coleridge's interest in states of inspiration and possession, whether among the North American Indians with their shamanistic traditions, the Obi of the West Indies, or the oracles recorded by the writers of classical Greece. It was fairly commonplace to point out parallels between ancient religious practices and contemporary shamanism: the *Essai sur la religion des anciens Grecs* begins by comparing the Pelasgians, the hunter-gatherers who were the first known inhabitants of Greece, to the aboriginal peoples of North America, and Condorcet comments indirectly and more patronizingly on the medicine men ("sorciers") among peoples fixed in earlier stages of development (19).

David Cranz, a Moravian minister, records in his *History of Greenland* some of the beliefs and spiritual practices of the aboriginal people of that country. Cranz advances something like Bryant's theory of relics of the patriarchal faith, scattered among the peoples of the earth: "Almost all heathen nations know something of Noah's Flood, and the first missionaries found also some pretty plain traditions among the Greenlanders; namely, that the world once overset, and all mankind, except one, were drowned; but some were turned into fiery spirits." Cranz notes that the Greenlanders hold a "Sun-feast" at the time of the winter solstice, and that they believe the sun and moon have "their tutelary residents, who were once men."[30] But what apparently most attracted Coleridge's attention is the description

---

und dem Gebiete der Sinne schwebet, da sie beide mit einander zu verbinden und im Endlichen das Unendliche zu erringen strebt, wie kann es anders seyn, als dass das, was sie erstrebt und errungen hat, die Zeichen seines Ursprungs an sich trage, und selbst in seinem Wesen jene Doppelnatur verrathe? Und in der That lassen uns die wesentlichen Eigenschaften, und gleichsam die Elemente des Symbols, jene doppelte Herkunft deutlich erkennen. [*Symbolik und Mythologie*, 1:56, 58]).

30. David Cranz, *The History of Greenland,* 1:204–5, 209. Coleridge quotes Cranz's book in the notes to "The Destiny of Nations" (*CPW,* 1:135).

of the initiation and oracular utterances of the Greenland shaman, or *angekok*. In Cranz's description, we already breathe some of the atmosphere and even hear the very language of "The Rime of the Ancient Mariner":

> If a Greenlander will be an *Angekok*, i.e. a sorcerer or diviner, he must procure one of the above-mentioned spirits of the elements for his *Torngak* or familiar spirit. . . . The Greenlander must retire from all mankind for a while into some solitary recess or hermitage, must spend the time in profound meditation, and call upon Torngarsuk to send him a torngak. At length, by abandoning the converse of men, by fasting and emaciating the body, and by a strenuous intenseness of thought, the man's imagination grows distracted, so that blended images of men, beasts and monsters appear before him. He readily thinks these are real spirits, because his thoughts are full of spirits, and this throws his body into great irregularities and convulsions, which he labours to cherish and augment. . . . [A]fter he has begun to sing, in which all the rest join with him, he begins to sigh and puff and foam with great perturbation and noise, and calls out for his spirit to come to him, and has often great trouble before he comes. But if the spirit is still deaf to his cries, and comes not, his soul flies away to fetch him. During this dereliction of his soul, he is quiet, but by and by he returns again with shouts of joy, nay with a certain rustling, so that a person who was several times present, assured me, that it was exactly as if he had heard several birds come flying first over the house, and afterwards into it. But if the Torngak comes voluntarily, he remains without in the entry. There our angekok discourses with him about any thing that the Greenlanders want to know. Two different voices are distinctly heard, one as without, and another as within. The answer is always dark and intricate. (1:209–11)

In this remarkable description, particularly in the self-induced trance and the two distinct voices, we have a compelling indication of the Mariner's shamanic origins and perhaps of the importance of *his* voices.[31] Moreover, remote places like Greenland were not the only source of evidence of the poets' reliance on self-induced trance. According to Bryant, there was such evidence in the very heart of classical Greece:

31. Paul Magnuson is wrong, I think, when he describes the voices of the spirits as "senseless chatter" (*Coleridge and Wordsworth: A Lyrical Dialogue*, 81). Donald P. Kaczvinsky, in "Coleridge's Polar Spirit: A Source," argues for Cranz's book as that source but does not mention the "two voices" passage.

Jamblichus takes notice of many ways, by which the gift of divination was to be obtained. *Some, says he, procure a prophetic spirit by drinking the sacred water, as is the practice of Apollo's priest at Colophon. Some by sitting over the mouth of the cavern, as the women do, who give out oracles at Delphi. Others are inspired by the vapour, which arises from the waters; as is the case of those who are priestesses at Branchidae.* He adds, *in respect to the oracles at Colophon, that the prophetic spirit was supposed to proceed from the water. The fountain, from whence it flowed, was in an apartment under ground; and the priest went thither to partake of the emanation.* . . . . The river, into which this fountain ran, was sacred, and named Halesus; it was also called Anelon; An-El-On, Fons Dei Solis. Halesus is composed of well known titles of the same God. (1:205–6)

Here, in a passage linking the prophetic spirit of the ancient oracles with the fountain, sacred river, and sun, an image cluster whose significance for the composition of "Kubla Khan" has been ably documented by John Beer, we can surely see one of the main motives for Coleridge's interest in narratives of trance and possession.[32] Like "Kubla Khan" and many other poems of the 1790s, "The Rime of the Ancient Mariner" emerges from Coleridge's concern with the validity of trance and other extraordinary mental experiences, with the justification of the poet's calling, and with finding a believable history of religious belief. In the second half of this chapter, I trace the development of the seer figure in earlier poems before examining the narrative of the Mariner himself.

"Religious Musings," with its extravagant praise of Priestley and Hartley, its abhorrence of "superstition," and its espousing of a primitive Christianity without priests, bishops, or the Trinity, may seem an unpromising place to begin; but it contains several pointers to the course of development that culminates in the Mariner. The questions "What is poetry *for?*" and "What does the poet *do?*" are answered, implicitly, by the description of the race of philosophers and bards who spread out over the world as it shakes off the grosser products of imagination. The poem describes the mode of life of the earliest humans as if the imagination were not yet awakened:

32. See *Coleridge the Visionary,* 218, 236–37. The passage I have quoted from Bryant is not cited by Beer, I believe; but the reader should bear in mind Beer's own warning about claims for the "sources" of the poem ("The Languages of *Kubla Khan,*" 225).

> In the primeval age a dateless while
> The vacant Shepherd wander'd with his flock,
> Pitching his tent where'er the green grass waved.
> (*CPW*, 1:116)

Then imagination conceived "new desires," which first led to property and thence to warriors, lords, and priests. This apparently ranks imagination on the side of reaction, among the threefold enemy of enlightened thought: war, aristocracy, and religion. But imagination, we learn, is not always to be negative in its effects: the desires conceived by imagination are a *divinely ordained* discontent, urging us on in the march of human progress. In the present age, imagination is able to rise above these temporary expedients and prophesy a new age of equality and freedom. The argument is echoed in *The Watchman*: "Providence, which has distinguished Man from the lower orders of Being by the progressiveness of his nature, forbids him to be contented. It has given us the restless faculty of *Imagination*" (*Watchman*, 131). The prophets of the new age will be poets, endowed with something like the magical powers of an Orpheus to

> tame the outrageous mass, with plastic might
> Moulding Confusion to such perfect forms,
> As erst were wont,—bright visions of the day!—
> To float before them.   (*CPW*, 1:118)

Such images of the inspired Orphic poet, frequent in Coleridge's poetry before his first meeting with Wordsworth, and often juxtaposed with images of rivers and the sea, link "Kubla Khan" and "The Rime of the Ancient Mariner" with Gray's Bard, who delivers his lament for Wales from the rock that "Frowns o'er old Conway's foaming flood." The lines Coleridge added to the 1794 version of the "Monody on the Death of Chatterton" (published with Chatterton's Rowley poems) contain a similar Romantic image, but with the added implication that poetic inspiration is a kind of trance, or madness.

> Here, far from men, amid this pathless grove,
> In solemn thought the Minstrel wont to rove
> ·
> And here, in Inspiration's eager hour,
> When most the big soul feels the mad'ning power,
>   These wilds, these caverns roaming o'er,

> Round which the screaming sea-gulls soar,
> With wild unequal steps he pass'd along.
> (CPW, 1:129–30 and n)

Coleridge's new philosopher-poets resemble Gray's and Macpherson's bards, with a strong infusion of Orphic magic, more than they resemble the tormented Ancient Mariner, but the "mad'ning power" that takes hold of the poet and lifts him up to envision the depths of the sea is very close to the shaman's power, as recorded by Cranz; and the Mariner's torments evidently draw on the picture Cranz gives of the shaman's procedures for invoking his Torngak.

In the lines Coleridge contributed to *Joan of Arc* (1796) which later formed part of "The Destiny of Nations," the shaman's trance appears as an instance of Fancy, "the power / That first unsensualises the dark mind." The shaman or "Greenland Wizard," when his people return empty-handed from their hunt and famine threatens, must travel in spirit over "an horrible abyss" into the palace of the evil spirit who lives at the bottom of the sea so that through magic he can free the sea creatures she has captured:

> Or if the Greenland Wizard in strange trance
> Pierces the untravelled realms of Ocean's bed
> Over the abysm, even to that uttermost cave
> By mis-shaped prodigies beleaguered, such
> As Earth ne'er bred, nor Air, nor the upper Sea:
> Where dwells the Fury Form.   (CPW, 1:135)

In the spirit of the syncretic mythographers, "The Destiny of Nations" asserts that such "phantasies" embody a kind of ancient pretheological wisdom, in that they teach reliance on a higher power, preparing the way for more systematic forms of religious belief. Coleridge is as knowing and superior, in his own way, as Alexander Pope, who in the "Essay on Man" described the "poor Indian" as one of "untutor'd mind" who "Sees God in clouds, or hears him in the wind"; but there is an interest in alternative possibilities here that Pope never admitted.[33]

The idea that the earliest poets could enter a state of trance, either by hypnotizing themselves through some form of chant, drum-

---

33. "Essay on Man," Epistle 1, lines 99–100 (*Poems*, 508).

ming, or other music, or by drinking intoxicating waters or inhaling volcanic vapors, was clearly more attractive to Coleridge than the more straightforward Enlightenment notion that the early poets simply described the wonders of nature. Trance and similar states suggested a reason for the prevalence of spiritual experience in accounts of religions other than Judaism and Christianity. They constituted a kind of alternative revelation, and one that by analogy might enable us to understand the biblical revelation better. Perhaps, too, they were more in keeping with the self-image of a poet who described himself in a letter as steeped in "Faery Tales, & Genii &c &c" (*CL,* 1:354). But the investigations of Dupuis and other mythographers placed in question the unknowable origins of myth and—inevitably—the credibility of *any* revelation built on miracles and the supernatural. Volney, to devastating effect, incorporated in *Les Ruines* a contest between the apologists for the various religions, showing that *every* religion can claim its miraculous portents, its history of dreams, trances, and visions, and its codes of law delivered by divine authority.[34] As earlier Enlightenment writers realized, the more resemblances were discovered between biblical narratives of prophetic afflatus or visionary trance and those "out-of-body" experiences common in other religious traditions, the more problematic were claims of special status for biblical "miracles." It was not the actual experience of divine portents or possession by spirits but the manner in which that experience was interpreted within a faith community and the vocabulary of vision, the stock of images shared by successive prophets and seers within a given culture, that became the basis for one or another religious tradition to claim supernatural experiences.

At this point, comparative mythology, through the "mythological school" of biblical critics, brought a new perspective to biblical studies and (for the believer, at any rate) made necessary a new way of understanding the authority of Scripture. Biblical revelation was no longer thought to be static and remote from history but was something (as McGann puts it) "expressed and later re-expressed through commentary, gloss, and interpretation by particular people at different times according to their different lights."[35] There can be

34. Volney, *Les Ruines,* chaps. 21 and 22 (156–217).
35. McGann, *Beauty of Inflections,* 144.

no such thing as an objective and timeless account of a miracle, a prophecy, or a conversion experience. McGann shows that already in *The Watchman* (1796) Coleridge demonstrates an acute historicist awareness of the way the text of the New Testament reflects the policies, superstitions, and cultural prejudices of the early Christian communities. He is already, that is, showing more than a passing interest in the approach to biblical studies we now associate with the term "Higher Criticism"; and his rapidly developing sense of the importance of historical, cultural factors to religious witness is (McGann persuasively argues) part of the context of "The Rime of the Ancient Mariner."

Comparative mythology lies behind "The Rime of the Ancient Mariner," as has been recognized. What has not been fully recognized, however, is that by showing superstitious belief in the very process of formation, the poem comes close to putting in question *all* extrapolations from psychic experience, including its own. We are already in a world in which apparently similar symbols recur within shifting, ambivalent codes, in which truth is not universal but is always already coded for validity within a particular belief system, and in which the same series of events can be reinterpreted (its hierarchies inverted, its sequences reversed) to support a different scheme of values. Coleridge's Mariner is of his time, for all the ostensible medievalism of the poem, precisely because he is launched into a world that appears to operate by codes he is not used to. In his passive susceptibility to the impressions borne in upon him by the sea, sky, sun, moon, stars, and wind, he resembles the primitive man postulated by Enlightenment mythographers, one without religious or cultural predisposition (despite his appeals to Jesus and Mary), responding to the activity of the elements and forming them into his narrative so as to lay the groundwork of a new mythology. Critics have been eager to discover a systematic mythmaking within the poem: a "Coleridgean" philosopheme in which the sun signifies Understanding and the moon Imagination, or a Christian parable of sin and redemption, or a depiction of "the travail of a soul passing from self-consciousness to imagination," or a symbolic exploration of the nature of love.[36]

36. Robert Penn Warren's classic essay "A Poem of Pure Imagination" proposes this reading of sun and moon. The journey from self-consciousness to imagination is suggested by Geoffrey H. Hartman, *Beyond Formalism:*

Such explanations ignore the historical debate about mythology and religious history within which the poem took shape and to which it is in some sense a response. The Mariner fits so well into the myth critics' schemes of explication because he was designed that way: he is a product of the same syncretic mythographical traditions that produced Frazer, Weston, and twentieth-century myth criticism itself. But this does not amount to saying that the poem actually initiates or reflects a mythology. If a consistent mythology could be extracted from the poem, it would probably be quite close to the *religion universelle* of Dupuis. But the image-making mechanisms of the poem are so near the surface, and the figure of the Mariner so clearly human and fallible, tormented and bewildered, a prophet without any of the pious deodorizing, the gilt embellishments, of a later hagiographic tradition, that any potential for a new mythology crumbles under careful examination.[37] In its radical indeterminacy the poem actually subverts the myths it appropriates, whether from the orthodox mythography of Bryant or the revolutionary, nature-sentiment mythography of Dupuis.

Interpreters such as Robert Penn Warren, searching for a Christian understanding of the poem, have understandably stressed the Mariner's frequent appeals to Mary and to Jesus, his recollection that the albatross was hailed as if it were a "Christian soul," the "shriving" by the hermit, and so on. Clearly, the Mariner has tried to create a redemption story out of his experiences. But this story is stretched to fit an account of the striking appearances of nature that uses language not specifically Christian, language much closer to that of the mythographers representing what they imagine to have been the simple, immediate perceptions of "early man." His unreflective

---

Literary Essays 1958–1970, 306. The suggestion that the poem is about the nature of love is mine (see *Coleridge and the Idea of Love*, 63–65).

37. Coleridge himself, trying to retrieve the poem from wrongheaded criticism and equally wrongheaded praise, wrote of his contributions to *Lyrical Ballads* (the first and most notorious of which was "The Rime"): "The excellence aimed at was to consist in the interesting of the affections by the dramatic truth of such emotions, as would naturally accompany such situations, supposing them real. And real in *this* sense they have been to every human being who, *from whatever source of delusion*, has at any time believed himself under supernatural agency" (*BL*, 2:6, emphasis added).

and even superstitious Christianity, that is, has not taken away the Mariner's "primitive" ability to mythologize. Enlightenment theorists held that (in the representative words of Priestley) "it is natural to suppose that the first words which mankind, in the early ages of the world, would invent and apply, would be names for sensible objects; as of animals, vegetables, the parts of the human body, the sun, moon, &c. because these are the things that would first occur to their observation."[38] It is not hard to see that these and similar lines from the poem both reflect such a language theory and subtly undercut it:

> "The Sun came up upon the left,
> Out of the sea came he!"

> "The Sun's rim dips; the stars rush out:
> At one stride comes the dark."

> "The upper air burst into life!
> And a hundred fire-flags sheen,
> To and fro they were hurried about!
> And to and fro, and in and out,
> The wan stars danced between."
> (CPW, 1:187, 195, 199)[39]

The problematic status of such perceptions and, even more, of the phantom appearances the Mariner reports (the Spectre Ship, the seraph band) is not part of the "staging," nor is it mere decoration. We are not dealing here with certain *events* that are *poetically narrated*: the whole point of the Mariner's narrative is the impossibility of separating event from interpretation. To experience something is to supply the metaphors necessary to represent the experience to ourselves; in other words, to mythologize it. The similarity between the Mariner's hearing two voices while he is in his "swound" and the

38. Joseph Priestley, *A Course of Lectures on the Theory of Language, and Universal Grammar*, 50.

39. Werner W. Beyer has traced the first example to a line in Wieland's *Oberon*, "Die Sonne kam, die Sonne wich" ("Coleridge, Wieland's *Oberon*, and *The Ancient Mariner*," 404). If this borrowing is admitted, it does not, I think, materially affect my argument. Beyer's larger claim is that the elemental, uninhabited landscapes of certain scenes in *Oberon* provided Coleridge with the stark imagery he needed for "The Rime."

experiences of the Greenland shaman described by Cranz indicates that the psychic basis of *all* such experiences of visionary dreaming, possession, and revelation, is dubious.

The mythographers' technique of postulating a simple, precivilization man endowed with the five senses but with no existing system of belief, in a world of startling meteorological and astronomical phenomena, is reflected in the Mariner's narrative at lines 105–6: " 'We were the first that ever burst / Into that silent sea' " (*CPW*, 1:190). Even the simple anthropomorphism suggested by the references to the sun as "he," and of lines such as " 'And now the STORM-BLAST came, and he / Was tyrannous and strong' " (*CPW*, 1:188), establishes the worldview of the Mariner and crew as primitive, according to the models of ancient man current in eighteenth-century learned discourse. When the slaying of the albatross appears to bring about the first series of torments, the ship fixed in the "silent sea" and the crew dying of thirst, another frequently postulated source of myth comes into play: " 'some in dreams assuréd were / Of the Spirit that plagued us so' " (*CPW*, 1:191). The ancients, as is clear from Cicero's *De divinatione* or even from the story in Genesis 40 of Joseph and the two servants of Pharaoh—one of whom is condemned to die after they have dreamed different dreams—held that the truth of dreams was implacable and irreversible, and this was the common ground of eighteenth-century scholarship. And like all the later "supernatural" occurrences narrated in the poem, the presence of the Spirit is vouched for by the Mariner alone on the basis of his own or others' visionary experience. It is only "in dreams" that the Spirit is revealed as the cause of the crew's sufferings. The interpretation gains extra authority, in the 1817 version, from the writer of the gloss, who invokes learned authorities (Josephus and Michael Psellus) to assure us of the Spirit's authenticity; but we should not lose sight of the built-in contingent nature of this and later supernatural manifestations. Men in the last agonies of thirst, seeing phosphorescent fires dance on the still water around them, hallucinate the presence of a vengeful spirit nine fathoms beneath the ship. The dreams, so interpreted, form the basis of the revenge plot that structures the Mariner's narrative. The plot itself, and the redemption scheme that several critics have discovered in the poem, may be a way to make sense of a given sequence of events, but we should recognize that such interpretation begins with pure conjecture. Moreover, the Mariner does not expound this sequence of events close to the time; he is retelling his tale perhaps decades later, and the reader can see in his account some of the marks of events reinterpreted to harmonize with a more comfortable theology, particularly, later in the poem, with the Wedding-Guest's more orthodox ideas and fears about ghosts and spirits. The vivid sense perceptions of earlier parts of the narrative give way to penance, angels, seraphs, and shriving. As Raimonda Modiano has shown, "After the intervention of the Wedding Guest in Part IV . . . the Mariner is increasingly tempted to find Christian equivalents in his mysteriously demonic universe."[40]

The Mariner is already singled out as the scapegoat-prophet of the ship's crew when at the beginning of Part III he looks westward—the compass point associated with death—and sees, or dreams he sees, the approaching Spectre Ship, a "sign" as the gloss calls it. The approach of the ship is in an obvious sense the approach of death. The black bones of the woman's "fleshless Pheere" (in the 1798 version) associate him with the already black lips of the thirst-tormented crew. The Nightmare Life-in-Death may be in part an evocation of Demeter in her dark, "destroyer" aspect, as Warren Stevenson has suggested: Bryant's *New System* contains a description of Demeter in an ark, as psychopomp, dicing with Rameses for the souls of the dead.[41] The dice game, in which the Nightmare Life-in-Death (according to the later interpretation added by the glossator) "wins" the Mariner, Death having to be content with the rest of the crew, is the anticipatory explanation of what follows, the shaman's prediction, halfway between a prophecy and a judge's sentence.

The Mariner's physical appearance and manner, the repeated "thus spake," his "strange power of speech" (*CPW*, 1:208), as well as his enforced solitude, fasting, "intenseness of thought," and "distracted" imagination, associate him with the ghost seer, shaman, or prophet. So do his "glittering eye," linked, as John Beer has shown,

40. Raimonda Modiano, "Words and 'Languageless' Meanings: Limits of Expression in *The Rime of the Ancient Mariner*," 52. On the "two modes of language," see 51–52.

41. Warren Stevenson, *Nimbus of Glory: A Study of Coleridge's Three Great Poems*, 79–80. The reference is to *A New System* 3:346. Demeter was often pictured as having a horse's head. However, I question Stevenson's argument that Demeter also presides over the "redemptive" part of the poem.

with hypnotic powers and the presence of quasi-magical electrical forces,[42] and his hearing the "two voices" during the "swound" caused by the sudden lurch of the ship:

> "How long in that same fit I lay,
> I have not to declare;
> But ere my living life returned,
> I heard and in my soul discerned
> Two voices in the air."
>   (*CPW*, 1:202)

We are prepared for these further hallucinatory experiences by the description of the noises of the cracking ice, in the extreme southern reach of the voyage: " 'It cracked and growled, and roared and howled, / Like noises in a swound!' " (*CPW*, 1:189). *Before* the Mariner commits his crime, that is, the noises heard in a swound may be described simply as noises. *Afterward*, a pattern is imposed on them; they become meaningful. In such a state of disordered consciousness, John Beer has suggested, "the mind might be thought to be more open to the impact of forces subsisting in the primary consciousness."[43]

The exchange between the Mariner and his hearer at the beginning of Part IV— " 'Fear not, fear not, thou Wedding-Guest! / This body dropt not down' "—reminds us that the Mariner is not a ghost, a revenant, as the Wedding-Guest fears, but a living man who has returned from extreme, out-of-body experiences to communicate his tale. Behind the moral conversion worked in the Mariner by the simple act of blessing the water snakes (not quite as Babbitt dourly put it, by admiring them) lies the pattern uncovered by the eighteenth-century mythographers' researches: primitive man endowing his fellow creatures with magical or godlike powers. The conversion is not so much pagan as prereligious, like the workings of Fancy described in "The Destiny of Nations," "peopling air" or projecting human fears and hopes on to outward things, preparing the way for superstition that in turn "[Seats] Reason on her throne"

42. See John Beer, *Coleridge's Poetic Intelligence*, 91–92, 220, and chap. 7 passim.

43. Beer compares the Mariner's trance to the conversion experience of the evangelical preacher John Newton, who experienced a state of delirium during a sea voyage. The polar voyage of the Mariner "acts as an equivalent to delirium in disordering the senses." See *Coleridge's Poetic Intelligence*, 153.

(*CPW*, 1:134). Like all the benevolent and malevolent powers that operate in the Mariner's narrative, the act of blessing comes from the dreamworld·or subconscious.

The "roaring wind" that now comes up resembles another of the trappings of the shaman, as described by Cranz. The Mariner has visited the abode of the dead, or so it seems to him: "'I thought that I had died in sleep, / And was a blesséd ghost'" (*CPW*, 1:199). He hears, or intuits, the two voices interpreting his sufferings as the vengeance of the Polar Spirit; he has been taught the crime-suffering-expiation pattern that his experiences are to take. He has no authority to declare himself saved—or damned. Although the Pilot's boy judges him to be the Devil, and the pious Hermit crosses his brow as a gesture of protection against possible evil, he remains merely *homme moyen sensuel,* not a messiah nor a devil but an ordinary man chosen from others for ultimately inexplicable reasons to suffer extraordinary events, and now, as a result, endowed with "strange power of speech."

It is interesting to note that Coleridge revised some parts of the poem to achieve greater realism—for example, cutting out the more grotesque parts of the Spectre Ship passage and even (in *Sibylline Leaves*) changing "The furrow followed free" to "The furrow stream'd off free," because the latter more accurately described the actual appearance of a ship's wake from the ship itself (*CPW*, 1:190n). He did not, however, tamper with the essential dream-experiences of the Mariner and the crew. That is, Coleridge showed no interest in rendering the Mariner's "supernatural" experiences less incredible. Wordsworth's "Peter Bell," insofar as it was to demonstrate that massive moral changes could occur in the mind of the simple man even in the absence of supernatural agency, was a little beside the point. There are no guaranteed supernatural events in "The Rime of the Ancient Mariner." There are only events dreamed, or natural phenomena interpreted, as supernatural. On the other hand, the poem does not support the contention of Volney that man's miseries can be overcome if only all peoples would study the immutable laws of Nature, and govern their behavior and social organization accordingly, harmonizing human life with universal natural law. The universe depicted in the poem is too capricious—the sun and moon each being at one moment· benign, at another moment vengeful. More than this, too much depends on the Mariner's own passions and state of mind. The sea serpents appear to him as slimy creatures, and at another time they are beautiful and blessed. The rules that govern the Mariner's reception of these impressions—if the term "rules" can be applied to any process so apparently arbitrary—have nothing to do with "natural" laws, but emerge from deep within his own psyche. Coleridge's poem certainly draws on the reports of naturalists, such as Johann Reinhold Forster, whose observations made during Cook's second voyage around the world were recounted by his son, but at the same time it attempts to rebut the claim of science to be able to provide, on its own, encyclopedic explanations: the human observer is too much part of the observation.[44]

The effect of the poem, then, is to place in question the credibility of belief systems founded on purported supernatural experience, and of French writers' appeals to "natural law" as well. Like Shelley's "Mont Blanc" a generation later, "The Rime of the Ancient Mariner" is a radically indeterminate poem about the very nature of myth that returns the reader virtually to a zero base of skepticism. This is an extraordinarily brutal and capricious universe. The element of chance introduced into the Mariner's narrative by the dice game undermines any attempt to view it as affirming a guaranteed order, either an order ensuring that crimes against nature are avenged by a tutelary spirit within nature itself, or a Christian soteriological order. The achievement of the poem is exactly that it shows the radical contingency of both these ex post facto explanations and of any others. In the words of a recent critic: "The poem raises questions about the *adequacy* of our moral categories for interpreting our place in the world."[45] The poem reflects and questions eighteenth-century models of the origin of myth and of religious belief. It

44. Arnd Bohm points out that Georg Forster, Johann's son and the author of *A Voyage Round the World,* clearly a source for "The Rime," was aware of the danger that science would amass a large body of data and have no means to make sense of it. Bohm suggests that Coleridge may have read Forster's account to see whether Forster criticized the "minute enquirers" of this sort of blinkered science. See Arnd Bohm, "Georg Forster's *A Voyage Round the World* as a Source for *The Rime of the Ancient Mariner:* A Reconsideration," 364.

45. David S. Miall, "Guilt and Death: The Predicament of *The Ancient Mariner,*" 635. The element of chance introduced by the dice game, and the ruthlessness of a universe in which two hundred men die because they

does so by placing the hypothetical primitive man of Enlightenment theory in an environment where sun, moon, wind, stars, and
other natural phenomena work on his senses and appear to form
themselves into patterns of "benevolent" and "malevolent," punitive
and redemptive action. The figure of the Mariner as primitive man
who interprets these dreams and phenomena owes much to the
conjectural "primitive man" that eighteenth-century mythographers
adopted as a model. The poem's demonstrable indebtedness to theories of the postdiluvian spread of sun worship, especially to Bryant's
New System, is essential to, but does not exhaust, its meaning. The
Mariner is a type of the seer, prophet, shaman, witch—those figures
who in all religious traditions have been the origin of mythological
systems, bringing back new visions of heaven and hell from beyond
the borders of the rational.

The poem also exemplifies the process that takes place as the
seer reenters society. The obvious agents of this process are the
Wedding-Guest, as surrogate for the reader, and the glossator, who
provides one reading of the Mariner's experiences. The glossator's
reading is not necessarily a *wrong* one, but its evident elaboration
of the raw data of the Mariner's story, ably pointed out by Kathleen
Wheeler, demonstrates the more clearly just how overdetermined
such readings are.[46]

The Wedding-Guest is singled out by the Mariner as the recipient
of his narrative: "He holds him with his skinny hand" (*CPW,* 1:187).
Like the inexplicable and somehow disturbing belief that the albatross *loved* the Mariner, conveyed to him in his "swound" by one of
the two oracular voices he hears, the sudden irruption of the gaunt,
suffering figure of the Mariner into a wedding party, singling out one
of a group of three guests to be his pupil, disciple, or victim, and—
by the end of the poem—to be a changed man, sadder and wiser,
recalls the essential *unreasonableness* of religious experience, which

---

condone the Mariner's crime, are emphasized by E. E. Bostetter in "The
Nightmare World of *The Ancient Mariner.*"

46. See Kathleen Wheeler, *The Creative Mind in Coleridge's Poetry,* 46:
"The gloss is constantly disrupting the balance and pushing the reader into
one specific response or reading." On the poem as an instance of a narrative
of "superstition" brought within the ambit of a Christian ideology, see also
McGann, *Beauty of Inflections,* 162–63.

so scandalized the fastidious taste of eighteenth-century scholars. There are reasons why the Wedding-Guest may have "deserved" to hear the Mariner's tale, but they are really beside the point: the choice of the Wedding-Guest as hearer is arbitrary, like so much else in the poem. The Mariner begins his tale not as part of a learned cosmological explanation, nor as a lesson in natural piety, but in response to the Hermit's terrified question:

> " 'Say quick,' quoth he, 'I bid thee say—
> What manner of man art thou?'
>
> Forthwith this frame of mine was wrenched
> With a woful agony,
> Which forced me to begin my tale;
> And then it left me free."
>   (CPW, 1:208)

The Mariner cannot say *who he is*, except by narrating the whole experience; and the recurrence of this seizure, not some priestly vocation nor the need to proselytize, determines when and where the tale will next be told and who its hearer will be. The response of the Wedding-Guest, who "went like one that hath been stunned / And is of sense forlorn," may be passive and irrational, but it is more true to the spirit of the narrative than that of the glossator, who comments only that the Mariner's agony forces him "to teach, by his own example, love and reverence to all things that God made and loveth" (CPW, 1:209). This reflects the Mariner's parting advice to the Wedding-Guest, that prayer is the best response to a loving God: "He prayeth best, who loveth best."

Many readers (myself included) have made the mistake of reading this line through the distorting lens of the gloss and, even more, of nineteenth-century sentimentality, as if it were a lapse into the sententiousness of a needlework sampler. This is to overlook what the line implicitly repudiates, however, which is the kind of religious orthodoxy that instructs the believer to love only God. In the dialectic marked out by Dupuis' and Bryant's readings of myth, it is actually closer to the stance of a Dupuis, since it proposes that religious feeling is more properly directed toward the visible, natural world than to an invisible deity, and that without love of the visible world, prayer is actually insincere. For a Christian interpreter, this is alarmingly close to the sentiments of the French philosophes d'Holbach and Condorcet. On the other hand, however, the Mariner is far from proselytizing on behalf of a new "religion of nature." He is the bearer not of a theological doctrine but of a mere tale, though one that challenges established systems of thought. It is clearly not the moralizing stanzas that stun and bewilder the Wedding-Guest, but the tale itself, which places in question the strategies and evasions of such interpretations.

By raising so bluntly, through its very inaccessibility and later deft use of an explanatory gloss that explains nothing, the whole issue of how experiences of trance, vision, hallucination, and speaking in tongues are tamed, contextualized, interpreted, and so brought within the safe ambit of human institutions, "The Rime" puts myth back at the center of literature for the English Romantics. It also initiates a new style of *reading*, asking of its readers a new awareness of the process of interpretation itself. Its ostentatiously anachronistic, antirational form, the traditional ballad as preserved by Bishop Percy, is only the most overt sign of its imperviousness to rational questioning. This fact alone puts it in a category quite different from Blake's myth, which for all its apparent eccentricity is fundamentally reasonable, normative, humanistic. In the last few years of the eighteenth century, Romanticism, at least as personified in the mind of S. T. Coleridge, pushes forward to new territory, where inward experience is seen to be inaccessible, untranslatable, finally incommunicable, and the reader has to ask not "What reflection of truth can I find here?" but "What structure of thought can I devise that will enable me to interrogate this work?"

Two

Imaginative Animism in Wordsworth's 1798–1799 *Prelude*

For considerably more than a decade, a composite text of Words-worth's autobiographical recollections largely written in the years 1798–1799 has been widely available to readers, first in an edition published in 1977 by Cornell University Press and then in the Norton Anthology and the Norton Critical edition of *The Prelude*. Since these verses are readily identifiable as early drafts of sections of *The Prelude*, they have become known, with good reason, as "the Two-Part *Prelude*."

Many critics have attended to the relationship between this "version" and the later versions of 1804, 1805, and 1850, although disagreement persists about the status of the 1798–1799 text—is it legitimate to regard it as "a poem" or a "version" at all, for instance, since Wordsworth obviously never sanctioned its publication? My intention is to track in some detail instances of the reception of myth in Romantic poetry, however, and evaluative criticism is not a principal aim, so the legitimacy of regarding the Two-Part *Prelude* as a poem in its own right need not directly concern us here. Rather, in this chapter I suggest that the emphasis critics have placed on the 1798–1799 text as ancestor or precursor of the later versions has tended to obscure its contemporaneity. By this I mean in particular the extent to which, besides being an early "version" of *The Prelude*, the 1798–1799 text is a good example of late-eighteenth-century descriptive and reflective verse, "mythological" in the sense that its landscape is peopled with spirits and genii in the manner of Thomson, Akenside, Collins, and Burns, a literary mode that Northrop

Frye has designated "imaginative animism."[1] Its actual contemporary context, in other words, is not the 1805 *Prelude*, still less the 1850, but other poetry of the "age of sensibility," including Wordsworth's own "An Evening Walk" (1793).

The neglect of what I have called the contemporaneity of the 1798–1799 *Prelude* perpetuates what is arguably a false or misleading characterization of Wordsworth's imaginative animism as a sign of his poetic immaturity, even as a mere stylistic quirk, soon to be thrown off as the real Wordsworth emerged. But these verses are not only chronologically, but stylistically, as close to the language of "An Evening Walk"—which no less a critic than Coleridge admired, albeit with reservations—as they are to the 1805 *Prelude*. Until we learn to read them as an eighteenth-century text, a work of the "age of sensibility," as well as the ancestor of the 1850 *Prelude*, we shall not do them justice. More important, reading the extensive use of imaginative animism as a legitimate and not "un-Wordsworthian" literary mode of the period (the 1790s) will give us a much better understanding of Wordsworth's early attitude to local myth and folklore—which remains positive and generous, even as he gradually abandons his sympathy with it in favor of a more philosophical explanation of nature's powers in the 1805 and 1850 versions.

In considering the languages of *The Prelude*, therefore, I do not intend to argue for the superiority or inferiority of the Two-Part *Prelude* to any of the later versions—the five-book "1804," the thirteen-book "1805," or the fourteen-book "1850" version. In any case, criticism seems now to be advancing beyond debate about the relative merits of the three or four main versions. My analysis is, rather, in the spirit of Thomas McFarland's suggestion that the meaning of *The Prelude* is in the "tension" between its different versions, and John

---

1. One might object here that the use of imaginative animism in *The Prelude* is not, strictly speaking, "work on myth," because no actual identifiable narrative is involved. Although Wordsworth does not transmit to us a complete, traditional north-country narrative about genii or spirits, he is certainly drawing on memories of those narratives, and such borrowings are an example of the way he "works on" myth, precisely by fragmenting and decontextualizing its narrative elements. Such narratives would also fulfill the requirement that they have to do with "the inner nature of the universe and of human life." (See Wheelwright's proposed definition of myth, cited in my Introduction.)

Beer's remark that *The Prelude* is *"in itself* a process, embodying, in its various texts, stages in Wordsworth's interpretation of his own experience."[2]

To speak of "development" or of "stages" at all, perhaps, is to suggest an inherent value judgment. What comes later in any developmental process, we tend to assume, must be superior to earlier attempts. There are good reasons why many critics have preferred the 1850 *Prelude,* but the merits of "1805" have been proclaimed with equal fervor, and there is a respectable and growing list of admirers of "1798–1799." Those who prefer the fourteen-book *Prelude* often use such terms as "polish" and "maturity" while those who defend the earlier versions find in them greater "authenticity," "vividness," "verve," and so on. Avoiding such judgments for the moment, I examine the language and imagery of some passages in the 1798–1799 *Prelude,* as well as some revisions Wordsworth made in the 1805 and 1850 versions, without necessarily claiming "authenticity" for the early version or "maturity" for the later.

The reader who comes to the Two-Part *Prelude* expecting to find the evolutionary ancestor of the 1805 or 1850 text is in for a shock. This is altogether a darker, bleaker, and more mysterious poetic environment. Yet it would be quite wrong to say that the great narrative theme of the later versions—what M. H. Abrams has called the "secular theodicy," which is most explicit in the fourteen-book *Prelude*—is absent from the 1798–1799 version.[3] What is remarkable is that the argument about "God," "Nature," and "Mind," which by 1850 became the unifying theme and manifest *raison d'être* of the whole work, is in 1798–1799 much less integrated with the narrative. It is confined, in fact, to Part 2 of the 1798–1799 text and really

2. Thomas McFarland, *Romanticism and the Forms of Ruin: Wordsworth, Coleridge, and Modalities of Fragmentation,* 237; John Beer, *Wordsworth and the Human Heart,* 91. On the development of *The Prelude* and the status of the 1798–1799 version, see Jack Stillinger, "Textual Primitivism and the Editing of Wordsworth"; Kenneth Johnston, *Wordsworth and The Recluse,* 53–78, 105, 119; Stephen Gill, "Wordsworth's Poems: The Question of Text," 188–90; Stuart Peterfreund, *"The Prelude:* Wordsworth's Metamorphic Epic"; and Jonathan Wordsworth and Stephen Gill, "The Two-Part Prelude of 1798–99."

3. M. H. Abrams, *Natural Supernaturalism: Tradition and Revolution in Romantic Literature,* 95.

becomes explicit only in the last two hundred lines of the poem (lines 310–514 of the "reading text" established by Stephen Parrish).[4] As Jonathan Wordsworth puts it, Part 1 "stands—and stands perfectly well—with no discussion of first principles."[5]

Conversely, the folkloric or "pagan" imagery that survives in only one or two passages of the fourteen-book *Prelude*—1.464-66 and 12.9-31, for instance—is everywhere in the 1798-1799 version, especially in the first part. De Selincourt and Darbishire's edition of the 1805 and 1850 texts contains the following remarks, which are misleading, I think, because they fail to take account of the fact that literary conventions of the time would have given a certain legitimacy to the invocation of folkloric beliefs in reflective and descriptive poetry:

> It is interesting to notice that when Wordsworth began to write *The Prelude* he still delighted to conceive of Nature not merely as the expression of one divine spirit, but as in its several parts animated by individual spirits who had, like human beings, an independent life and power of action. This was obviously his firm belief in the primitive paganism of his boyhood . . . ; and long after he had given up definite belief in it, he cherished it as more than mere poetic fancy. The passages which illustrate this are chiefly found in the readings of MS V. . . . But though the "Spirits of air" reappear in the D text of [12.9-12], he would doubtless have regarded them, at that time, as merely "a pretty piece of Paganism." (*WPrelude*, 517)

More recent critics (Stephen Gill, Kenneth Johnston, Jonathan Wordsworth) have continued to disparage the "primitive paganism" of the early manuscripts as somehow unworthy of the epic task the poet had undertaken. The de Selincourt–Darbishire note represents the "pagan" elements of *The Prelude* as a relic of boyhood, "cherished" as more than poetic fancy perhaps, but still viewed by

---

4. Quotations from the Two-Part *Prelude* are from *The Prelude, 1798–1799*, ed. Stephen Parrish (cited as *WPrel 1799*), using, except where otherwise indicated, Parrish's "reading text" based on Dove Cottage MSS U and V. These fair copies of the poem are in the hands of, respectively, Mary Hutchinson and Dorothy Wordsworth. See the editor's "Preface" and "Introduction," vii–ix, 3–36, for essential information on the history of the manuscripts and the editorial principles involved in establishing the "reading text."

5. Jonathan Wordsworth, *William Wordsworth: The Borders of Vision*, 74.

Wordsworth as a way station on the road to mature poetic capability. Kenneth Johnston is only slightly less scathing, referring to the spirits of Nature in the Two-Part *Prelude* as "conventional," "fairylike," and "patently artificial."[6]

Reading the Two-Part *Prelude* without these critics' developmental expectations, however, one is struck by the predominance of such primitivist modes of expression, as if they—and not a philosophical argument—were the thread that unifies the drafts into a single narrative. It is hard to resist the conclusion that the animism of the early versions of *The Prelude* has been judged, anachronistically and unfairly, by Coleridgean standards of what constitutes truly imaginative poetry—dismissed, that is, as "poor stuff." Coleridge, as is well known, objected strenuously to the Greek poets' habit of endowing natural objects with tutelary spirits, and contrasted their polytheistic style with the "genuine Imagination" displayed in Hebrew poetry:

> The Greeks in their religious poems address always the Numina Loci, the Genii, the Dryads, the Naiads, &c &c—All natural Objects were *dead*—mere hollow Statues—but there was a Godkin or Goddessling *included* in each—In the Hebrew Poetry you find nothing of this poor Stuff—as poor in genuine Imagination, as it is mean in Intellect— / At best, it is but Fancy, or the aggregating Faculty of the mind—not *Imagination*, or the *modifying*, and *co-adunating* Faculty. (*CL*, 2:865–66)

Since the theme of the "growth of the poet's mind" is already present and articulated in the Two-Part *Prelude*, and many of the interventions and visitations credited to "Nature" in the later versions are ascribed to the spirits, genii, and other pagan beings in the 1798–1799 version, it looks as if more is involved here than Wordsworth "delight[ing] to conceive of Nature as . . . animated by individual spirits." Wordsworth himself, describing the Pedlar's boyhood, hints that those supernatural beings who "peopled" the dark northern woods were the reason for the Pedlar's relative independence from books as a source of imaginative stimulation:

> for many a Tale
> Traditionary round the mountains hung;
> And many a legend, peopling the dark woods,

6. Kenneth Johnston, "Wordsworth and *The Recluse*: The University of Imagination," 62; *Wordsworth and* The Recluse, 56.

Nourish'd Imagination in her growth
And gave the mind that apprehensive power
By which she is made quick to recognise
The moral properties and scope of things.[7]

In expanding the story of the Pedlar to its form in *The Excursion,*
Wordsworth intended to work out just how a preternaturally quick
and unruly imagination is brought to the point where it can communicate with other minds, even perform a useful social function.
At the same time, the poet is reluctant to abandon the authority
implicit in his claim to possess extraordinary gifts. This passage from
The Excursion, then, may be an important clue to the role played
by "traditionary tales" of spirits and genii in the early versions of
The Prelude.

In an essay first published in 1956, Northrop Frye proposed a
theory of the literature of sensibility which can help us to understand Wordsworth's adoption of imaginative animism in these early
drafts of *The Prelude.* Frye notes in the work of Collins, Fergusson,
Burns, and the Wartons "an imaginative sympathy with the kind
of folklore that peoples the countryside with elemental spirits." The
value of such imaginative animism, Frye suggests, is that it maintains
a certain level of emotional involvement on the reader's part, and
he connects this literary use of animism with that "concentration
on the process of writing" that was characteristic of the "age of
sensibility," when maintaining a reader's empathy with the author
took precedence over creating a perfected aesthetic object.[8]

For an instance of animism used in this way, that is, adopted in a
self-conscious way as a means of making contact with the reader on
an emotional level, we might turn to Collins's "Ode on the Popular
Superstitions of the Highlands of Scotland, Considered as the Subject of Poetry," addressed to the Scottish author John Home. The
ode was written in 1749 and first appeared in print in 1788.

There must thou wake perforce thy Doric quill,
    'Tis Fancy's land to which thou sett'st thy feet;
    Where still, 'tis said, the fairy people meet

7. "The Pedlar," MS E, in *The Ruined Cottage and The Pedlar,* ed. James
Butler, 396; cf. *Excursion,* 1.163–69 (*WPW,* 5:13).
8. Northrop Frye, "Towards Defining an Age of Sensibility," 150.

Beneath each birken shade on mead or hill.
. . . .
'Tis thine to sing how, framing hideous spells,
   In Skye's lone isle the gifted wizard seer,
   Lodged in the wintry cave with
Or in the depth of Uist's dark forests dwells;
How they, whose sight such dreary dreams engross,
   With their own visions oft astonished droop,
When o'er the watery strath or quaggy moss
   They see the gliding ghosts unbodied troop.[9]

Collins's "Ode" was unquestionably known to the young Wordsworth, for there are several references to it in the notebook shared by William and Christopher Wordsworth (reprinted by Z. S. Fink in *The Early Wordsworthian Milieu*).[10] Fink also cites (36), as likely sources of Wordsworth's evocations of the spirits in "An Evening Walk," Milton's *Paradise Lost*, 4.680–88; Beattie's *The Minstrel*, book 1, stanzas 35–36; and the following lines from Thomson's *The Seasons*:

Here, frequent, at the visionary hour,
When musing midnight reigns on silent noon,
Angelic harps are in full concert heard,
And voices chaunting from the wood-crown'd hill,
The deepening dale, or inmost sylvan glade.
           ("Summer," lines 556–60)[11]

Early in his poetic career, as Fink points out, Wordsworth may well have shared folkloric beliefs similar to those referred to by Thomson, Akenside, Collins, and Beattie, and taken pleasure in remembering Lake District traditions that resembled those mentioned by his favorite poets. When he invokes the genial spirits of a place, as he does in lines 325–58 of "An Evening Walk" (1793 version), Wordsworth is thus following a well-established literary tradition, enlivening his descriptions of the northern landscape by drawing on tales of supernatural beings dwelling among the hills and "fairy holms"; but he is

9. *The Poems of Thomas Gray, William Collins, Oliver Goldsmith*, 503, 505–6. The line "Lodged in the wintry cave with" is printed as in Lonsdale's text, and is apparently incomplete.

10. See Z. S. Fink, *The Early Wordsworthian Milieu*, 88, 98, 101, 135.

11. On Wordsworth's indebtedness to Collins, see also Mary Jacobus, *Tradition and Experiment in Wordsworth's Lyrical Ballads* (1798), 88–90.

also claiming a certain role as a Cumbrian poet, recording some of the folklore of his own region.

The whole passage modulates skillfully—in a style that owes much to Thomson and Collins—from the "far-off minstrels of the haunted hill," who "Tune in the mountain dells their water lyres," via a Spenserian allusion (the fading light of evening is compared to "Una shining on her gloomy way"), to this piece of animated picture-making:

> —'Mid the dark steeps repose the shadowy streams,
> As touch'd with dawning moonlight's hoary gleams,
> Long streaks of fairy light the wave illume
> With bordering lines of intervening gloom,
> Soft o'er the surface creep the lustres pale
> Tracking with silvering path the changeful gale.
> —'Tis restless magic all; at once the bright
> Breaks on the shade, the shade upon the light,
> Fair Spirits are abroad; in sportive chase
> Brushing with lucid wands the water's face,
> While music stealing round the glimmering deeps
> Charms the tall circle of th'enchanted steeps.
> —As thro' th'astonish'd woods the notes ascend,
> The mountain streams their rising song suspend;
> Below Eve's listening Star the sheep walk stills
> It's drowsy tinklings on th'attentive hills;
> The milkmaid stops her ballad, and her pail
> Stays it's low murmur in th'unbreathing vale;
> No night-duck clamours for his wilder'd mate,
> Aw'd, while below the Genii hold their state.
>
> (*WPW*, 1:31–32)

In this kind of writing, the question of belief hardly arises. The poet in no way affirms his own belief in the genii and spirits; after all, he is clearly identified on the title page of the 1793 quarto as "W. Wordsworth, B.A., of St. John's, Cambridge," a designation that seems to present him as one educated beyond the point of continuing to entertain boyhood folk beliefs. Rather, the genii and spirits are introduced in such a way as to invite the reader to imagine how the landscape *might* be experienced *if* he or she believed in them. They play a role comparable to the one given them in Dorothy Wordsworth's Grasmere journal, where she records that the waves on the lake were "like a dance of spirits that rose out of the water," or that a tree by the lake was "like a Spirit of water."[12] In "An Evening Walk," as in the journal entries, there is an implied sense that romantic landscape itself stimulates such beliefs. This directly connects the reader's sophisticated pleasure in "playing at" superstition with the middle-class discovery of the picturesque, in which the cultivated observer enjoys the landscape without having to make a real moral, emotional, or material commitment to it. As with other manifestations of the sensibility movement, this taste for "playing at" superstition has a certain "democratic" (or at least anti-aristocratic and anticlassical) element to it, though criticism should not ignore the element of patronage shown toward rural society by the university-educated, city-dwelling writers and readers who took up the beliefs of country people as a source of aesthetic pleasure, with no real cost attached, as some tourists would admire rural scenery from the comfort of their carriages. Raymond Williams has shown how in this period mountains and forests became, for those who could afford to tour them, "objects of conspicuous aesthetic consumption: to have been to the named places, to exchange and compare the travelling and gazing experiences, was a form of fashionable society."[13]

It is true that the role of the sophisticate dabbling in local folklore is strangely at odds with the poetic voice in the opening lines of "An Evening Walk." Personification and vaguely classicizing diction hardly prepare us for the later appearance of apparitions and other local phenomena. In the first hundred lines of the poem, the poet's youth is surrounded by such readily recognizable figures as Mirth, Transport, Life, Impatience, Reflexion, Content, Memory, and Quiet: "link'd with thoughtless Mirth I cours'd the plain," "Memory at my side, I wander here," "Quiet led me up the huddling rill," and so on (lines 31, 43, 71; WPW, 1:6, 8). Even the swans—later to play such an important role in "Home at Grasmere"—are here decorously attended by the appropriate baroque minor deities, "tender Cares and mild domestic Loves" (line 207; WPW, 1:22). From this baroque decoration and the rather different ghostly horsemen, the subject of local superstition (lines 175–90), we move to a more

12. Dorothy Wordsworth, *Grasmere Journals*, entries for June 2, 1800, and November 24, 1801.
13. Raymond Williams, *The Country and the City*, 160.

animistic imagery as "The far-off minstrels of the haunted hill," the "Fair Spirits" and the Genii, make their appearance.

The fact that these visions instantly disappear like the spirit procession conjured up by Prospero ("No wrack of all the pageant scene remains," line 360) and are followed by a moralizing couplet about the transience of human pleasures, warns the educated reader against taking them too literally; yet while they enjoy a brief permitted imaginary existence, the visions animate the landscape and invite the reader's emotional involvement in it. The magic is clearly a flourish of artistic skill and not what the shepherds and milkmaids of Grasmere would mean by "magic," but the pleasure aimed at is the reader's participation in imagining the landscape animated by spirits as if belief were possible. The surface of the lake does not merely ripple and shine but is brushed by magic wands; the cliffs are enchanted, the woods astonish'd.

The major difference between this use of the genii and spirits and the use made of them in the 1798–1799 *Prelude* lies precisely in the kinds of belief invoked. It is not that the 1798–1799 *Prelude* demands that the reader believe in spirits, nor even that the later work goes far beyond the conventional in its evocation of polytheistic beings and presences. What the later work does ask of us is just that we believe that the narrator, as a boy, believed in supernatural beings. That is, the reader is not merely invited to flirt with imaginative animism, as in "An Evening Walk"; rather, it becomes the agent of the poet's own perceptions and youthful development. Imaginative animism is reworked to become part of the poet's own myth, and therefore demands far more of the reader's imaginative response as part of a total response to the poet's representation of his own earlier self. Unlike the pleasing holiday-tour glimpses of folk beliefs in the Collins poem and in "An Evening Walk," which are in some sense presented for the reader's pleasure like those mountain scenes that had already become (in Raymond Williams's phrase) "objects of conspicuous aesthetic consumption," the imaginative animism of the *Prelude* raises in the critical reader's mind a question about whether the perceptions and imaginings of even the most highly educated literary intelligence are not in some sense derivative from his or her early social environment, including those toys of the sophisticated middle-class reader, folk beliefs and "superstitions." This is the radicalism of the early versions of the

Prelude: that it forces a revaluation of what is important in education and personal development, and, by implication, it asks what value can attach to the beliefs of a man's childhood (and of the rural society in which he spent that childhood) when they come to be viewed through the distancing lens of a sophisticated literary medium.

In the Two-Part *Prelude*, then, what is at stake in the first instance is not a philosophic description of the universe but the analysis of the poet's own imaginative development. The literary version of the widespread country belief that the night landscape is haunted by supernatural beings is combined with another tradition of the "age of sensibility," that of locating the source of poetic inspiration in the utter solitude of a remote wilderness, as in the following lines by Joseph Warton, addressed to Fancy:

> Say, in what deep and pathless vale,
> Or on what hoary mountain's side,
> 'Midst falls of water you reside,
> 'Midst broken rocks, a rugged scene,
> With green and grassy dales between,
> 'Midst forests dark of aged oak,
> Ne'er echoing with the woodman's stroke,
> Where never human art appear'd,
> Nor ev'n one straw-rooft cott was rear'd,
> Where NATURE seems to sit alone,
> Majestic on a craggy throne.[14]

In developing this idea of seeking Fancy, or poetic inspiration, among such secluded natural spots, Wordsworth in the Two-Part *Prelude* clearly goes far beyond earlier poets' reassessment of folkloric tradition as a subject for poetry, and his own topographical use of imaginative animism in "An Evening Walk." It is especially noteworthy that the "Powers," "Genii," and "Familiars" apostrophized in the Two-Part *Prelude* are credited not only with the educative process that forms the theme of all versions of *The Prelude* but also with the authorization of poetic language. Wordsworth ascribes to animistic spirits and powers the initiating, exemplary act of making caves, trees, hills, and woods stand for, figure forth, the feelings he experienced.

14. Joseph Warton, *Odes on Various Subjects* (1746), 6–7.

Ye Powers of earth! ye Genii of the springs!
And ye that have your voices in the clouds
And ye that are Familiars of the lakes
And of the standing pools, I may not think
A vulgar hope was yours when ye employed
Such ministry, when ye through many a year
Thus by the agency of boyish sports
On caves and trees, upon the woods and hills,
Impressed upon all forms the characters
Of danger or desire, and thus did make
The surface of the universal earth
With meanings of delight, of hope and fear,
Work like a sea.
                    (*WPrel 1799*, Part 1, lines 186–98)

The point here is not so much that Wordsworth explicitly apos-
trophizes "pagan" or animistic powers as if he literally believed in
their existence. Rather, I want to stress that the powers and genii,
through their "voices," and their ability to "[Impress] upon all forms
the characters / Of danger or desire," to make the earth vivid with
"meanings of delight, of hope and fear," are made to seem the forces
that authorize Wordsworth's narrative, by providing him with the
necessary models of writing. In later versions of *The Prelude* the
reciprocity of mind and nature (familiar to us from "Tintern Abbey"
and "There Was a Boy") will again take the form of a specifically
linguistic transference, as J. Douglas Kneale shows. The authority
Wordsworth seeks is ascribed to the "written" as well as to the "spoken" language of Nature, to Nature's "characters" as well as to her
"voices." "Wordsworth transfers these two forms of human language
to nature," writes Kneale, "and then receives them again, as though
nature were linguistically prior."[15] The impact of these forces is
explicitly linguistic and textual. "Characters"—conjoined as the word

15. J. Douglas Kneale, "Wordsworth's Images of Language: Voice and
Letter in *The Prelude*," 352. Kneale discusses only the 1805 and 1850 versions, however. Bradford K. Mudge makes the more general argument that
"for the romantics in general and Wordsworth in particular, the generation
of meaning or self-expression initially involves problems of origination and
authority, as signification—whether transcendental or not—seeks first a
substantiating source, a pre-linguistic 'signified,' and then a legitimizing
articulatory power, an authorizing will." Mudge refers to this "source" as an

is with the verb "impressed"—suggests not the emotional colorings of a vague mood but the textuality with which the genii and familiars invest the "surface" of earth, enabling the boy Wordsworth, in the pauses of his "boyish sports," to decipher or "read" the "meanings" of his various passions. (In a similar way, the Pedlar can "read / Unutterable love" in the silent faces of the clouds, and in the mountains can "see the writing" that expresses his religious faith [MS B, *The Ruined Cottage and The Pedlar*, 157, 159]).

In the 1805 version, interestingly, two key words—"voices" and "meanings"—have already been eliminated: only "impress'd" and "character" remain.

> Ye Presences of Nature, in the sky
> Or on the earth! Ye Visions of the hills!
> And Souls of lonely places! can I think
> A vulgar hope was yours when Ye employ'd
> Such ministry, when Ye through many a year
> Haunting me thus among my boyish sports,
> On caves and trees, upon the woods and hills,
> Impress'd upon all forms the characters
> Of danger or desire, and thus did make
> The surface of the universal earth
> With triumph, and delight, and hope, and fear,
> Work like a sea?   (1.490–501)

As in the early manuscript version of "Nutting," then, the animistic spirits do not merely embellish but in some sense authorize the narrative. This assertion cannot rest on one isolated passage, however. The effect is cumulative. Invocations of the mysterious pagan presences occur frequently enough in the Two-Part *Prelude* to provide a general context for the narrative episodes, and frequently these apostrophes to polytheistic spirits give a different sense to passages that in later versions are introduced by apostrophes to Nature, or to a single deity such as the "Spirit of the Universe." In such a context, the "strange utterance" of the wind blowing through the young boy's ears as he hangs perilously on a rock face (*WPrel 1799*, 1.64), the "voice / Of mountain-echoes" that accompanies his

---

"Ur-poetry" ("Song of Himself: Crisis and Selection in *The Prelude*, books 1 and 7," 3).

excursion in the stolen boat (lines 91–92), the "murmurs" and the "voice" of the River Derwent flowing by his parents' home (lines 3, 5), and "The ghostly language of the ancient earth" heard as the boy shelters from the storm under some jutting rock (2.358—earlier in a description of the Pedlar), seem part of a total environment, not merely an eerie moment, as is the case in Thomson's line, quoted above: "And voices chaunting from the wood-crown'd hill." The fact that the lines about the "ghostly language" are from an earlier fragment about the Pedlar perhaps indicates that Wordsworth associated growth in mental powers with the general ability to receive or project the "language," to ascribe significance to natural sounds. The poet seems to absorb the language spoken to him and *for* him by the very close and vividly conceived company of gods and spirits. As Kneale has it, *"In the language of Wordsworth the sound of waters tends to the image of voice,"* and such a voice not only "haunts" Wordsworth, Kneale suggests, but in some sense "usurps" his own, human voice (354).[16] The boy who "stood alone, / A naked Savage in the thunder shower" is presented as a young shaman, his body stripped for a closer experience of the power of spirits. (Wordsworth seemed fond of the image, as he repeated it in "Stanzas Written in My Pocket-Copy of Thomson's *Castle of Indolence*.") Though the image is still present in "1805," it is considerably weakened. The arresting statement, "[I] stood alone, / A naked Savage," becomes

> [I] stood alone
> Beneath the sky, as if I had been born
> On Indian Plains, and from my Mother's hut
> Had run abroad in wantonness, to sport,
> A naked Savage, in the thunder shower.
> (1.300–304)

The narrator of 1798–1799 represents such moments as raw contacts with elemental spirits, and finds in them sources of visionary power,

16. Kneale's emphasis: he is troping Hartman. In the Lucy poems, I argue in Chapter 3, it becomes necessary for Wordsworth to circumscribe and delimit his own human voice against this "usurping" voice from Nature. On the "ghostly language" passage, see also Magnuson, *Coleridge and Wordsworth*, 224–26.

and not just pretty fantasies of childhood. This is made explicit in Part 2:

> I would stand
> Beneath some rock listening to sounds that are
> The ghostly language of the ancient earth
> Or make their dim abode in distant winds.
> Thence did I drink the visionary power. (2.356–60)

Still more significantly, the passages in the Two-Part *Prelude* that anticipate the developmental argument of the thirteen-book and fourteen-book versions were evidently conceived in a similar vein, as tributes to the powers of the "spirits." The key passage is this:

> The mind of man is fashioned and built up
> Even as a strain of music: I believe
> That there are spirits, which, when they would form
> A favored being, from his very dawn
> Of infancy do open out the clouds
> As at the touch of lightning, seeking him
> With gentle visitation; quiet Powers!
> Retired and seldom recognized, yet kind,
> And to the very meanest not unknown;
> With me, though rarely, [in my early days]
> They communed: others too there are who use,
> Yet haply aiming at the self-same end,
> Severer interventions, ministry
> More palpable, and of their school was I.
> (*WPrel* 1799, 1.67–80; cf. MS V transcript, 233, 235)

Wordsworth appears to mean something quite specific by "of their school was I"—that as a boy he was peculiarly subject to the visitations of these severer powers; that he seemed to have been *singled out* by the spirits responsible for inducing feelings of terror and awe. The observation seems to mark his special affiliation to these powers. The musical analogy at the beginning of this passage also links the theme that is to achieve such importance in Part 2, the growth of the poet's mind, with the primitive music of such manifestations of nature as the wind, the mountain echoes, and the murmurs of the river. The spirits "form" their favored being much as a musician composes a melody, combining a variety of tones and timbres, harmony and discord. (The effect of the 1805 version, which replaces "spirits" with

"Nature" and "of their school was I" with "and so she dealt with me,"
is quite different.)

The language of imaginative animism here does more than maintain the reader's emotional involvement with the moods of the author (the role Frye ascribes to imaginative animism in the work of
Collins and the Wartons). Since the writing of "An Evening Walk,"
Wordsworth has learned that to use the technique of imaginative
animism in this way may involve the reader with the subjectivity of
a momentary perceptual experience, the truth of feeling, but could
not initiate him or her into the real subject matter the Two-Part
Prelude was beginning to propose for itself—the earliest origins of a
poetic sensibility and the growth of the poet's mind. Wordsworth's
spirits, familiars, presences, and genii do not merely appear on cue,
as it were, to spook the reader. They are represented as having transformed the appearances of Nature into a text in which the young boy,
under their tutelage, read "meanings of delight, of hope and fear."
They are also represented as having governed the boy's intellectual
and emotional growth, interpreting and linking his strongest passions
with the "beautiful and permanent forms of nature" (WPW, 2:387).
The very fact that both "The Pedlar" and later versions of *The Prelude*
ascribe this function to Nature or to the Spirit of the Universe
suggests how important was the discovery of the function itself, and
how well the language of imaginative animism served Wordsworth's
own myth of the growth of his poetic power.

This theme—the claim that the gentle visitations of the quiet
powers, and the "severer interventions" of the "ministry of fear,"
influenced the young boy's mind and developed in it the capacity to
contemplate powers beyond those immediately apparent in nature—
is the thread that links the several episodes of Part 1. The passage
just quoted leads into the narrative of the boat-stealing, which in
the 1798–1799 version begins "They guided me: one evening, led
by them, / I went alone into a Shepherd's boat," changed in the
1805 version to "One evening (surely I was led by her) / I went alone
into a Shepherd's Boat" (1.372–73), and in "1850" to "One summer
evening (led by her) I found / A little boat tied to a willow tree"
(1.357–58). Successive versions direct the reader's interest more and
more toward the story itself. But in the process, the intervention of
nature's powers is lessened in prominence until it is summarized in
the matter-of-fact syllables "led by her." More is at issue here than

tidying verbose language. The revisions involve and perhaps result from a reinterpretation of the significance of the episode.

In "1805," Wordsworth adds seven lines to the first part of the description, scrupulously naming the precise location (Patterdale), the occasion (he has gone on a ramble from the village inn during school holidays), and the act of theft itself: "I unloos'd her tether and embark'd" (1.382). "1850" drops these lines, but substitutes others, still mentioning the theft: "Straight I unloosed her chain, and stepping in / Pushed from the shore" (1.360–61). In contrast, "1798–1799" has a dreamlike quality, as if the act were truly compelled, as if it had happened before the boy realized it:

> They guided me: one evening, led by them,
> I went alone into a Shepherd's boat,
> A skiff that to a willow-tree was tied
> Within a rocky cave, its usual home;
> The moon was up, the lake was shining clear
> Among the hoary mountains: from the shore
> I pushed, and struck the oars, and struck again
> In cadence, and my little Boat moved on
> Just like a man who walks with stately step
> Though bent on speed. (WPrel 1799, 1.81–90)

There is here much less of a sense that the boy has committed a theft, but still, as the boy rows across the lake, a "huge Cliff" lifts its head from behind the top of the ridge on which he has fixed his gaze, and follows him as he rows. As in "Nutting," the transgression lies more in the fact that he seems to be tempting the spirits of the place, pretending to be someone he is not. This surely is the meaning of the lines "It was an act of stealth / And troubled pleasure; not without the voice / Of mountain-echoes did my boat move on" (1.90–92). In a curious way, the boy Wordsworth in his "elfin" pinnace is represented as having invaded the territory of the spirits by the act of pushing the boat from shore. By this logic, Wordsworth can introduce without qualification the startling statement that the huge cliff "strode" after him:

> I struck, and struck again,
> And, growing still in stature, the huge cliff
> Rose up between me and the stars, and still

> With measured motion, like a living thing,
> Strode after me.   (*WPrel 1799*, 1.110–14)

The 1850 version introduces a qualification here that makes the narrative marginally more acceptable to the skeptical mind, but considerably weakens its psychological impact:

> I struck and struck again,
> And growing still in stature the grim shape
> Towered up between me and the stars, and still,
> For so it seemed, with purpose of its own
> And measured motion like a living thing,
> Strode after me.   (*WPrelude*, 1.380–85)

At the end of the episode, there is in the 1798–1799 *Prelude* a further apostrophe to the powers that oversaw the theft of the boat, and the eerie manifestation of apparent warning as the cliff towers over the retreating boat:

> Ah! not in vain ye Beings of the hills!
> And ye that walk the woods and open heaths
> By moon or star-light, thus from my first dawn
> Of childhood did ye love to intertwine
> The passions that build up our human soul,
> Not with the mean and vulgar works of man,
> But with high objects, with eternal things,
> With life and nature, purifying thus
> The elements of feeling and of thought,
> And sanctifying by such discipline
> Both pain and fear, until we recognise
> A grandeur in the beatings of the heart.
>   (*WPrel 1799*, 1.130–41)

In "1805" and "1850," the apostrophe is to the "Wisdom and Spirit of the universe!" (1.428; 1.401).

Still more striking in its unadorned, unexplained form is the story of the man drowned in Esthwaite Lake, placed in book 5 of the 1805 and 1850 versions but in the Two-Part *Prelude* placed soon after the account of boyhood card games and other indoor pastimes (lines 198–233 of Part 1). In its original location in the 1798–1799 version it is the first of three narratives dealing with death. There is no palliation of the stark image of the drowned man: the poet, almost as if appalled at the recollection, hurries on to speak of other "accidents":

> Twilight was coming on, yet through the gloom
> I saw distinctly on the opposite shore
> Beneath a tree and close by the lake side
> A heap of garments, as if left by one
> Who there was bathing: half an hour I watched
> And no one owned them: meanwhile the calm lake
> Grew dark with all the shadows on its breast,
> And now and then a leaping fish disturbed
> The breathless stillness. The succeeding day
> There came a company, and in their boat
> Sounded with iron hooks and with long poles.
> At length the dead man 'mid that beauteous scene
> Of trees, and hills, and water, bolt upright
> Rose with his ghastly face. I might advert
> To numerous accidents in flood or field. . . .
>   (WPrel 1799, 1.266–80)

The terror implied here is left undiminished, just as it is without explanation. There is no reference to the forests of romance or streams of fairyland as having in some sense prepared the boy for the horror of the dead man's appearance.

The incident near the moldered gibbet, although introduced by the familiar reference to "spots of time," is bare of any reference to later, happier times (in 1798, of course, Wordsworth was yet to revisit that site with his bride-to-be, Mary Hutchinson), nor is there yet present the notion of the *mind* being revealed as "lord and master" in such visionary experiences. Curiously, too, as Wordsworth revised the "spots of time" passage in 1803–1805, he made the imagination appear more and more vulnerable, as Kenneth Johnston points out. The Two-Part *Prelude* speaks of the "fructifying" virtue of these spots of time; in the first drafts of "1805" this becomes "vivifying" virtue; and finally (in the last 1805 version and in "1850") they are credited with a "renovating" virtue.[17] It is as if, in 1803–1805, Wordsworth found that he had spoken with too much confidence of the imagination's early growth, and saw that if its powers were traced too straightforwardly to the early boyhood experiences there would be

17. Johnston, *Wordsworth and* The Recluse, 105.

no dramatic tension in the later narrative "Imagination and Taste, How Impaired and Restored."

In Part 2 of the 1798–1799 *Prelude*, all these visitations and manifestations of the spirits and invisible powers are gathered up into a passage that hymns the "one life," a theme that grows in importance in later versions of the poem, at least partly because of Coleridge's influence. Yet in these first manuscripts, the poet's vision of the "one life" seems to come more naturally and cumulatively out of the stories of various intervenient, polytheistic powers. The creatures that leap and run, the powers that are "to the human eye / Invisible," all share "one life," but are more than merely different manifestations of it: they are granted more independence of action—like Darwin's genii and Priestley's monads—and the creative spirit is immanent in them, rather than transcendent.

H. W. Piper is inclined to question the claim Wordsworth makes here (and in the 1805 *Prelude*, 2.429–30, 3.121–29) that in his seventeenth year (1786–1787) he had already recognized the "one life," and that he refined this belief while at Cambridge. Piper prefers to date the "one life" belief from 1794, when Wordsworth was occupied with revising "An Evening Walk," and he ascribes Wordsworth's interest in it to his involvement with Unitarian and Girondin groups, many of which embraced a pantheistic faith: "Wordsworth was in touch during 1792 and 1793 with a number of men who held a doctrine of life in natural objects very like that which first appeared in his poetry in 1794 and in these men the doctrine went hand in hand with the radicalism which Wordsworth had now adopted."[18]

Jonathan Wordsworth and John Beer date the period of Wordsworth's enthusiasm for pantheistic ideas even later, linking it to the influence of Coleridge.[19] Even if this formal or philosophical pantheism was actually a product of the 1790s rather than of Wordsworth's late adolescence, however, in the 1798–1799 *Prelude* the poet's recognition of the "one life" is emphatically presented—in some lines that

18. H. W. Piper, *The Active Universe: Pantheism and the Concept of Imagination in the English Romantic Poets*, 62, 72.

19. Jonathan Wordsworth, *The Borders of Vision*, 22; "On Man, on Nature, and on Human Life," 17; John Beer, *Wordsworth and the Human Heart*, 77, 113, 210. See also *The Ruined Cottage and The Pedlar*, ed. James Butler, 176–77.

are lifted and adapted from the February–March 1798 version of *The Pedlar*—as the culmination of successive boyhood experiences with spirit powers and presences:

> wonder not
> If such my transports were, for in all things
> I saw one life and felt that it was joy.
> One song they sang, and it was audible,
> Most audible then when the fleshly ear,
> O'ercome by grosser prelude of that strain,
> Forgot its functions, and slept undisturbed.
> (WPrel 1799, 2.458–64)[20]

The 1805 version shows few substantive changes in these lines, but in "1850" the orientation is dramatically different. The unifying divine power is now distinctly transcendent, and the love that permeates the various creatures and invisible powers is love of the unseen God, not of their own joyous existence.

> Wonder not
> If high the transport, great the joy I felt,
> Communing in this sort through earth and heaven
> With every form of creature, as it looked
> Towards the Uncreated with a countenance
> Of adoration, with an eye of love.
> One song they sang, and it was audible. (2.409–15)

Both versions continue somewhat defensively, with a half-retraction of the claim: "If this be error, and another faith / Find easier access to the pious mind" (2.465–66). But the meaning of the implied retraction is quite different in each case. In the 1798–1799 *Prelude*, Wordsworth is apologizing for the pantheism of the "one life" statement, but also for the animism implied in the lines that precede it. In "1850," the reference to the "one life" is gone, and the apology is much vaguer, apparently repudiating as overenthusiastic or possibly heterodox the poet's early excitement at the "one song" of Nature.

20. Compare the draft of *The Pedlar* in Dove Cottage MS 16, excerpted in WPrel 1799, 159: "Wonder not / If such his transports were for in all things / He saw one life & felt that it was joy." See also Jonathan Wordsworth, *The Borders of Vision*, 378–79, 384.

We must not forget, either, that the issue here is less a way of naming or invoking the beauties of Nature than an entire poetic, for the poet claims that these powers shaped his imaginative faculties and continued to fuel his poetic endeavors. The "strain" the poet hears, in these lines, is obviously meant to recall the "strain of music" that is fashioned like the mind of man (*WPrel 1799*, 1.67–68). Wordsworth's story in these episodes has clearly come to be about the growth of a poet's mind, fostered by the spirits and familiars that are represented as nature's "under-agents." Part 1 of the Two-Part *Prelude* deals with (in Kenneth Johnston's phrase) these "solitary, free-spirited relations with Nature," but Part 2 deals with "socially determined relations."[21] To make his narrative more explicitly "philosophical," Wordsworth has to introduce into the Two-Part *Prelude* a different language, one of interpretation and analysis more appropriate to "W. Wordsworth, B.A., of St. John's, Cambridge," and it is this that comes to the fore in the second part of the 1798–1799 version. Wordsworth learned this language, scholars have suggested, from Coleridge, but also from Hartley, Burke, Gerard, and other late-eighteenth-century theoreticians.[22]

The passage beginning "Bless'd the infant Babe," the focus of this interpretive-analytical theme in Part 2, blends the language of perception theory—"elements," "object," "faculties," "forms," "sensations," "intercourse of sense"—with more overtly figurative language that seems to have been carried over from the animistic passages of the poem.[23] Now, however, it is not nature but the hypothetical mother of this hypothetical babe who communicates the impulses: "powers," "feelings" which "pass into his torpid life / Like an awakening breeze," "virtue which irradiates and exalts."

> Bless'd the infant Babe
> (For with my best conjectures I would trace
> The progress of our being) blest the Babe

21. Johnston, *Wordsworth and* The Recluse, 66.

22. On Hartley, see Arthur Beatty, *William Wordsworth: His Doctrine and Art in Their Historical Relations*, 63–72; and Sue Weaver Westbrook, "The Influence of David Hartley's *Observations on Man* on Wordsworth's Post–1802 Poetry and Aesthetics," 8–14.

23. On Coleridge's influence on the "Bless'd the infant Babe" passage, see Beer, *Wordsworth and the Human Heart*, 85–89.

Nursed in his Mother's arms, the Babe who sleeps
Upon his Mother's breast, who when his soul
Claims manifest kindred with an earthly soul
Doth gather passion from his Mother's eye!
Such feelings pass into his torpid life
Like an awakening breeze, and hence his mind
Even in the first trial of its powers
Is prompt and watchful, eager to combine
In one appearance all the elements
And parts of the same object, else detached
And loth to coalesce. Thus day by day
Subjected to the discipline of love
His organs and recipient faculties
Are quickened, are more vigorous, his mind spreads
Tenacious of the forms which it receives.
In one beloved presence, nay, and more,
In that most apprehensive habitude
And those sensations which have been derived
From this beloved presence, there exists
A virtue which irradiates and exalts
All objects through all intercourse of sense.
                    (WPrel 1799, 2.267–90)[24]

Obviously this passage does not represent any experience that the adult Wordsworth could be conscious of remembering. Rather, it is what may be called—in a phrase from E. H. Gombrich—a "relational model."[25] It attempts to describe a Coleridgean "primary consciousness," "the first / Poetic spirit of our human life" (2.305–6). As such, it is the first *extended* treatment of the theme of the growth of a poet's mind, but it is not an isolated passage. Its language— that of philosophical analysis, of epistemology—occurs often in Part 2 of the 1798–1799 *Prelude,* as the poet starts to integrate his developmental theme with the language evocative of natural powers that predominated in Part 1. What he earlier explained in terms of spiritual powers acting on the poet, or sometimes left without any explanation, is treated as a mental characteristic or habit, the

24. Compare 187, 189, 191 in Parrish's edition (MS RV, fols. 5^v–6^v).
25. E. H. Gombrich, *Art and Illusion: A Study in the Psychology of Pictorial Representation,* A. W. Mellon Lectures in the Fine Arts (1956), quoted in E. H. Gombrich, "Representation and Misrepresentation," 196.

"observation of affinities / In objects where no brotherhood exists / To common minds" (2.433–35).

Even this modest claim, however, is not as far removed from imaginative animism as might appear, for there was a recent precedent for using spirits and genii to give color to a "philosophical" argument about the subtle affinities of consciousness with phenomena of nature. This philosophical and quasi-scientific use of imaginative animism was to be found in the work of Erasmus Darwin. Darwin's long poem *The Botanic Garden* (1789–1791) advances the theory that the world developed under the guiding influence of various natural forces, which Darwin represents as the spirits. *The Botanic Garden* was among Coleridge's favorite books in the 1790s, and he combined Darwin's "genii" with Joseph Priestley's theory of monadic powers to create a picture of the world in which, as Priestley put it, "a source of infinite power and superior intelligence" is served by "inferior beings," each of which "has a consciousness distinct from that of the supreme being."[26] It is likely that Coleridge discussed this theory with Wordsworth—for one thing, it has an evident bearing on the universe of "The Rime of the Ancient Mariner."

Combining the language of philosophical psychology and such imaginative sympathy with the supernatural, Wordsworth provides an after-the-fact reinterpretation of imaginative animism, or, more accurately, of its continuation into the period of late adolescence. For the function of Wordsworth's narrative has now subtly changed. As David P. Haney has said of the 1805 and 1850 version of *The Prelude*, the poem begins by establishing the child as "an atemporal figure other to the writing poet," and this fiction gives rise to its opposite, a youth who is *in* time and who is the predecessor of the poet himself: "that same child . . . slowly manifests his identity with the speaking poet."[27] We can see this beginning to happen in Part 2 of the 1798–1799 version:

26. *Disquisitions concerning Matter and Spirit* (1782), quoted in Piper, *The Active Universe*, 37. Part 2 of Darwin's poem, *The Loves of the Plants*, appeared first, in 1789; Part 1, *The Economy of Vegetation* (the more theoretical section), in 1791.

27. David P. Haney, "The Emergence of the Autobiographical Figure in *The Prelude*, Book I," 63.

> My seventeenth year was come,
> And whether from this habit rooted now
> So deeply in my mind, or from excess
> Of the great social principle of life
> Coercing all things into sympathy,
> To unorganic natures I transferred
> My own enjoyments, or, the power of truth
> Coming in revelation, I conversed
> With things that really are.
>   (WPrel 1799, 2.435–43)

The experiences of this period are told in terms not entirely dis-similar from those used in Part 1, but they are now evaluated, as it were, publicly, or at least in the presence of Wordsworth's im-mediate auditor, Coleridge. Repetition is the technique used most extensively in Part 1, and it is noticeable that at this stage of com-position Wordsworth has not quite solved the problem of gracefully introducing a series of essentially similar episodes (see the awkwardly apologetic passage in Part 1, lines 247–58, wisely omitted in later versions). In Part 2, though, Wordsworth has just one story to tell—the story of "the growth of mental power / And love of Nature's works" (1.257–58).

The story of the gradual detachment of an individual conscious-ness from the undifferentiated ego of the infant, its existence swal-lowed up in the mother's, is of course the classic narrative of psycho-analysis. Richard J. Onorato and other critics have seen an analogy between this process and the process of poetic maturation outlined in *The Prelude*.[28] One passage often quoted in support of this view is that in which Wordsworth, according to Onorato, very obliquely refers to the death of his mother:

> I was left alone
> Seeking this visible world, nor knowing why:
> The props of my affections were removed

28. See, for example, Richard J. Onorato, *The Character of the Poet: Wordsworth in* The Prelude, 17, 25, 52, 56–57, 61–63, 72–73, 161–62, 171–72, 268; David Ellis, *Wordsworth, Freud and the Spots of Time: Interpretation in* The Prelude, 44, challenging Onorato's emphasis on the death of Wordsworth's mother; and McFarland, *Romanticism and the Forms of Ruin*, 148.

And yet the building stood as if sustained
By its own spirit. (*WPrel 1799*, 2.322–25)

This passage raises again in more urgent form the question of origins which haunts the entire second part of the 1798–1799 *Prelude*. Kenneth Johnston comments perceptively that Onorato's account of the psychological struggle enacted in *The Prelude*, so far from being condescending toward Wordsworth, shows rather how Wordsworth's sense of the transcendent was painfully *earned*, rather than merely given. In none of the versions of *The Prelude* is there a direct and easy development from childhood fears to adult faith. Rather, the 1798–1799 *Prelude* already shows how the emotions created by childhood experiences must later be worked through again, but with new meanings attached to them.[29]

The passage referring to the death of Wordsworth's mother is actually part of a verse paragraph or movement, in manuscript V (pp. 297–303), which ends as follows:

I deem not profitless these fleeting moods
Of shadowy exaltation, not for this,
That they are kindred to our purer mind
And intellectual life, but that the soul
Remembering how she felt, but what she felt
Remembering not, retains an obscure sense
Of possible sublimity to which
With growing faculties she doth aspire,
With faculties still growing, feeling still
That whatsoever point they gain, they still
Have something to pursue.
                    (*WPrel 1799*, 2.361–71)

These moods of shadowy exaltation, then, develop the "purer mind" of "Tintern Abbey" and later versions of *The Prelude* by creating in the mind of the young individual an *expectation* of "sublimity," an expectation that, in adult life, can no longer be fulfilled by experiences of the same kind (hearing "the ghostly language of the ancient earth"). The individual thus influenced develops, in psychoanalytic terms, from the infantile undifferentiated ego to the fully developed adult self-consciousness, or, in theological terms, from spiritual sleep

29. Kenneth Johnston, "The Idiom of Vision," 7.

to the recognition of transcendence. What was presented in "Nutting" as a form of apostasy, willful and violent, is now (in the 1805 and 1850 *Prelude* versions) rationalized as a necessary stage in the development of Imagination. The boy's violent action in ravaging the hazel bower was "wrong," it now seems, mainly because it was an attempt to hurry things, a premature repudiation of the gentle Powers and Stewards while they still had something to tell him.

This "rationalization," however, does not detract from the disturbing fact that "Nutting" represents or travesties nature as a passive, if not a willing, virginal victim, sacrificing itself so that the boy may achieve self-consciousness. Neil Hertz's astute question concerning the autobiographical moment, the moment of self-consciousness, in Wordsworth—"Who pays?"—may here be answered provisionally and limitedly: "Nature pays."[30] In the same spirit, I think, Wordsworth suggests in book 4 of *The Excursion* that even the "gross fictions" of the Greek polytheistic religion were able to elicit a certain awe among the Greek people. The polytheistic Greeks thus enjoyed some glimmerings of a purer and more worthy faith: "a thought arose / Of Life continuous, Being unimpaired" (4.755). Wordsworth here interprets the development of religious doctrine in terms of his own imaginative development as first set out in the Two-Part *Prelude*, and again, an early "primitive" belief is excused and partly rehabilitated (whatever its cost) because it prepared the way for a later saving doctrine.

This is where the tension between different versions of *The Prelude* is especially interesting. What can justly be described as the taming of some parts of the Two-Part *Prelude* in the 1805 and 1850 versions—the sentimentalizing of some episodes (the skating episode, the drowned man episode, the young boy's relationship to the River Derwent) and the frequent reinterpretation of the genii, familiars, and spirits in terms of abstract "Nature" and a theology of transcendence—raises far-reaching questions about the relationship of literary romanticism to its predecessor, the "age of sensibility."

Clearly, to say that this examination of the Two-Part *Prelude* reveals the poem to be "really" about the young Wordsworth's contacts with polytheistic beings—the godkins and goddesslings of which Coleridge spoke so contemptuously—would be to read it naïvely,

30. Neil Hertz, *The End of the Line: Essays on Psychoanalysis and the Sublime*, 223.

ignoring the conventions on which Wordsworth drew. We do not have to become polytheists in order to read *The Prelude*. Rather, the Two-Part *Prelude* belongs to what Albert Cook has designated as the fourth phase of the evolving interrelationship between myth and literature, a phase in which "assumed disbelief" in mythic beings is combined with "byplay of communicative suggestion."[31] I would also argue that the communicative suggestion in this poem, the use of animistic beings as the authorizing powers of the narrative, works surprisingly well. The tension that exists between different versions of *The Prelude* is not a matter of maturing poetic power, or increasing clarity of philosophical ideas, or of relative literary merit. There are lame passages in all three versions, and fine passages in all three versions. Rather, it is a matter of the interpretation and reinterpretation of certain experiences selected as formative—experiences accessible to Wordsworth at the time of writing primarily by means of certain eighteenth-century literary traditions.

Commenting on the work of two of Wordsworth's predecessors, William Collins and Thomas Warton, Geoffrey Hartman has said that "between the time of Gray and that of Wordsworth . . . the fate of poetry seemed to depend on poetry's revaluation of its founding superstitions."[32] I have tried to show that this "revaluation" is a key element in the origination of one of the key High Romantic texts, Wordsworth's *Prelude*. On the evidence of the Two-Part *Prelude*, I think we have to revise considerably our understanding of Wordsworth's *Prelude*, both as a paradigm for "natural supernaturalism" and as what we have learned from M. H. Abrams to call the definitive theodicy of British Romanticism. A "post-Abrams" theory of Romanticism must in some way find room for the intimate dependence of the understanding of nature in the fourteen-book *Prelude*— a reinterpretation, as I have tried to show, of an interpretation—on the literary primitivism, or imaginative animism, that is the controlling trope of the Two-Part *Prelude* of 1798–1799. In doing so, too, the theory may acquire a measure of cultural openness, as critics realize that the theology of transcendence that characterizes Wordsworth's maturity has a closer connection to animistic beliefs than they have been prepared to admit.

31. Albert Cook, *Myth and Language*, 58.
32. Hartman, *Beyond Formalism*, 311.

Three

Wordsworth and the Defeminizing of Pastoral

Wordsworth's poetry has gained increasing attention from feminist critics in the past decade.[1] In contrast to Coleridge, whose women often disturb and disrupt the course of poetic narrative or prophetic afflatus (Sara in "The Eolian Harp," the "woman wailing" in "Kubla Khan," Geraldine in "Christabel"), Wordsworth to a remarkable extent succeeds in eliding the feminine, so that when the Wordsworthian landscape includes a female figure, even the best critics "see" her only with an effort. Even Lucy, as has often been pointed out, is not only silent but very difficult to visualize. Some male critics, as a consequence, have simply conflated Wordsworth's female figures with the landscapes they blend into. Consider, as an illustration, the following discussion of the "spots of time" episode in *The Prelude* (1850), book 12, lines 225–61:

> Pool, beacon, and woman are, in fact, perceived singly and with the sharpness of individually engraved signs.... The experience... remains etched in [Wordsworth's] mind, as freshly visible among the moldering effects of time as the name under the gallows.

1. However, many, perhaps most, feminist analyses of Wordsworth understandably focus on his relationship to his sister Dorothy. See, for example, Margaret Homans, "Eliot, Wordsworth, and the Scenes of the Sisters' Instruction"; Thomas Vogler, "'A Spirit, Yet a Woman Too!': Dorothy and William Wordsworth"; Marlon B. Ross, "Naturalizing Gender: Woman's Place in Wordsworth's Ideological Landscape"; and Susan J. Wolfson, "Individual in Community: Dorothy Wordsworth in Conversation with William."

> Yet without this transference to nature—the fixity of the memorial writing being repeated in the fixtures of nature (pool, beacon, girl) and so engraved on the mind—the event could not have reached through time.[2]

The ease with which this usually alert critic moves from describing the woman as a "sign" that, along with the pool and the beacon, is "perceived singly," to calling her one of three "fixtures of nature"— not to mention his conflation of "girl" and "woman," which simply takes over Wordsworth's usage (the 1798–1799 and 1805 texts both have "girl," then "woman"; the 1850 version replaces "woman" with "Female")—suggests that this is less a case of critical blindness than a forgivable, though unexamined, response to some feature of Wordsworth's text. Had the figure been male, however, one can imagine a very different style of critical commentary. In short, the poem does not invite us to consider the woman's presence as having its own significance, separable from that of pool and beacon. She is part of a scene, even a "fixture of nature." One may quibble about the word "fixture," as applied to her, since in all versions she is a figure of energy, forcing her way with difficult steps against the blowing wind. But the poet registers her presence simply as part of the composition, the "keeping," of the scene imprinted on his mind.

The very elusiveness of the woman's presence, and Wordsworth's hesitation over the terms "girl," "woman," and "Female," have attracted the interest of at least one psychoanalytic critic. Richard Matlak suggests that in the "spots of time" episode the young Wordsworth "fantasizes the mother's presence," a projection revealed by the change from "girl" in the earlier part of the passage to "woman" some lines later.[3] In a "feminist" variation of this argument, Thomas Vogler similarly suggests that "the logic of Wordsworth's narrative requires a return to the mother" (249). Pointing to the recurrent appearances of Dorothy in association with the spots of time, he suggests that Dorothy and nature are both mother surrogates. Dorothy is the enabling presence that bestows on Wordsworth the "feeling of coherence" which *he* associates with childhood experiences of nature, but Vogler (basing his interpretation on Melanie Klein's theory of the infant's relationship to its mother) ascribes it to the adult's drive to reconstruct an idealized mother-figure.

2. Geoffrey H. Hartman, *Wordsworth's Poetry 1787–1814*, 216–17.
3. Richard Matlak, "The Men in Wordsworth's Life," 395.

What such psychological interpretations fail to explain adequately is why, if the presence of a beloved woman is so important to recovering the primal "feeling of coherence," there has to be in Wordsworth's poetry as a whole the progressive muting and elision of the feminine that has attracted the attention of many feminist critics. For all its modernity, Wordsworthian pastoral ultimately traces its ancestry (through a long line of descent) to the Theocritan mountain idyll, a genre that should authorize a greater prominence for "the feminine" than most other classical genres. The Idylls of Theocritus are haunted by female presences: the powerful goddess Aphrodite (Daphnis' tormentor and the "enemy of man"), Persephone, Helen, Berenice (mother of Ptolemy), and other mythical or semi-mythical figures. Women are the speakers and main players in Idylls II, XV, and XVIII, and have a large role (not always just as objects of desire) in several others. One modern critic of Theocritus goes so far as to suggest that he is unusually sympathetic to women.[4] It is partly for this reason that it seems possible to speak of the "defeminization" of the idyll in Wordsworth.

In this chapter, then, I will try to show how many of Wordsworth's poems, from "Tintern Abbey" to the Lucy poems, elide and absorb their females into a background that the poet's imagination can then assume the privilege of interpreting. In doing so, I shall argue, Wordsworth is in part revising a myth tradition: specifically, the group of traditions we associate with the Theocritan idyll. Rather than fantasizing an absent female, or merely continuing the classical gendering of some of nature's powers as female, these poems tend toward the "defeminizing" of classical pastoral, rejecting the mythologizing of nature as Venus or Demeter, and even turning nature, in a curiously sinister way, into a successful *male* rival for the affections of the human female.

There is a remarkable claim for the permanent relevance of Theocritus' Idylls in a letter that Dorothy and William co-wrote while in Germany. William discusses the comparatively ephemeral value of poetic depictions of city life, with its "wearisome unintelligible obliquities" and "transitory manners," as compared to depictions of rural manners, which are intrinsically more enduring because "connected with the permanent objects of nature." This argument obviously

4. See Anna Rist, *The Poems of Theocritus*, 132, 162.

anticipates the 1800 Preface, which lends additional significance to the discussion of Theocritus that follows. Wordsworth proceeds to take the poems of Theocritus as an example of the way that poetry about rural manners remains interesting for many centuries:

> The reason will be immediately obvious if you consider yourself as lying in a valley on the side of mount Ætna reading one of Theocritus's Idylliums or on the plains of Attica with a comedy of Aristophanes on your hand. . . . But I may go further read Theocritus in Ayrshire or Merionethshire and you will find perpetual occasions to recollect what you see daily in Ayrshire or Merionethshire read Congreve Vanbrugh and Farquhar in London and though not a century is elapsed since they were alive and merry, you will meet with whole pages that are uninteresting and incomprehensible.[5]

The importance of this appeal to a classical precedent should not be exaggerated. Wordsworth does not name any specific virtues of the Theocritan idyll that might account for its continuing interest, other than the occasions it provides for recollecting "what you see daily in Ayrshire or Merionethshire." Still less does he indicate that he might have seen Theocritus as a possible model for his own poetry. Nevertheless, the reference to Theocritus here, in close juxtaposition with the phrase about "permanent objects of nature" that is such a key term in the Preface, might at least indicate that the Sicilian inventor of the idyll symbolizes to Wordsworth a certain promise of permanence for his own poems, and perhaps a point of reference, at however great distance, by which his work might be understood. Wordsworth's negative view of Restoration comedy (not to mention Aristophanes) strikes us today as quirky, reflecting the prejudice of his time, but that helps to bring out my point. Looking for an example of the enduring vigor of poetic descriptions of rural life, Wordsworth finds one in Theocritus, who is accordingly praised for his depiction of simple rural manners "connected with the permanent objects of nature"—a connection not nearly so apparent to modern critics, who generally see Theocritus as having little interest in forms of nature as such. But as Fink points out, Wordsworthian pastoral is modeled not so much on classical sources themselves as on those sources as mediated by Milton, Thomson, and the topographical writers of the

5. *The Letters of William and Dorothy Wordsworth*, 1:255. The letter is to Coleridge.

eighteenth century, so that the Wordsworthian mountain idyll is "a kind of localization in the Lake district of Virgilian, Horatian, and Thomsonian themes" (67).

I begin with one of the Poems on the Naming of Places, "To M.H.," since it exemplifies Wordsworth's using the Theocritan idyll at its most apparently classical. The word "idyll" derives from "eidyllion," meaning "little picture," and seems especially appropriate to this poem:

> Our walk was far among the ancient trees:
> There was no road, nor any woodman's path;
> But a thick umbrage—checking the wild growth
> Of weed and sapling, along soft green turf
> Beneath the branches—of itself had made
> A track, that brought us to a slip of lawn,
> And a small bed of water in the woods.
> All round this pool both flocks and herds might drink
> On its firm margin, even as from a well,
> Or some stone-basin which the herdsman's hand
> Had shaped for their refreshment; nor did sun,
> Or wind from any quarter, ever come,
> But as a blessing to this calm recess,
> This glade of water and this one green field.
> The spot was made by Nature for herself;
> The travellers know it not, and 'twill remain
> Unknown to them; but it is beautiful;
> And if a man should plant his cottage near,
> Should sleep beneath the shelter of its trees,
> And blend its waters with his daily meal,
> He would so love it, that in his death-hour
> Its image would survive among his thoughts:
> And therefore, my sweet MARY, this still Nook,
> With all its beeches, we have named from You!
>   (WPW, 2:118)

There is no claim that the "still Nook" was one of Mary's favorite places; no incident is related; and yet the beech grove (in one manuscript, poplar grove) is to be named for Mary as if it were entirely natural to link a sheltered woodland spot and a woman's name. At first sight, then, this poem seems to maintain the classical tradition of associating a magical or secluded place with a woman's presence. The word "therefore" in the penultimate line suggests a logic other than the logic of biography or history, which would have applied if the poem told us that Mary frequented this spot. Nor is the logic of mythopoeia at work, however, despite the idyllic tone of the poem and its Theocritan allusions. If anything, the poet has reversed the usual pattern by which a place is mythologized through the discovery in it of a mythic presence, a *genius loci* or guardian spirit. Here, the poet addresses Mary as a being who is *not*, apparently, in relation to the beech grove until he, the speaker, establishes that relation. Mary is endowed with a "title" to the beech grove, rather than the other way around. Moreover, the poet subtly establishes nature as the originating poetic power, of which he purports to be merely the interpreter.

The first two lines of the poem lead us to expect chaos, an untouched wilderness. These woods are without paths or roads, and the phrase "far among the ancient trees" adds the notion of a journey to origins, to a place outside human history, never yet transformed into human meaning. As in "Nutting," this pleasant excursion is presented as a miniature version of grander expeditions, such as those of Bartram (quoted in Wordsworth's note to "Ruth," WPW, 2:510). Yet Nature surprises us, and the verse enacts the interpretive process that ensues, the process of "seeing-as." There is thick shade ("umbrage"); the shade has "checked" the wild growth of weeds and saplings, as if purposively (an earlier version has the shade "shutting out the light / From weed and sapling"); and the resulting stretch of clear turf is described as a "track" (the terms "road" and "path" have already been tried and dismissed).[6] The purposiveness imputed to Nature here is reemphasized with the statement that the track *"brought us* to a slip of lawn." Nature makes the first metaphor in the poem. A length of "soft green turf" is, or is turned into, a "track."

What Wordsworth has done here, I suggest, is to link his own poetic, metaphor-making activity closely with the primeval and therefore authoritative processes of a hypostatized nature.[7] The middle section of the poem contains a veritable cornucopia of poetic figures,

6. See Kelley Grady and Martha Michael, "A New Manuscript of Wordsworth's 'To M.H.,'" 39.

7. Frances Ferguson uses the term "authorize" of nature, in a rather different, more somber sense. See *Wordsworth: Language as Counter-Spirit*, 47–48. See also J. Douglas Kneale's convincing treatment of Wordsworth's

but there is no female presence, no hint of a nymph or dryad. The poet animates the scene—he populates it with imaginary flocks and herds, he adds an equally imaginary herdsman, who would have had to make a stone basin for these flocks and herds to drink from were not the pool already so well formed, and its margin so firm, and he further humanizes the place by metaphor, simile, synecdoche, and metonymy (the pool is a *"bed* of water," the flocks and herds might drink *"as from* a well," the herdsman's *"hand"* would have made the basin, the dell is a "glade *of water"*). These images are part of traditional pastoral. The spring of water, arching trees heavy with fruit, and soft green lawn come straight from the Idylls of Theocritus.[8] Yet this abundance of figural language all appears to claim the authority of Nature itself, since it was after all Nature, through the "thick umbrage," that "made" the track which "brought" the poet and his companions to the spot. The length of soft green turf seen as a track—a purely fortuitous circumstance, turned by the poet's perception into a special provision, an arrangement for the explorers' benefit—sets a precedent for the pool seen as a well, the slip of lawn seen as a field, and by extension the peopling of this landscape with imaginary flocks, herds, and herdsman.

The absence of any mythologized female figure means that the only way in which the description of the grove admits a "female" presence at all is in the hypostatizing of "Nature," here gendered as feminine; her primary relationship is to the poet, and her function is to authorize the poet's use of language. The line "The spot was made by Nature for herself" might suggest that Wordsworth and his companions are intruders, but the rest of the poem indicates that they are intruders permitted to share Nature's secrets primarily because they share *her* apparent interest in metaphor, in putting things in place of other things. The recluse who is mentioned in the next few lines personifies this primitive gift. He is one of Wordsworth's "silent poet" figures, one of the "Poets that are sown / By Nature" (like the hermit in "Tintern Abbey," and John Wordsworth in "When,

---

tropes of voice, in *Monumental Writing: Aspects of Rhetoric in Wordsworth's Poetry*, 82–83.

8. In particular Idylls I, VI, VII, although a closer source could be Coleridge's "This Lime-Tree Bower My Prison." See Thomas McFarland, *Originality and Imagination*, 132.

to the attractions of the busy world"), who lives, breathes, and drinks the place Nature made for herself (*WPW*, 5:10 [*Excursion*, 1.77–78]; *WPW*, 2:122). He does not so much build his cottage as "plant" it, and the pool that was previously pictured giving refreshment to flocks and herds is now a Pierian spring that slakes the poet's thirst for inspiration. The poetry that results is an unspoken poetry, but the imaginary recluse does achieve the all-important first step *toward* poetry, a vivid recollection of the dell: "in his death-hour / Its image would survive among his thoughts."

Such "silent poet" figures, as Jonathan Ramsey has perceptively suggested, indicate Wordsworth's "recurrent frustration with the limitations of even the best articulate language."[9] Here I would only add that the presence of the imaginary recluse prepares us for the poet's abandonment of his own attempt at an "articulate language" in favor of a human signified—Mary. The naming of the dell "for" or "from" Mary, or the identification of Mary as *the thing the dell signifies*, follows immediately on the evocation of a recluse mutely dying with the image of the dell in his mind. A subtle power shift takes place here, an eliding of what there is of "feminine" in Theocritan pastoral. Rather than representing himself as the recipient of some feminized power in the natural scene, Wordsworth lays claim to the dell, interprets it, and finds its meaning to be "Mary." He assumes the prerogative of articulating what the dell "means." It is the imputed power of the dell to create poetry, that is, the way the dell is made to *seem to* initiate Wordsworth's own poetic processes, that leads Wordsworth to single it out as a signifier for Mary. If the act of naming in the last two lines of the poem ostensibly treats the name "Mary" as the signifier and the dell as the signified (the dell being named "from" or, in the 1802 and 1805 versions, "for" Mary), it only partly disguises the fact that the preceding description has already established the dell as the signifier and Mary herself as the thing signified. Mary's personal qualities (quietness, resourcefulness, self-possession, her association with shelter and refreshment) *do* evidently reinforce the association, but in this context they amplify, on a human level, the claims for the secretly creative powers of nature, rather than providing the rationale for the identification of a woman with a place. We may legitimately associate the recluse figure with the early descriptions

9. Jonathan Ramsey, "Wordsworth's Silent Poet," 271.

of the Pedlar (later, "Wanderer") who learns to love humankind by attending to the beneficent influences of untouched nature. In "To M.H.," however, nature though not physically despoiled is not empty of human meaning or prelinguistic. Rather, in an extraordinarily skillful way Wordsworth dramatizes Nature as the original *maker*, her poetry being the pristine pastoral kind that makes paths for human beings out of uncultivated turf, fields for their pastures out of wild lawn, and wells out of woodland pools. The meaning of this activity is finally a human meaning, "Mary," but Mary is not invoked as a poet, even of the silent kind, nor as a spirit of the place or potent presence. She is represented, rather, as the human terminus or final cause of Nature's poetic activity. The effect is not to bestow control of the place on Mary or to call up any other female presence; control remains with the male speaker, who claims the power to interpret the dell while he makes it authorize his own speech.

The poem is therefore an unusual kind of work on myth. As Frances Ferguson has argued, Wordsworth is well aware of the human arbitrariness of metaphor, our acts of naming one thing "for" or "from" another. For Wordsworth, Ferguson suggests, mythology demonstrates how inevitable, and distinctively human, is this search for a "natural cause" of human fortunes.[10] In this sense Wordsworth's claiming the "right" to interpret the dell is aggressive just as the despoliation of the hazel tree in "Nutting" is aggressive. What Wordsworth has done in "To M.H.," on a small scale, is to reinterpret and actually reverse an ancient pastoral and mythological tradition: the identification of a blessed place, a *locus amoenus*, with a person. The subtext of "To M.H." is that nature, in itself, is empty of meaning.

"Tintern Abbey" is a poem of greater depth than "To M.H." partly because it lays more emphasis on the speaker's ambivalent attitude toward the language of nature's forms. Three elements within the poet's life (as represented in the poem) are in tension: "nature and the language of the sense" (line 108); the element of the sublime, which raises the poet above the natural or chthonic language and seems to initiate a process of freeing or detaching the poet from nature (line 94); and between these two, the interpretive effort of the poet himself, which is constantly portrayed as an experience of perplexity

10. Ferguson, *Wordsworth: Language as Counter-Spirit*, 62.

and difficulty—"gleams of half-extinguished thought," "recognitions dim and faint," "sad perplexity" (lines 58–60). If it is true that, as Harold Bloom has claimed, "Tintern Abbey" is Wordsworth's attempt to assert the Muse of Nature over against the Muse of Milton, it is also true that the Muse of Nature in "Tintern Abbey" is a highly fugitive and inscrutable being.[11] Much of the poem is defensive in tone, its enthusiasm guided and controlled, its sentiments often disowned almost as soon as they are expressed. Jeffrey Baker rightly places "Tintern Abbey" in a highly sophisticated tradition of poetry that purposely overreaches itself in order to disown its own affirmations, thereby subtly reaffirming them.[12] In such a work, "nature" is hardly a simple presence whose influence can be straightforwardly affirmed.

Critics interested in the Lockean heritage of Wordsworth, such as Arthur Beatty and C. C. Clarke, have taken the phrase "language of the sense" as evidence of Wordsworth's interest in exploring Lockean ideas, emphasizing that it is a language of the *sense*.[13] Before the philosophical question of whether empiricism or idealism had the greater role in Wordsworth's development can be settled, however, something must be said about the particular claim Wordsworth is making by using the term "language" of sensory images. The commonsense way to interpret the line "In nature and the language of the sense" is to take the "and" as disjunctive. Nature, on the one hand, and the language of the human senses, on the other, provide in their interrelationship the "anchor," "nurse," "guide," and "guardian" of the poet's "moral being." But Wordsworth is surely saying the opposite: that "nature" and "the language of the sense" are really *one* thing, that in the state of awareness of "something far more deeply interfused" invoked in these lines, there is no way of telling what the eye and ear "perceive" and what they "create." In the words of C. C. Clarke, in "Tintern Abbey" "thoughts take on something of the objectivity of cliffs and secluded scene, and these latter the subjectivity of thoughts" (45). The boundary between subject and object dissolves. The language that is being praised here is at least as much the language of nature, then, as it is the language of the sense.

11. Harold Bloom, A *Map of Misreading*, 61.
12. Jeffrey Baker, *Time and Mind in Wordsworth's Poetry*, 59–60.
13. See Arthur Beatty, *William Wordsworth*, 91, 98; and C. C. Clarke, *Romantic Paradox: An Essay on the Poetry of Wordsworth*, 41–42.

To use such a phrase, however, is to raise a series of questions about the relationship of empiricism to idealism, certainly, but also— I suggest—about the origins Wordsworth claims for his own use of language. The occurrence of the word "nature" in this phrase is the culmination of a long rhetorical movement that begins twenty lines earlier, as Wordsworth is explaining that he does not mourn the loss of the aching joys and dizzy raptures of his early manhood:

> For I have learned
> To look on nature, not as in the hour
> Of thoughtless youth; but hearing oftentimes
> The still, sad music of humanity,
> Nor harsh nor grating, though of ample power
> To chasten and subdue. And I have felt
> A presence that disturbs me with the joy
> Of elevated thoughts; a sense sublime
> Of something far more deeply interfused,
> Whose dwelling is the light of setting suns,
> And the round ocean and the living air,
> And the blue sky, and in the mind of man:
> A motion and a spirit, that impels
> All thinking things, all objects of all thought,
> And rolls through all things. Therefore am I still
> A lover of the meadows and the woods,
> And mountains; and of all that we behold
> From this green earth; of all the mighty world
> Of eye, and ear,—both what they half create,
> And what perceive; well pleased to recognise
> In nature and the language of the sense
> The anchor of my purest thoughts, the nurse,
> The guide, the guardian of my heart, and soul
> Of all my moral being.   (lines 88–111; WPW, 2:261–62)

The considerable power of these lines comes from a strategic abstractness that is very different from the pastoral topoi, evocative of Nature's own chthonic language, we traced in "To M.H." The strategy is a series of attempts at definition: what he has felt is a *presence* that disturbs with the *joy of elevated thoughts*, and a *sense sublime* of *something* that is then itself defined as a *motion* and a *spirit*. The "authority" of these lines, in other words, comes not from the supposed rhetorical precedent of nature itself but, rather, from the confession, implicit in the abstractness of the terms, that the experience is beyond the power of language to define, and can only be hinted at through such repeated attempts at definition. The lines are not primarily about an experience of nature, but are about the difficulties we face as we try to interpret and communicate such experience. They mark the point of transition so well defined by de Man in his explication of "The Boy of Winandermere" as "the transformation of an echo language into a language of the imagination by way of the mediation of a poetic understanding of mutability." The sensory object is absorbed into consciousness, transmuted into something that cannot be seen but can be imagined ("the light of setting suns," "the round ocean") and thereby, paradoxically, brought closer to pure being. De Man sees this as a gain: indeed, he finds the echo language of "The Boy of Winandermere" (he cites such phrases as "jocund din" and "mimic hootings") to be intentionally "flat and mechanical," and he praises Wordsworth as one of those writers who, like Rousseau and Hölderlin, "put into question . . . the ontological priority of the sensory object."[14]

Yet Wordsworth himself seems to post a warning against this movement away from the sensory object by insisting that he *is* still a lover of the meadows and the woods, and that the *anchor* of his moral being is "In nature and the language of the sense." The poem originates in a sensory experience, vividly recreated, although the key word "uncertain" appears here, as it does in "The Boy of Winandermere" ("that uncertain heaven"), as a subtle reminder of the fallibility of human interpretations:

> Once again I see
> These hedge-rows, hardly hedge-rows, little lines
> Of sportive wood run wild: these pastoral farms,
> Green to the very door; and wreaths of smoke
> Sent up, in silence, from among the trees!
> With some uncertain notice, as might seem
> Of vagrant dwellers in the houseless woods,
> Or of some Hermit's cave, where by his fire
> The Hermit sits alone.   (lines 14–22)

As in "To M.H.," an imaginary hermit or recluse, privy to the secret language of nature, is incorporated into the landscape as a

14. Paul de Man, *The Rhetoric of Romanticism*, 54, 53, 16.

surrogate, perhaps, for the poet's lost intimacy with the language of sensory objects. But "uncertain notice" is in a way a description of the whole opening section of the poem, since the poet is not seeing but seeing *again*. The powers of nature are still active—the waters "roll," their sound is a "murmur," the cliffs "connect / The landscape with the quiet of the sky," the hedgerows seem to overrun the landscape as if with a will of their own—but they do so within the context of the poet's aesthetically tuned observation. The landscape is a scene of writing, cultivated as much by the poet's eye as by the cottagers.[15] A second visit, especially given the carefully explained interval of five years and the view of the landscape is from *exactly* the same spot—"under this dark sycamore"—already suggests reinterpretation and uncertainty. The observer is the same, yet not the same; the landscape is the same, yet not the same. The very vocabulary of the passage—"seclusion," "landscape," "view," "hue"— is that of the painter, the professional landscape architect, or the experienced judge of landscape, rather than of the rapturous lover of the wilderness. We are involved in the more reflective, analytical process described (after the fact, of course) in the 1800 Preface.

The emphasis on reflection and interpretation continues in the next three verse paragraphs. The "serene and blessed mood" (lines 35–49) is owed not to a moment, or to a felt presence such as is invoked in "Nutting" and "To M.H.," but to "These beauteous forms," mental forms abstracted from the immediate experience and spot of time. The language continues to be that of a professional critic of landscape ("forms," "harmony," "picture," "paint"). The poet has "learned / To look on nature" with the "music of humanity" (that is, de Man suggests, history) in mind, not as "in the hour / Of thoughtless youth."

The motion the poem sets up, then, is not from the articulation of a chthonic or primal language to a dramatized overcoming of that language, as in "Nutting," but from an already self-consciously "aesthetic" language to the language of transfiguration and exaltation, adopted in the climactic passage, lines 93–111. Yet there is considerable nostalgia for a time before either aestheticism or the "joy / Of elevated thoughts" was known to the poet, a time when

15. On this question, see Kjell Morland, "The Disturbing 'Presence': A Central Problem in Wordsworth's 'Tintern Abbey,' " 39.

nature was "all in all" and he explored the hills and woods—"wherever nature led"—with energetic enthusiasm. What has happened to the original language corresponding to this rapturous phase of the poet's relationship with nature? Evidently, it has been distanced, and, I would argue, subtly revalidated, by its association with Dorothy in the extraordinary final paragraph of the poem.

> . . . in thy voice I catch
> The language of my former heart, and read
> My former pleasures in the shooting lights
> Of thy wild eyes. Oh! yet a little while
> May I behold in thee what I was once,
> My dear, dear Sister! and this prayer I make,
> Knowing that Nature never did betray
> The heart that loved her.
> (lines 116–23; WPW, 2:262)

The prayer Wordsworth speaks, "yet a little while / May I behold in thee what I was once," cannot but have a certain elegiac quality, despite the elaborate statement about a compensatory exchange that precedes it. Nature has given him first the "aching joys" of unreflective communion and then, as these diminished, something still more precious: a "sense sublime" of the very presence of Being itself—which is why he still sees Nature as the "nurse," "guide," and "guardian" of his moral being. There is a progression, the poem tries to assure us: Nature's privilege is to lead us "From joy to joy," and each stage is presumably an advance on the preceding one. Counter to this claim, however, is the irrepressible feeling that "The language of my former heart"—now an attribute of Dorothy, not of the poet himself—must have been more vivid and enchanting, if the poet is so anxious to see this language kept alive in the voice of his sister.

Despite its personal tone, "Tintern Abbey" is in many ways a very public poem, as Jeffrey Baker suggests. It is an announcement that the poet has emerged from a period of intense solitary distress and suffering into the shared, common griefs of humanity, but with an important if qualified message about the compensations and higher insights life holds in store—not unlike the Ancient Mariner, or Wordsworth himself in the much later "Elegiac Stanzas": "A deep distress hath humanized my Soul" (WPW, 4:259). It is all the more revealing, then, that the poem ends with a passage that seems more a sorrowful farewell to "The language of my former heart" than a celebration of the poet's new role as witness to the developmental powers of Nature, her ability to "lead / From joy to joy." The role of Prophet of Nature, which Coleridge so insistently pressed on Wordsworth, seems to be one that Wordsworth took on reluctantly, if dutifully. As we know, he frequently reverted, in the next few years, to attempting to re-create that rapturous communion with nature—supposedly inferior to the sober pleasures of later life— which in "Tintern Abbey" he bequeathed forever to Dorothy. As Paul de Man says of the stories of "deprivation" and subsequent "compensation" in *The Prelude*, "the question remains . . . how trust- worthy the ensuing claim of compensation and restoration can be" (73–74). By symbolically handing over one kind of poetic language to Dorothy—which he later returns to reclaim, as it were, in "Nutting" and some early episodes of *The Prelude*—Wordsworth seems to signal his wish to believe that this language is appropriate to a sensibility of a less exalted kind, different from that which he now possesses. Yet even this public signal fails to convince us that the poet really considers Dorothy's sensibility to be less mature and less developed than his own. Her experience of nature will continue to be direct and unmediated:

> let the moon
> Shine on thee in thy solitary walk;
> And let the misty mountain-winds be free
> To blow against thee.   (lines 134–37)

She will continue to read that pristine language, a language au- thorized by nature itself and not by the "purer mind" or "elevated thoughts" supplied by the poet's allegedly more self-conscious, re- flective faculty. Whatever lingering regrets there may be in the sub- text of "Tintern Abbey," the poem remains predominantly a poem of farewell. A later and more final version of this farewell can be seen in "Nutting" and "Three Years She Grew."

The "dear nook" described in "Nutting" as "a bower beneath whose leaves / The violets of five seasons re-appear / And fade, unseen by any human eye" (lines 30–32; WPW, 2:212) shares the pas- toral and metaphor-generating aspects of the beech grove, or poplar grove, in "To M.H." Although Wordsworth likens the "green stones" in this hazel bower, "fleeced with moss," to a "flock of sheep," the simile is almost unnecessary; he appears to be doing no more than re-articulating Nature's transformation of the stones, since Nature gives the stones their green "fleece." The violets are "unseen by any human eye"—suggesting that they *are* seen, though not by human eyes—and the rivulets, or "fairy water-breaks," "murmur," both images suggesting that this is a place where trees, flowers, water, and stones communicate to each other. The spot is already inhabited. (The notion of its being populous with spirits is encouraged by one manuscript version of the poem, which states: "They led me, and I followed in their steps, / Tricked out in proud disguise." [*WPW*, 2:211n], and the phrase "Tricked out" may even suggest that the boy explorer is somehow bamboozled into doing what the spirits wish him to do, namely, invade the bower.[16]) In another early version, in some lines discarded even before Wordsworth sent Coleridge a draft of the poem, Wordsworth more explicitly described Nature's powers or presences as being of two kinds: those who took particular charge of the poet's inspiration, stimulating his imagination even in full sunlight, and those who restored and refreshed his mind in the shelter of "groves" and "shades."

> Ye gentle Stewards of a Poet's time!
> Ye Powers! without whose aid the idle man
> Would waste full half of the long summer's day,
> Ye who, by virtue of its dome of leaves
> And its cool umbrage, make the forenoon walk,
> When July suns are blazing, to his verse
> Propitious, as a range o'er moonlight cliffs
> Above the breathing sea—And ye no less!
> Ye too, who with most necessary care
> Amid the concentration of your groves
> Restore the springs of his exhausted frame,
> And ye whose general ministry it is
> To interpose the covert of these shades,
> Even as a sleep, betwixt the heart of man
> And the uneasy world, 'twixt man himself,

16. For this reason, I dissent from Jeffrey Baker's view that the "timeless" quality of the bower is *immediately* destroyed once the boy invades it. "The virgin scene," Baker says, "is already raped by the eye that sees and the consciousness that counts" (*Time and Mind in Wordsworth's Poetry*, 47).

> Not seldom, and his own unquiet heart,
> Oh! that I had a music and a voice
> Harmonious as your own, to tell the world
> What ye have done for me.   (WPW, 2:504–6)

In "Nutting," however, the Stewards and Powers have made no path or track for the human explorer. Critics have frequently pointed out the Edenic imagery of the scene—the hazel trees "with tempting clusters hung," the term "bower," and the suggestion that it is enclosed, even protected, by the "tangled thickets" and "pathless rocks" which surround it.[17] Less often noticed is the way in which the Powers themselves are represented as manipulative makers of metaphors, as magicians or tricksters. They turn stones into green-fleeced sheep, rivulets into murmuring "fairy water-breaks," and an unvisited, protected nook into an apparently virgin scene, a paradise, which is nevertheless haunted, a place of witchcraft, like Acrasia's bower. The function of these Powers is comparable to the way metaphor itself works in this poem. In creating the bower, the Powers exemplify figurative speech and wordplay as Wordsworth often deploys them—seeking to transcend the division between mind and world by finding "terms in which he can speak simultaneously of mental and physical."[18]

When Wordsworth the boy puts on his "disguise of cast-off weeds" to journey out into the woods, then, he is not only aping manhood—a suggestion surely reinforced by the choice of phrase to describe the "weeds" (they had been "husbanded, / By exhortation of my frugal Dame")—but also inviting the duplicitous Powers to share their best poetic tricks with him. Like the shaman who wears a caribou hide to attract, befriend, and control the spirits of the forest, Wordsworth as a boy (the poem suggests) puts on a trickster's "motley" that is already halfway to the costume of a wild man, "More ragged than need was!" Nature does, at first, cooperate. The "wise restraint" and voluptuous suspension of threatening desires exercised by the young explorer are learned from the restraint amid exuberance of the bower itself:

17. See Baker, *Time and Mind in Wordsworth's Poetry*, 47; Kneale, *Monumental Writing*, 161.
18. Keith Hinchliffe, "Wordsworth and the Kinds of Metaphor," 100.

> not a broken bough
> Drooped with its withered leaves, ungracious sign
> Of devastation; but the hazels rose
> Tall and erect, with tempting clusters hung,
> A virgin scene!—A little while I stood,
> Breathing with such suppression of the heart
> As joy delights in; and, with wise restraint
> Voluptuous, fearless of a rival, eyed
> The banquet.   (lines 17–25)

The boy is indulging a particular, human pleasure, that of con-templating "after long / And weary expectation" the imminent ful-fillment of his hopes. This fulfillment is described in human terms, as a "banquet" and as an anticipated sexual release. Yet Wordsworth encourages us to see these "human terms" as already implicit in the scene itself. In his reconstruction of the experience, just as in "To M.H.," Wordsworth is mythologizing, if in a minimal way, imposing on nature a gender scheme, in which the primary relationship of nature is to the poet himself. The hazel bower is figured as a "virgin" and "tempting" scene, one that (supposedly) invites erotic response.

This mythopoeic harmony between the human and the natural, established by imputing the human power of "seeing-as" to nature, breaks down, however. The boy Wordsworth seems about to slip into a mood of absolute receptivity and passivity. Just when the human and the natural are so much in harmony that the heart is "of its joy secure," the passive anticipation becomes impatience:

> Perhaps it was a bower beneath whose leaves
> The violets of five seasons re-appear
> And fade, unseen by any human eye;
> Where fairy water-breaks do murmur on
> For ever; and I saw the sparkling foam,
> And—with my cheek on one of those green stones
> That, fleeced with moss, under the shady trees,
> Lay round me, scattered like a flock of sheep—
> I heard the murmur and the murmuring sound,
> In that sweet mood when pleasure loves to pay
> Tribute to ease; and, of its joy secure,
> The heart luxuriates with indifferent things
> Wasting its kindliness on stocks and stones,
> And on the vacant air.   (lines 30–43)

One way of knowing nature, erotic and Edenic, is replaced by another, a knowledge that *is* power, including the power to destroy. The images of the natural scene suddenly become "indifferent things," "stocks and stones," and "vacant air," *mere* things, on which human "kindliness" is wasted. "Vacant" suggests that whatever seemed to be present has now vanished, or withdrawn, turning the pastoral organicism of lines 15–40 into a longing for self-aggrandizement through "victory" over nature. The phrase "stocks and stones" comes from Milton's well-known sonnet "On the late Massacher in *Piemont*":

> Avenge O Lord thy slaughter'd Saints, whose bones
>   Lie scatter'd on the Alpine mountains cold,
>   Ev'n them who kept thy truth so pure of old
>   When all our Fathers worship't Stocks and Stones,
> Forget not.[19]

The idyllic scene has suddenly been repudiated as if it were no better than crude paganism. The boy enacts a conquering of nature, which is not only a moment of triumph, carried out with perhaps more violence than need was, but a display of crusading zeal, the act of a young prophet triumphantly pursuing idolaters and destroying the groves of idols. If, as suggested in a recent neo-Freudian study of his poetry, Wordsworth's poetic vocation comes to necessitate "the incorporation of the father's word into a superego, a strong conscience that will propel Wordsworth into the role of a more dutiful son," it is the Miltonic register that most frequently encodes this sense of patrilineal inheritance and, more, the poet's self-identification with the strong conscience of his Puritan poetic ancestor.[20] None of this would be very interesting, however, were it not for the way the maternal or pre-Oedipal myth actually resists erasure despite the violence the poet deals out to it, as here in "Nutting." After the boy has smashed the bower open to the "intruding" sky, the erotic compact that existed—as the poem claims—between the boy and the spirits of the bower, when he lay with his cheek on a green stone and listened to the murmur of the rivulets, has supposedly been destroyed. The intrusive, all-seeing sky has been let in. The imagery suggests that it was the seclusion of the bower—the fact that it was

19. John Milton, *Works*, 1, part 1:66.
20. See Laura Claridge, *Romantic Potency: The Paradox of Desire*, 101.

hidden from the sky—that made it a spot congenial for poetry, a place like the beech grove of "To M.H.," possessing a sort of chthonic power of its own, and administering the "care" Wordsworth ascribed to the spirits in the earlier version of the poem, who

> Amid the concentration of your groves
> Restore the springs of his exhausted frame . . .
>   . . . whose general ministry it is
> To interpose the covert of these shades
> Even as a sleep, betwixt the heart of man
> And the uneasy world.

Now that the bower is open to the sky, the boy is "rich beyond the wealth of kings," but the compact with the spirits is broken. I do not think we can identify the "spirit in the woods," the spirit Dorothy is enjoined to respect, with the intrusive, judgmental presence suggested in the phrase "the intruding sky." The sky presence is more paternal, stern, coercive; the chthonic deity of the woods is elvish, playful, restorative. Yet Wordsworth's sin, in ravaging the bower, is not so much greed as apostasy, and the entire poem—as the unpublished lines make clear—is meant to persuade Dorothy not to be guilty of a similar apostasy. In appealing to Dorothy, in the published version,

> Then, dearest Maiden, move along these shades
> In gentleness of heart; with gentle hand
> Touch—for there is a spirit in the woods

Wordsworth is clearly warning her against acts of devastation, invoking the elvish spirit-presence whose restorative ministry in the paradise-bower he had brutally rejected.[21] The unpublished lines

21. Frances Ferguson has argued that the boy of "Nutting" is a romance hero whom nature allows to find the object of his quest far too easily—a point with which I would agree—and that his turning against nature is a result of his "enraged frustration at having followed nature until she turned *him* into a literary property" (*Wordsworth: Language as Counter-Spirit*, 75). I am not sure about this. The boy's rending of the bower seems to me more a trampling of the idols than an assertion of existential freedom, and I do not think Ferguson fully accounts for the use made of Dorothy (who is, I admit, more prominent in the manuscript versions than in the published version).

demonstrate how he sees a reflection of his own past cruelty and boyish mischievousness in Dorothy now, representing *her* as a potential "enemy of nature":

> If I had met thee here with that keen look
> Half cruel in its eagerness, those cheeks
> Thus [   ] flushed with a tempestuous bloom,
> I might have almost deem'd that I had pass'd
> A houseless being in a human shape,
> An enemy of nature.   (WPW, 2:505)

As in "Tintern Abbey," where Wordsworth sees in the figure of Dorothy what he was once, so here Wordsworth wishes Dorothy to remain maidenlike so as to preserve the relationship, the compact, he once enjoyed with "Nature," to keep open a channel of communication with the Stewards and Powers, to read his own "former pleasures" in Dorothy's charmed intimacy with the spirit of the woods. The destruction of the bower has become emblematic of a rejection and mutilation that is precisely the rejection and mutilation of a *language*, which is also a way of knowing: the chthonic language that the boy Wordsworth heard as he toyed with the spirit of the woods, listening to "the murmur and the murmuring sound." As in "To M.H.," in seeming to accept the authority of nature's oracular utterance, Wordsworth is in fact claiming the adept's privilege of "interpreting" nature's language.

The actual lines describing the moment of the boy's intimacy with the spirit of the woods do not themselves embody the lost chthonic language. As in "To M.H.," again, the priority of this language is asserted, but its content is inaccessible and can only be invoked by a series of icons (hazels, flowers, fairy water-breaks, sparkling foam, green stones). "Nutting" is more complex a poem than "To M.H." because the rejection of that earlier language is acted out, and it takes place at the end of the very sentence that begins by invoking some of these pastoral icons. The spiritual rejection of the bower is already accomplished in the transformation of the icons of a pastoral paradise into "indifferent things . . . stocks and stones . . . the vacant air." All that remains is for the physical mutilation to take place—as it soon does—and confirm the new interpretation of the hazels and green stones as indifferent, meaningless idols.

Both "To M.H." and "Nutting," then, posit a primal, chthonic language as authority in some sense for the poet's use of metaphor and other poetic figures. In both poems, at least one human intermediary represents the "naturalistic continuities":[22] the hermit, and more ambivalently Mary herself in "To M.H.," Dorothy in "Nutting." In the latter poem, the primal language is lost to the poet not because of an apocalyptic act of destruction (that act merely sets the seal on the attitudinal transformation that has already taken place) but because of a prior rereading of the sights and sounds that were the signs of this language, a rereading that turns them into mere "stocks and stones." In the early draft version of "Nutting," the primal language is an attribute of certain presences or powers, some of whom take special interest in the restoration and refreshment of the poet and some of whom take special interest in stimulating and inspiring him.

In "Three Years She Grew," the poet seems to have passed beyond the conflict evoked in "Nutting" to a new, more austere and limited conception of the natural underpinnings of poetic speech. The poem invites interpretation according to two distinct codes, one of which is the tradition of pastoral elegy. Frances Ferguson treats the Lucy poems as combining the genres of love poem, epitaph, and elegy, but in "Three Years She Grew," elegy predominates, more even than in "I travelled among unknown men" (which Ferguson explicitly compares to "Lycidas"). The speaker of the poem names a person, "my Lucy," whose death purports to be the occasion for the poem, and as Daniel Cottom says of all the Lucy poems, "the voluptuous elaboration of [the speaker's] vision of death is precisely what defines him as a lover."[23] At this level the subject matter of the poem appears to be the common one of personal loss:

> She died, and left to me
> This heath, this calm, and quiet scene;
> The memory of what has been,
> And never more will be. (*WPW,* 2:216)

As is usual in pastoral elegy, the poem promises immortality to the mourned beloved and invokes a state appropriate to her imputed

22. The phrase is Kenneth Johnston's, in *Wordsworth and* The Recluse, 294–95.
23. Frances Ferguson, "The Lucy Poems: Wordsworth's Quest for a Poetic Object," 534, 542; Daniel Cottom, *The Civilized Imagination: A Study of Ann Radcliffe, Jane Austen, and Sir Walter Scott,* 48.

qualities. Here, however, the type of immortality the poem anticipates is defined not by the speaker but by "Nature," which through
the device of prosopopoeia announces its intention to possess the
woman-child and form her, having singled her out as exceptional in
her beauty:

> "A lovelier flower
> On earth was never sown;
> This Child I to myself will take;
> She shall be mine, and I will make
> A Lady of my own."

A different, apparently conflicting code is at work. An interpreter
seeking the right context for lines 2–36 of the poem, the lines spoken
by "Nature," would likely recall the myth of Korè/Persephone and
her abduction by the god of the underworld. The ancient metaphor,
woman-as-flower, reveals here its violent underside. Woman is a thing
grown, and something therefore to be harvested, plucked, or gathered, like Blake's Oothoon, who plucks the flower-nymph, the Marygold, at the Marygold's own invitation, but is herself instantly
plucked, ravished, by Bromion. Wordsworth's poem, like Blake's *Visions of the Daughters of Albion*, renews and makes transparent the
well-known reference to the Persephone myth in book 4 of *Paradise Lost*:

> that faire field
> Of *Enna*, where *Proserpin* gathering flours
> Her self a fairer Floure by gloomie *Dis*
> Was gatherd, which cost *Ceres* all that pain
> To seek her through the world.[24]

Irene H. Chayes, without noting the Miltonic parallel, shows
Lucy's resemblance to Persephone in a 1963 essay. But she sees
Wordsworth's Nature as wholly benevolent, a Demeter or Ceres
figure, and she does not appear to feel that Lucy's death involves
any degree of violence. In fact, she describes the Persephone myth
itself as embodying a "fortunate fall." Likewise, J. R. Watson sees an
earth-mother or "terra genetrix" myth in the Lucy poems "I travelled

---

24. Milton, *Paradise Lost* 4.268–72 (*Works*, 2, part 1:116).

among unknown men" and "A Slumber Did My Spirit Seal."[25] To a reader alert to the violence that is explicit in the Korè myth, and that Milton does not attempt to disguise, the lines spoken by Nature in "Three Years She Grew" sound much more like the declaration of a ravisher, Hades (Milton's "Dis"), than like a mother gathering her child to her breast: " 'She shall be mine, and I will make / A Lady of my own.' " Frances Ferguson is right when she sees Nature in "Three Years She Grew" as a "Plutonic male." The poem seems to draw upon a myth in which Nature is a violent, dark, masculine deity, Hades rather than Demeter, bent on consolidating its power by the forceful abduction and rape of a woman. This interpretation of Nature as Pluto (or Hades) is in no sense strained or unclassical. Andrew Tooke's popular *Pantheon*, familiar to every eighteenth-century schoolboy, explains that "Pluto" signifies "wealth" because, as Cicero stated in *De natura deorum*, "all the natural Powers and Faculties of the Earth are under his Direction; for all things go to the Earth, and proceed from thence."[26]

As Judith Ochshorn has pointed out, the Persephone myth was at least partly about a struggle for the rule of the underworld, the abode of the dead, as male deities increasingly took over from female ones in the Greek pantheon: "Having at his side the daughter of the powerful Demeter may have been necessary to Hades in order that he might more effectively or legitimately rule the province of the dead" (79). Just as Hades makes Korè his queen, naming her Persephone and

25. Irene H. Chayes, "Little Girls Lost: Problems of a Romantic Archetype," 590; J. R. Watson, "Lucy and the Earth-Mother," 198. The parallel with Korè/Persephone is also noted by Northrop Frye, *Fables of Identity*, 125.

26. Ferguson, "Lucy Poems," 544; Tooke, *Pantheon*, 282. According to John Jortin, *Tracts, philological, critical, and miscellaneous*, 1:67, the "Rector terræ" mentioned by Lucan in *De bello civili*, 6.697 ("Rector Terræ, quem longa in secula torquet / Mors dilata deum") is Pluto/Hades. A psychoanalytic treatment of the Lucy poems might suggest that the feared Plutonic male Nature of "Three Years She Grew" is a shadowy type of the "phallic mother" uncovered in Freudian analysis. One such study hints at this possibility; see Claridge, *Romantic Potency*, 37, 41. Contrary to what modern readers might expect, perhaps, mythology does not uniformly represent the earth as beneficent mother. It is interesting to note James Frazer's point that Demeter was at enmity with Earth, which lured Persephone to her death (*The Golden Bough*, 396).

sharing his power with her, Nature in Wordsworth's poem promises Lucy "an overseeing power / To kindle or restrain," and particularly gives her rule over the secret sources of life, its hidden places and murmured sounds.

The unusual role given to Nature is not the only striking feature of Wordsworth's poem, however. It is a common expectation that elegy hold out the promise of immortality for the person mourned. The speaker in "Lycidas," for example, pronounces its hero the immortal "Genius of the shore" near which the real Henry King drowned. This immortality is usually earned rather than simply bestowed, however, for it is a reward for the beloved one's virtues and especially for the gift of poetic eloquence, now untimely silenced. Milton's elegy advertises its secondariness. The elegist's own immortality may be the ulterior goal, but the overt function of the poem is to praise the eloquence of the deceased poet, hinting that the mourner's strain is an inferior, rougher rhyme. John Dryden's ode "To the Pious Memory of the Accomplisht Young Lady Mrs Anne Killigrew, Excellent in the two Sister-Arts of Poesie, and Painting" is distinctly condescending about her poetic gift, ascribing it to her good fortune in having had Henry Killigrew for a father— "Thy Father was transfus'd into thy Blood: /So wert thou born into the tuneful strain"—but even Dryden acknowledges Mrs. Killigrew's equal right of access to the Muse and cedes to her the honor of leading the celestial choir at the Last Judgment.[27]

Wordsworth's poem is innovative, therefore, with respect to at least one norm of elegiac tradition. The departed Lucy is promised immortality, because of her silence rather than because of her eloquence, unlike Henry King or Anne Killigrew. The poem achieves a powerful sense of Lucy's nearly mythic stature, her closeness to natural forces, by violating the expectation that her powers of utterance or at least her moral virtues or personal qualities will be celebrated. But at the same time it is impossible for the modern reader not to recognize that Lucy becomes a sign without having ever been a maker of signs—a poet—or having displayed what could be called a personality. She is depicted only in relation to sun and shower and not in relation to other human beings. As Ferguson says, "There may be a fundamental category mistake in seeing her as a human

27. John Dryden, *Works, 3, Poems 1685–1692,* 110, 115.

being."[28] This curious dehumanization of Lucy through her total silencing has led Laura Claridge, a neo-Freudian critic, to suggest (rightly, I think) that the Lucy poems encapsulate particularly well Wordsworth's anxiety over the claim he wishes to make to a self-engendered or autochthonous poetics. The anxiety stems from his realization that ceding linguistic priority to silent Nature—in other Wordsworth poems, mythically encoded as female—entails the risk of his own re-absorption into and destruction by maternal potency (the "phallic mother"):

> At the same time that Wordsworth's fear of a phallic woman invades his poems, we also sense a subtle denial of women's social power in such complex texts as the Lucy poems, for example, where Lucy is assigned repeatedly to a mute, presocial order. No one but the speaker knows Lucy—no one but Mother Earth. It is Lucy's threat to burst into meaning—to laugh, as the woman of "To Joanna" does, in a betrayal of her proper place—rather than remain content to be assigned to "Being," that activates the keen sense of anxiety in these poems. (41)

If such an anxiety drives the Lucy poems, it is most apparent not in the mere presence of the Persephone myth in the poems—a relatively elementary feature, often noted by critics—but in the fundamental way the myth is reinterpreted. In its received form—in book 5 of Ovid's *Metamorphoses*, for example—the Persephone myth is a myth of recurrence. Persephone, like nature's vital, vegetative powers of growth, will not be consigned to the underworld forever, but divides her time equally between that concealed world and our own. Persephone's enthronement as queen of the underworld, in the classical myth, at least assures her the right to return to earth for six months each year.

Lucy is to take on natural powers after her death, too, for Nature decrees that

"The Girl, in rock and plain,
In earth and heaven, in glade and bower,
Shall feel an overseeing power
To kindle or restrain."

But this does not include the power to return to her previous existence or to communicate with the human world in any other

28. Ferguson, "Lucy Poems," 534.

way than through the inarticulate sounds of nature. She will embody "the silence and the calm / Of mute insensate things"; she will live with Nature. The speaker is given no promise of her return in any form. She leaves him only "The memory of what has been, / And never more will be."

If Lucy's future is to be so clearly linked with natural, "vital" forces, what is her function as sign? Why is she treated as everlastingly distinct from Nature, as Nature's companion, Nature's lover, even Nature's pupil (the 1802 version of the second stanza begins "Her teacher I myself will be, / She is my darling."), but not as one with Nature? What functions are left to Lucy, if unlike Persephone she is never to return?

Lucy's only two remaining functions are being absent and being possessed. The sign "woman" in "Three Years She Grew" means "that which is capable of being possessed," either by a human lover—the speaker—or by Nature, personified as a rival lover and as a more successful one. Nature speaks in the poem from imputed love and admiration for Lucy. It is a tribute, if a rather sinister one. But Lucy has no Demeter to search for her, no distinctive human qualities except for a vaguely defined beauty, and no future existence except as an invisible, silent companion to "Nature," here personified as male underworld god. Lucy's absence, then, is not an affirmation of the contiguity and interdependence of earth and underworld, the link expressed in the classical myth by Persephone's yearly return to earth. Nor can it be read as the untimely silencing of a memorable human voice, or the loss of a paragon of womanly virtue. What Lucy's absence does do is to empower the speaker of the poem. Her absence is the purported occasion for the poem, which is partly about the speaker's own remoteness from the immortality he promises to "his" Lucy, about his inability to bring Lucy back, and thus about the ineffectiveness of his human speech. The speaker, unlike Shelley in "Adonais," does not anticipate reunion in some future stage of existence with the one he mourns: Lucy's realm is closed to him. The immortality he promises to Lucy is not comparable to that Milton envisions for Henry King, either: it is not a poet's immortality. The situation of the poem's speaker is the limited span of mortal life. Here my reading diverges from that proposed by Ferguson. In her view, "Nature's suppression of Lucy's voice—which amounts to an appropriation of her spirit or breath—also constitutes a suppression of the poet's voice." I would argue that it constitutes only a *limitation* of the poet's voice, a self-limitation, in fact, that nevertheless leaves the poet the undisputed master of a realm from which the rival immortality of natural processes has been banished.[29] Lucy's departure from the scene signifies a boundary line between human and natural life, as between human speech (ineffective, unable to recall Lucy) and the speech of Nature, which is apodictic, potent: "Thus Nature spake—The work was done."

In this respect, too, the poem strikes a distinctly modern note by turning the perpetual recurrence that was part of the ancient myth into perpetual absence. It associates woman as sign with the vegetative powers of earth, with fecundity and even a kind of immortality. Yet it sharply distinguishes this immortality from the speaker's own expectations of *his* future life, indeed from his earthbound human existence as a person.[30] The poet preserves his power of speech, in effect, by circumscribing it carefully within the human and setting against it not woman's speech but an impersonation of the potent speech of Nature. The woman's silence and absence leave the speaker in lonely dominance within the now merely mortal world that remains to him.

The speaker, then, has to identify womanhood as mute and insensate in order to preserve a differentiation between the "human" and the "natural." To counter the fear of seeing his individuality overwhelmed by the natural world the speaker must sacrifice "his" Lucy, Persephone-like, to the impersonated otherness of the nonhuman. Woman in "Three Years She Grew" signifies absence and that

29. Ferguson, "Lucy Poems," 544–45. My point here is somewhat different from Anne K. Mellor's argument that in his poetry in general "Wordsworth has actually usurped Nature's power, leaving her silenced, even absent" (*Romanticism and Gender,* 18). I would argue that Wordsworth is in a constant rivalrous battle with "Nature," and that in the Lucy poems, figuring nature as a male rival, he divides the field with it, reluctantly finding that he cannot have both Lucy (or what she represents) and his own poetic voice.

30. Marlon Ross's essay, to which I am indebted, makes a similar point: "The tendency in Western culture is to position the female closer to nature than the male . . . as the masculine mind wields its reason to construct society and civilization, the woman stands as a constant reminder of his inescapable relationship to nature, of the base first nature that can never be eradicated" ("Naturalizing Gender," 401).

which is possessed, not because it is in the nature of woman to be possessed or absent, but because the speaker's utterance can only be originated in and by the absence of the feminine. In the final stanza of the poem, the speaker recognizes this as an irreparable loss, a diminishment of the human realm: something is gone that "never more will be." Nevertheless, woman is reconstructed as the absent and the nonhuman (the natural/material) in order that the speaker may claim the prerogative of human utterance. The speaker, having lived an apocalyptic separation from Nature such as that described in "Nutting" and (in a more muted form) "Tintern Abbey," and no longer finding there an authorizing origin for his speech, sees that he must circumscribe or delimit part of the human if he is to exercise this prerogative. Woman is therefore transformed into a sign for what has to be distanced, by her exclusive association with the immortal but inarticulate processes of Nature. The delicate balance, which pastoral once permitted, between the powers ascribed to the goddess and the male poet's assumed privilege of interpreting her, has tipped in favor of the poet's prerogative of speech. The poet has to struggle anew to define his vocation and the relationship to nature that authorizes it. The poem in which this redefinition is most dramatically played out, entailing a renewal of the conflict adumbrated in "Nutting" between the patrilineal voice of self-conscious authority and the silently inspired spirit voices, which the poet can never quite let go, is "Home at Grasmere."

Four

Forgetfulness and the Poetic Self in "Home at Grasmere"

Since the publication in 1971 of M. H. Abrams' *Natural Supernaturalism*, these lines, with the preceding invocation to Milton's muse Urania, have been recognized as one of the towering peaks of English Romantic mythopoesis.

> Paradise, and groves
> Elysian, Fortunate Fields—like those of old
> Sought in the Atlantic Main, why should they be
> A history only of departed things,
> Or a mere fiction of what never was?
> For the discerning intellect of Man,
> When wedded to this goodly universe
> In love and holy passion, shall find these
> A simple produce of the common day.
> —I, long before the blissful hour arrives,
> Would chaunt, in lonely peace, the spousal verse
> Of this great consummation.[1]

Abrams' now classic study demonstrates that the Prospectus for *The Recluse* deserves this high rank for several reasons: its radical

---

1. Prospectus for *The Recluse,* from Wordsworth's Preface to *The Excursion* (1814), lines 47–58, in Abrams, *Natural Supernaturalism,* 467. The 1814 text (which Abrams prints in full) differs slightly from that given by de Selincourt, *WPW,* 5:3–6, which is based on Wordsworth's 1849–1850 text. However, in most of the rest of this chapter, for reasons soon to be explained, I refer not to the Prospectus as such but to various texts of "Home at Grasmere," from which the Prospectus was taken.

transformation of a native English visionary tradition that was linked to Jewish prophetic tradition and to the Greek myth of the celestial Aphrodite; its symbolic relocation of the human world–historical and eschatological drama in that apparently narrower but in fact sublimer sphere, the "Mind of Man"; and, not least, its use of the biblically sanctioned metaphor of the divine marriage to represent the process of the visionary transformation of the world, which is to be the result of the "blended might" of Mind and the external world. The idea of the sacred marriage derives from the Book of Revelation; Revelation in turn draws on the Tanach (Old Testament) prophetic tradition, which speaks of God's covenant with Israel in terms appropriate to the marriage-covenant, and, conversely, of the sins of Israel in terms appropriate to the reproach of an adulterous spouse. "Home at Grasmere" reenergizes the metaphor by secularizing the apocalypse to which it was applied. The poem thus marks Romanticism's decisive turn away from transcendence and toward the here-and-now.

Criticism of Wordsworth—and of Abrams—has not been lacking. Critics with a gnostic turn of mind have echoed Blake's angry dissent from the idea that the mind is fitted to the external world and the external world to the mind: "You shall not bring me down to believe such fitting & fitted I know better & Please your Lordship." Others have objected to Abrams' refusal to make room in his account of Romanticism for what he called the "ironic counter-voice" of Byron.[2] Byron's importance for any definitive account of Romanticism could hardly be denied, but the argument for his inclusion ranged wider: it was that Byron's ironic skepticism toward other poets' "vatic stance" was only the most dramatic case of a deep-seated malaise that affected all the major Romantics. They, too, labored under an acute sense of human limitations and the inevitable failure of inspiration, which led them to limit, qualify, undercut, and hedge around with ironic distancing any purportedly vatic utterance, as Carlyle does in *Sartor Resartus*, Keats in *The Fall of Hyperion*, and Coleridge in "The Rime of the Ancient Mariner."[3]

2. Annotations to Wordsworth's Preface to *The Excursion*, in William Blake, *The Complete Poetry and Prose*, 667; Abrams, *Natural Supernaturalism*, 13.

3. Anne K. Mellor cites these works, along with *Don Juan* and the odes of Keats, as examples of "open-ended and inconclusive structure," and argues that Byron, Keats, and Carlyle rejected the circular, return-

The position of Wordsworth's secularized apocalyptic in relation to the wider Romantic movement has been part of our critical agenda for some time, then. And because the longer poem from which the Prospectus was taken combines visionary intensity with the speaker's reflections on his own life decisions—a domestic story underwriting the High Romantic argument—this poem, "Home at Grasmere," has been canonized in a more than usually literal sense. It could be seen as the first part of a Wordsworthian "New Testament," suggests one critic: static in mode, priestly in function, consuming and completing the linear, Old Testament narrative of *The Prelude*.[4] Criticism of this kind, finding the value of the work in its delineation of the personal odyssey, or *Bildung*, of one actual, heroic individual, who is in some sense a surrogate for others, for the whole human race, has a precedent in the Romantics' own reinterpretation of Milton's *Paradise Lost*. Coleridge, for example, comes close to saying that the real story of *Paradise Lost* is that of John Milton:

> Observe, how the second and third book [of *Paradise Lost*] support the subjective character of the poem. In all modern poetry in Christendom there is an under consciousness of a sinful nature, a fleeting away of external things, the mind or subject greater than the object, the reflective character predominant. In the Paradise Lost the sublimest parts are the revelations of Milton's own mind, producing itself and evolving its own greatness. (*Lects 1808–1819*, 2:427–28)

Arguably, then, Abrams' approach, locating "Home at Grasmere" within a secularized Judeo-Christian tradition, at least places the poem in the right kind of context for assessing its superbly overreaching claims. But there is another kind of literary tradition at work here, one perhaps less favorable to preserving a "Romantic" interpretation of Romanticism. This is the tradition of mythological syncretism.

That "Home at Grasmere" is mythologically syncretic will hardly be denied, even though a precedent for this particular form of syncretism could have been Milton, or at least Milton as the Romantics

---

to-paradise structure of a "secularized Judaeo-Christian literary tradition" (*English Romantic Irony*, 6, 30). The deconstructive critique of Abrams' book was initiated by J. Hillis Miller, in "Tradition and Difference," *Diacritics* 2 (1972): 6–12. The other major study I have in mind here is Jerome McGann's *Romantic Ideology*.

4. See Kenneth Johnston, " 'Home at Grasmere': Reclusive Song," 25–26.

read him. Something interesting and important is happening to the mythological traditions Wordsworth draws on in "Home at Grasmere," and it has implications for our understanding of Romantic poetics as well as of the poem itself. I suggest here that the two traditions on which the poem draws—Jewish and Greek—pull in opposite directions throughout "Home at Grasmere," each of them broaching a different way of coming to knowledge and a different understanding of what it is to possess the visionary power. In attempting to construct his "master myth" from the syncretic combination of these two ancient traditions, the poet calls upon two *contradictory* ways of relating the mind to nature. This is the conflict between a neoclassical trope, the appeal for poetic inspiration to a power above and around the self, and a Christian desire to "save" fallen nature by treating it as textual, as a book the individual may "read." Both models of the mind-nature relationship assume the separation of man from nature, the second more obviously than the first.[5] But they involve quite different kinds of forgetting. The neoclassical technique for overcoming the mind-nature gap, most clearly seen in the famous apostrophe to Urania, aspires toward a form of anamnesis. It hopes to recover a lost union, to restore the lost source and origin of human powers, by forgetting the historical isolation or solipsism of the poet's present self. The nature-as-text analogy, on the other hand, preserves the contingency and isolation of the present self, permitting it the stance of acolyte and interpreter toward the book of nature. But in order to do this it must forget or repress the natural *origins* of the self, all those powers of nature that according to *The Prelude* "fashion" and "build up" the mind and contribute to the "spirit of the past" that the poet of *The Prelude* strives to recover "for future restoration."

This competition between two poetic epistemologies is a more serious matter than a mere failure to contextualize the poem or to choose between two styles of poetic imagery. It reaches to the main

5. "Self" is used in reference not to the historical William Wordsworth but to the poetic self figured within the poem. That the poem exists in more than one "version" merely emphasizes the extent to which discussion of poetic self opens up questions of the interdependency of self and text. I am indebted to Thomas Pfau's suggestion that self (in a poem) is best approached as a kind of figure. See "Rhetoric and the Existential: Romantic Studies and the Question of the Subject," esp. 508–9.

issue the poem raises—what kind of role and what special way of knowing the poet lays claim to. It threatens the poet's attempt to construct a secure and stable self, an attempt that culminates in the grand resolution of the marriage metaphor. This metaphor, finally so prominent in the Prospectus[6] and apparently a triumphant denial of solipsism, heralding the union of the "Mind of Man" with its partner, nature, actually succeeds in occluding rather than solving a conflict that has remained unresolved in the main body of the poem.

Rather than taking the Prospectus or "Home at Grasmere" as a key to unlock English Romanticism, then, I will examine critically what the lines Wordsworth used for the Prospectus achieve in the context established for them by the rest of the longer poem. In order to evaluate this achievement accurately, we must look at the contradictions that the main manuscript versions of the poem reveal and that the adoption of the marriage metaphor in lines 53–58 of the 1814 Prospectus tries to resolve. The published version of the Prospectus is a triumph of imaginative rhetoric over almost crippling poetic difficulties, faced and explored in the first nine hundred and fifty lines of the poem as it stood in 1806. Reading manuscript B of "Home at Grasmere" (the version Wordsworth worked on between March–April 1800 and September 1806) side by side with manuscript D (the version worked on after publication of *The Excursion* and largely completed in 1831–1832) enables us to see Wordsworth wrestling with these two contradictory positions.[7]

The fear that divides the poet's mind in "Home at Grasmere," and over which the marriage metaphor is meant to triumph, is fear of solipsism, the price of that seclusion or solitude on which the poem

6. "Finally" because, in the earliest surviving MS of the Prospectus, conveniently printed by Jonathan Wordsworth as an appendix to *The Borders of Vision*, 387–90, the marriage metaphor is given only ten words (lines 39–40), which grow to twelve *lines* in 1805–1806 (MS B); but it is there.

7. From this point, with exceptions to be noted, I refer to *Home at Grasmere: Part First, Book First, of* The Recluse, ed. Beth Darlington, abbreviated as *WHG*. Most references are to Darlington's parallel reading texts of MSS B and D (38–107), and are by line numbers. When it is necessary to refer to the editor's type-facsimile transcriptions of these and other relevant MSS, a page reference will be given. An admirable account of the textual history of "Home at Grasmere" is given in Darlington's "Introduction," 3–32.

bases so much of its claim to authority. "I was taught to feel, perhaps too much, / The self-sufficing power of solitude," he wrote in the 1798–1799 *Prelude*, and the phrase "perhaps too much" gives us a glimpse of Wordsworth's struggle to balance solitude, as a positive resource that strengthens and empowers the self, against the risk of a debilitating solipsism, the risk, even, of manic delusion.[8] That this fear was real enough to need confronting is apparent in the fragment entitled "Incipient Madness," probably written in the first half of 1797.[9] It portrays, in a first-person narrative, a man who in extreme grief and loneliness becomes obsessed with an object that, like himself (and the text that describes him), is a fragment: a shard of glass from a broken windowpane. For months, the man returns regularly to the ruined dwelling, to look at the piece of glass. Saving himself from this kind of desperate solipsism—not for his own sake, but as a surrogate for others—seems part of Wordsworth's purpose in "Home at Grasmere" and in *The Recluse*. It involves discovering how to cultivate "beauteous forms," instead of fragments that merely reflect one's own transient fragmentariness. Wordsworth had worked on this problem in the 1798–1799 *Prelude*; he had faced it before then, in the spring of 1798, drafting some lines for the consolatory reflections on Margaret's story in *The Ruined Cottage*. The sort of communion that a solitary has with objects of nature—"These quiet sympathies with things that hold / An inarticulate language"—may have a healthful effect, the passage suggests, softening and diverting into a more creative channel the potential violence of the feelings:

> Accordingly he by degrees perceives
> His feelings of aversion softened down
> A holy tenderness pervade his frame
> His sanity of reason not impaired.[10]

8. WPrel 1799, 56 (2.76–77). Thomas McFarland usefully distinguishes between "solitude of identity" and "solitude of alienation" ("Romantic Imagination, Nature, and the Pastoral Ideal," 16–17).

9. The fragment is printed in *The Ruined Cottage and The Pedlar*, ed. Butler, 468–75. See Kenneth Johnston's comments on the fragment, in *Wordsworth and* The Recluse, 35.

10. *The Ruined Cottage and The Pedlar*, ed. Butler, 261 (*The Ruined Cottage*, MS B, fol. 46ʳ). A different version of the lines appears in *The Excursion*, 4.1207–21 (see WPW, 5:148).

But the integrity of the self, "sanity of reason," has to be preserved when the "quiet sympathies" threaten to turn into something more debilitating. In "Home at Grasmere," Wordsworth returns to this struggle to balance sympathy with the self's integrity. One good illustration of the way Wordsworth tried to keep the notion of solitude from slipping into pure solipsism is the removal of the story of the adulterer (lines 469–532, MS B). This story, along with the counterbalancing description of the widower with six daughters (lines 533–606), was incorporated into *The Excursion*, book 6 (lines 1079–114), where the danger of solipsism has been contained by identifying it with the figure of the Solitary; but it is absent from manuscript D of "Home at Grasmere" (and of course from the posthumous printing). My argument need not, I think, involve too many conjectures about Wordsworth's reasons for shifting the story of the adulterous shepherd from "Home at Grasmere" to *The Excursion*. It will be sufficient to consider how disturbing, in a poem that in an early draft refers to "minds . . . wedded to this outward frame of things / In love" (*WHG*, MS B, lines 1000–1001) and in a later version concludes with lines heralding the "spousal verse" of the union of mind with nature, would have been the following:

> he himself
> A rational and suffering Man, himself
> Was his own world, without a resting-place.
> Wretched at home, he had no peace abroad,
> Ranged through the mountains, slept upon the earth,
> Asked comfort of the open air, and found
> No quiet in the darkness of the night,
> No pleasure in the beauty of the day.
> (*WHG*, MS B, lines 514–21)

Ostensibly, the man "suffered" because he did not take refuge in drink, remaining clearheaded and "rational" to the end; but when the approval and coadjuvancy of reason are so much a part of the larger theme, so much the thing sought, the shepherd's fate inevitably emerges as anti-Arcadian, a dark counterpart of the high pastoral or priestly role the poem's speaker takes. The shepherd's agony operates less as a warning of the dire consequences of breaking the social bond and the Seventh Commandment than as a reminder of the failure of nature, and of the mind's capacity for self-torture.

"[H]imself / Was his own world" echoes the words Milton gave Satan and that Emerson took up so enthusiastically, "The mind is its own place."[11] The shepherd's fate tells us that we receive but what we give. Reason here anchors and ironically confirms the selfhood of the shepherd, but this is a troubled and alienated selfhood, betrayed into crime and marked by the recollection of that crime: the selfhood of a Mortimer, a Manfred, or a Cain. The phrase "rational and suffering" emerges from this narrative, then, as a description not of a moral state, though the moral evidently *should* have been uppermost in the reader's mind, but of an incurably divided and solipsistic selfhood. In a context in which "reason" is more than once invoked as sanctioning the promptings of nature (MS B, line 82, MS D, line 72; MS B, line 942, MS D, line 734), this reminder of the cruel tribute reason exacted—the shepherd dies alone, not sustained by either faith or nature—would have been fatally disruptive. My interest is in the unlikely emergence, here in the tale of an adulterous shepherd, of reason as the self's nemesis. In manuscript B, it is an irony unmitigated by any moment of redemptive grace that the shepherd's story follows Wordsworth's own discovery of the *security* a rationally approved choice can bring. I refer to Wordsworth's choosing Grasmere as his home, and solitude as his way of life:

> But I am safe; yes, one at least is safe;
> What once was deemed so difficult is now
> Smooth, easy, without obstacle; what once
> Did to my blindness seem a sacrifice,
> The same is now a choice of the whole heart.
> If e'er the acceptance of such dower was deemed
> A condescension or a weak indulgence
> To a sick fancy, it is now an act
> Of reason that exultingly aspires.
> This solitude is mine; the distant thought
> Is fetched out of the heaven in which it was.
> (*WHG*, MS B, lines 74–84)

The tone of hard-won honesty cannot altogether conceal the potential instability of a self that needs "reason" to confirm its own blind earlier choice. "One" may be "safe" from external danger or

11. Milton, *Paradise Lost*, 1.254 (*Works*, 2, part 1:17).

distraction, but one may still be vulnerable to inner disharmony. The passage encapsulates the dilemma facing the poet: whether to be made "safe" by a heaven-borne reason, which approves the choice in this instance, or to follow, in the words of "Tintern Abbey," "Wherever nature led," risking seduction by a false appearance or an irrational attraction—by "sick fancy." If the self constructed and invoked in "Home at Grasmere" is the rational self of Christian humanism, the appeal to a neoclassical model of inspiration, to a power outside the self, seems likely to threaten its cohesion; on the other hand, if reason is *not* an integral part of it, the possibility arises of a division in the self. In the revised version, these lines are (again) omitted, being replaced by the simpler "On Nature's invitation do I come, / By Reason sanctioned" (MS D, lines 71–72). Yet our examination of manuscript B has alerted us to a difficulty that remains unresolved in manuscript D. Nature's invitation alone seems to be reason enough for a poet to choose Grasmere. The fact that reason also has to be invoked here betrays the possibility at least of a divergence between nature and reason, and once that is admitted, the choice looks less wholehearted than it should.

The distinction set up in both versions between good and bad solitude, or between solitude and solipsism, begins to look more like a distinction without a difference. Yet it is vital to maintaining the rationality of Wordsworth's choice to prove that the solitude of the city-dweller—one "by the vast Metropolis immured" (MS D, line 597)—is not inevitable, not part of the human condition in the modern age, but a misfortune or mistake that can be righted if one opts for "good" solitude, the solitude of the mountain and the lake. This question is closely connected with that of the poet's definition of his role. Ideally, the poet of Grasmere should be the mouthpiece for "The mind of Nature"—specifically, nature as embodied in the Vale of Grasmere—just as the poet of the 1798–1799 *Prelude* invests the genii and familiars of his boyhood remembrance with authority, and then invokes them as authorizing his narrative. Here, however, the problem is if anything more acute, since the subject is not "*a* life" but "life," and the developmental scheme of *The Recluse* demands that the imaginative animism of the early *Prelude* fragments be repudiated as naïve.

In a preliminary invocation (preliminary, that is, to the invocation of Urania), Wordsworth tries to solve this problem, of preserving the spirit of pastoral blessedness while subsuming its naïveté into a mature humanist discourse, one that acknowledges good *and* evil and makes way for the advent of reason. The invocation here breaks in unexpectedly, in the middle of the narrative of the widow and the fir grove. (The story and the poet's outburst are present in both manuscripts; the version given here is the later one.)

> Is there not
> An art, a music, and a strain of words
> That shall be life, the acknowledged voice of life?
> Shall speak of what is done among the fields,
> Done truly there, or felt, of solid good
> And real evil, yet be sweet withal,
> More grateful, more harmonious than the breath,
> The idle breath of softest pipe attuned
> To pastoral fancies? Is there such a stream,
> Pure and unsullied, flowing from the heart
> With motions of true dignity and grace,
> Or must we seek that stream where Man is not?
> (*WHG*, MS D, lines 401–12)

The primary opposition is evidently supposed to be between the moral consciousness, which embraces "solid good" and "real evil," and the "pastoral fancies" of the premoral consciousness. Yet the passage strives through its controlling metaphor to overcome that opposition, asking that a voice be found that is at once the "voice of life," knowing good and evil, and a "stream, / Pure and unsullied," with a power like nature's. In a late revision in manuscript D, Wordsworth changed "these things," referring to "motions of true dignity and grace," to "that stream," thereby repeating the image and emphasizing even more heavily the desire for a "natural" poetic voice.

This river-as-voice metaphor is the founding trope of classical poetic inspiration, Orphic and Neoplatonic, the trope of Renaissance pastoral (Spenser, Sidney, Waller, Denham), pretending that poets (as Plato argues in the *Ion*) cannot help themselves when in the command of inspiration, which flows uncontrolled, like a spring or a river (Hebrus, Helicon, Thames). It is reinforced by various anthropomorphic images: the vale not only promises or contains happiness but "is" happy: "Made for itself and happy in itself" (MS D, line 150). By a form of pathetic fallacy, solitude is said to be "in the sky" (MS D, line 133), and the very brooks and trees hold discourse with the new arrivals (MS D, line 167). The Vale has in itself the "sense / Of majesty and beauty and repose" (MS D, lines 142–43), and it can "embrace" the poet with a "smile . . . full of gladness" (MS D, lines 110, 116–17). Even the description of a house seemingly growing out of solid rock, in the narrative of the widower with six daughters, reinforces the impression that nature must participate actively and approvingly in human endeavors (MS B, lines 555–56).

This movement toward conflation of the human with the natural is offered as a kind of anamnesis, at once a recognition of origins and a recollection of forgotten knowledge. It is the mythologizing of human existence as autochthonous and of the earth as a living, conscious being, listening to human songs, smiling, blessing, succoring. In the words of the Wanderer,

> Upon the breast of new-created earth
> Man walked; and when and wheresoe'er he moved,
> Alone or mated, solitude was not.
> (*Excursion*, 4.631–33; WPW, 5:129)

The Wanderer does not seem to notice the incongruity of this autochthonous individual who walks on the breast of Mother Earth and hears "the articulate voice of God."[12] However, as Paul de Man points out, there is always in the search for origins an element of denial, of willed forgetting: "We can understand origin only in terms of difference: the source springs up because of the need to be somewhere or something else than what is now here . . . the ease with which we accept [origination] is indicative of our desire to forget."[13] Lest it be thought that this is only a recent poststructuralist perception, consider some lines from the Alfoxden Notebook (perhaps intended for *The Recluse*), which express the tendency of "consciousness of

12. Keats evades rather than solves the problem, in his evocation of anamnesis in *Hyperion: A Fragment,* by having the Titaness Mnemosyne appear in person to his poet-surrogate, Apollo. With this embodiment of memory before him, emerging from the "grassy solitudes" of a more classicized landscape, the idea of nature *listening* to his song does not seem so inappropriate. Apollo is also of a generation different from the Titans', one bound to succeed them; but in learning of his origins, as he does, it is still inevitable that he suffer.

13. De Man, *Rhetoric of Romanticism*, 4.

life" to slip into forgetfulness, the terrible power exerted by those same "beauteous forms" that at other times can be life giving:

> To gaze
> On that green hill and on those scattered trees
> And feel a pleasant consciousness of life
> In the impression of that loveliness
> Until the sweet sensation called the mind
> Into itself, by image from without
> Unvisited, and all her reflex powers
> Wrapped in a still dream [of] forgetfulness.
>   (WPW, 5:341)

This fragment, along with de Man's remark about the search for origins betraying indirectly a desire to forget the here and now, suggests a way of reading the Wordsworthian pursuit of a "natural" origin for human understanding and utterance as a flight from present consciousness—"what is now here"—and therefore, inevitably, despite the reiterated claims in *The Prelude,* a questioning of the whole developmental process. If present consciousness is not complete or stable, what is the point of the long, often painful process of maturation? In book 5 of *The Prelude,* Wordsworth recommends that a child be allowed to read tales of Fortunatus, Jack the Giant-Killer, Robin Hood, and St. George because "The child, whose love is here, at least, doth reap / One precious gain, that he forgets himself" (*WPrelude* [1850], 5.345–46). A child's "forgetting" himself or herself may suggest a widening of possibilities, an access of imaginative power, but an adult's suggests, I think, a narrowing, a retreat or abrogation.

Any moment of anamnesis involves a simultaneous forgetting or repression of what now is. The recognition of this iron law of exchange is embodied in the myth of Lethe, the river of forgetfulness, described by Æneas' father, Anchises, in his conversation with the hero in book 6 of the *Æneid.* The souls in Elysium are "Of future Life secure, forgetful of the Past"; in order to cleanse them of the stain of crimes committed in their previous existence, they have been "Compell'd to drink the deep *Lethæan* Flood: / In large forgetful draughts to steep the Cares / Of their past Labours, and their Irksom Years."[14]

14. John Dryden, *Works,* 5; *The Works of Virgil in English,* 560, 561.

Wordsworth's own version of the river of forgetfulness occurs just after the description of the mysterious disappearance of the two swans—possibly, although the speaker quickly tries to contradict the thought, killed by a shepherd (or by "the Dalesmen," in MS D). He continues,

> Thus do we soothe ourselves, and when the thought
> Is passed we blame it not for having come.
> What if I floated down a pleasant stream
> And now am landed and the motion gone—
> Shall I reprove myself? Ah no, the stream
> Is flowing and will never cease to flow,
> And I shall float upon that stream again.
> By such forgetfulness the soul becomes—
> Words cannot say how beautiful.
>   (*WHG*, MS B, lines 379–87)

The immediate reference is to the soothing thoughts that spring out of human suffering—specifically, to the notion that those who live in a holy place such as Grasmere "Must needs themselves be hallowed" (MS B, line 367). But the comparison to a river journey, the motion of which the traveler forgets, though its effect—the distance traveled— remains, widens the thought in a remarkable way. The river, in *The Prelude* so frequently a metaphor for personal growth, is also the river of forgetfulness. (Wordsworth does not use the name Lethe— his mythological allusions are rarely that explicit—but the absence of such specificity makes the passage that much more effective as an appropriation of that particular myth-element.) The stream may broaden and deepen as it leaves the source, but it becomes (in one sense) a different stream. A merciful forgetfulness of the past—not only of dalesmen with guns, but of one's own failures and errors, of the journey by which one has risen to a privileged vantage-point— underwrites the inarticulable beauty of the soul.[15] Moreover, it is precisely because the motion of the journey can be forgotten that the

15. Paul Magnuson argues that the "forgetfulness" in this passage is "a forgetting of earlier work" and that the flowing stream is present inspiration unencumbered by memories of past attempts at composition (*Coleridge and Wordsworth*, 233). He is clearly right to link the river with inspiration, the Helicon tradition, but he is forgetting the other river of classical mythology— Lethe—and this leads him to too narrow an interpretation. It is significant

journey has achieved its object. Tracing the history and seeking the origin of what one now is can sometimes be a debilitating exercise.

The perception is strikingly close to Nietzsche's ethic of forgetfulness, in its recognition of the truth in the ancient myth that there is no arriving at Elysian peace without first experiencing Lethe. In his essay "The Use and Abuse of History," which appears in *Thoughts out of Season* (second series), Nietzsche writes:

> In the smallest and greatest happiness there is always one thing that makes it happiness: the power of forgetting, or, in more learned phrase, the capacity of feeling "unhistorically" throughout its duration. One who cannot leave himself behind on the threshold of the moment and forget the past, who cannot stand on a single point, like a goddess of victory, without fear or giddiness, will never know what happiness is; and worse still, will never do anything to make others happy. . . . Forgetfulness is a property of all action; just as not only light but darkness is bound up with the life of every organism . . . life in any true sense is absolutely impossible without forgetfulness.[16]

In his essay "Nietzsche's Experience of the Eternal Return," Pierre Klossowski points out that forgetfulness is the essential accompaniment to the epiphanic experience that Nietzsche named "Eternal Return"—"the source and indispensable condition not only for the appearance of the Eternal Return but *for transforming the very identity* of the person to whom it appears." "Forgetting," Klossowski continues, "raises eternal becoming . . . to the level of being," for without it the boundaries of personal identity are dissolved. Present consciousness is predicated on the "forgetting" of other possible identities.[17] It is not simply a question of removing from

---

that this passage immediately follows the mysterious disappearance of the swans. Raimonda Modiano, agreeing that the allusion to Lethe indicates Wordsworth's desire to "exchange . . . an impure for a pure soul," adds that part of what has to be forgotten here is the "transgressive" relationship figured in the pair of swans. Pointing out that the swans, in the manuscript D version at least, are a masculine pair, Modiano suggests that their death could represent not (or not only) Wordsworth's inevitable renunciation of intimacy with Dorothy, but of intimacy with Coleridge ("Blood Sacrifice, Gift Economy and the Edenic World," 508–9).

16. Friedrich Nietzsche, *Complete Works*, 5:8–9.

17. Pierre Klossowski, "Nietzsche's Experience of the Eternal Return," 44, 45.

the burdened individual the almost intolerable consciousness of history. Nietzsche's discovery of forgetfulness, as Klossowski shows us, means that forgetting, the forgetting of other "possible identities," is implicated in the very existence from moment to moment of the consciousness of self.

If I am right in finding in "Home at Grasmere" a strain of proto-Nietzschean antihistoricism, then, it is arguably this antihistoricism, rather than the desire expressed in *The Prelude* to "enshrine the spirit of the past / For future restoration," that marks Wordsworth as a modern. Even Nietzsche does not want to render history and memory completely null, however. His objection is to "excess of history": "The unhistorical and the historical are equally necessary to the health of an individual, a community, and a system of culture."[18] What is disturbing, and intentionally so, to anyone used to the Christian-Hegelian notion that everything can ultimately be redeemed, synthesized, transformed, is the thought that action, consciousness, and culture itself may be impossible without "forgetting." It suggests a picture of human existence as a series of dark episodes and brief moments of illusory serenity—illusory, because based on the rejection of alternative possibilities of consciousness, on their being "written out of the script." It also disturbs our conception of Wordsworth in "Home at Grasmere" as priest, shepherd, prophet, since one other Wordsworthian figure who sees forgetfulness as a blessed release is the criminal, Mortimer. The fate he anticipates for himself is uncannily like that of the adulterous shepherd and not very different from that of Coleridge's Mariner:

> I will wander on
> Living by mere intensity of thought,
> A thing by pain and thought compelled to live,
> Yet loathing life, till heaven in mercy strike me
> With blank forgetfulness—that I may die.[19]

Despite its darker associations, however, the passage about the river of forgetfulness remained in manuscript D (with only minor changes), indicating that Wordsworth continued to think the agency

18. Nietzsche, *Complete Works*, 5:16, 10.
19. William Wordsworth, *The Borderers*, 294 (1797–1799 version, 5.3.271–75).

of forgetfulness significant in the formation of the moral being. But these lines amount to a surprising and extraordinary repudiation of the theme that gives narrative continuity to *The Prelude*, wherein the terrors and vexations of boyhood and youth are gratefully retrieved from memory as confirming the adult self. Now, it seems to be the *distance* between the two—between the early desiring and fearful self and the present, figured as a journey down the river of forgetfulness—that confirms the adult self.

It is not only the temporal origin of the self that is forgotten in "Home at Grasmere," however. In order for nature to be invoked at all, one must forget that nature itself cannot possibly inspire a being whose existence is cultural, not natural. To put it another way, invoking natural powers would presumably not be *necessary*, if there were not already an estrangement of the speaker from the originating power. The Christian form of this peculiar anxiety is most strikingly apparent in Rabanus Maurus' well-known medieval hymn:

> Veni, Creator Spiritus
> Mentes tuorum visita.
> Imple superna gratia
> Quae tu creasti pectora.

The Spirit is implored to "fill with heavenly grace the hearts thou hast created." But there is evidently a distance, for sinful humankind is alienated from its Creator. The hymn thus deftly reminds us both that humankind has separated itself from God ("altissimus Deus"), and the possibility of grace overcoming that distance. When such an invocation is secularized, as it is in the magnificent climax of "Home at Grasmere," the contradiction remains.

> Come, thou prophetic Spirit, Soul of Man,
> Thou human Soul of the wide earth that hast
> Thy metropolitan temple in the hearts
> Of mighty Poets.   (WHG, MS B, lines 1026–29)[20]

In revising these lines for the Prospectus, Wordsworth drops the more aggressively anthropocentric reference to the prophetic Spirit

20. Wordsworth changed "Come thou prophetic Spirit" in the 1814 Prospectus to "Descend, prophetic Spirit!" in the 1849–1850 *Poetical Works*. See Abrams, *Natural Supernaturalism*, 465.

as "Soul of Man," and puts the spirit at a further distance, making it inspire *nature*, not man—but it is nature still firmly anthropomorphized:

> Come, thou prophetic Spirit, that inspirest
> The human Soul of universal earth,
> Dreaming on things to come, and dost possess
> A metropolitan Temple in the hearts
> Of mighty Poets.   (WHG, MS D, lines 836–40)[21]

This revision clarifies and strengthens the allusion to Shakespeare's Sonnet 107:

> Not mine own fears, nor the prophetic soul
> Of the wide world dreaming on things to come,
> Can yet the lease of my true love control,
> Suppos'd as forfeit to a confin'd doom.
> The mortal moon hath her eclipse endur'd,
> And the sad augurs mock their own presage;
> Incertainties now crown themselves assur'd,
> And peace proclaims olives of endless age.
> Now with the drops of this most balmy time
> My love looks fresh, and Death to me subscribes,
> Since spite of him I'll live in this poor rhyme,
> While he insults o'er dull and speechless tribes.
>   And thou in this shalt find thy monument
>   When tyrants' crests and tombs of brass are spent.[22]

Wordsworth's allusion to this sonnet, which Jack Stillinger pointed out long ago, is not picked up by Abrams, though it is in its own way as stunning a recontextualization as the poet's earlier defiance of Jehovah, and the choir of shouting angels.[23] The prophetic soul of the wide world in Shakespeare's sonnet is clearly *not* a figure the poet

---

21. Darlington's text. But the lines were not actually written out in MS D; rather, at line 755 there is a direction, "see Preface to the Excursion," referring the reader to the printed text of the Prospectus (which ends the Preface).

22. William Shakespeare, *Complete Works*, 1326.

23. See Stillinger's notes to *The Recluse* in William Wordsworth, *Selected Poems and Prefaces*, ed. Jack Stillinger (Boston: Houghton Mifflin, 1965), 504.

expects to enlist to his aid. The mortal moon and even Shakespeare's own fears testify that such expectations are not natural, a reality ironically recognized in the line "Incertainties now crown themselves assur'd." It is only by a bold surrender of the poet's individuality to language (to the text of this poem) that Shakespeare's Death is made to subscribe to—set its seal on, witness, underwrite—him. Shakespeare's Death thus sets him apart from the poor "speechless tribes" who, like the crew of Coleridge's Ancient Mariner, are consigned to oblivion for the venial sin of having *said nothing*. Wordsworth's recontextualization of the prophetic soul dreaming on things to come actually outdares the daring of Shakespeare, for he apparently identifies his own poetic language with the language of universal earth. Death is not defied; it does not have to be, since it is an irrelevance, merely one of the "mutations that extend their sway / Throughout the nether sphere" (MS D, lines 845–46).

The passage is also, of course, a powerful humanizing of the "one common soul" that, in Anchises' monologue in the *Æneid*, animates the universe:

> Know first, that Heav'n, and Earth's compacted Frame,
> And flowing Waters, and the starry Flame,
> And both the Radiant Lights, one Common Soul
> Inspires, and feeds, and animates the whole.
> This Active Mind infus'd through all the Space,
> Unites and mingles with the mighty Mass.

Given further authority by Pope's lines in the "Essay on Man" ("All are but parts of one stupendous whole, / Whose body, Nature is, and God the soul"), this topos of the "active mind" of the universe was an eighteenth-century commonplace before the Romantics took it up.[24] What is new here, then, is not the universal soul as such but the humanizing of the soul of earth—or, more accurately, the rereading of the human element already implicit in the words "mind" and "soul" as literal truth, not analogy or figure. The key to this rereading, I think, is the new importance Wordsworth gives to the idea of the language of Nature as an interpretable *text*.

24. Dryden, *Works*, 5:560; Pope, "Essay on Man," Epistle 1, lines 267–68 (*Poems*, 514). Besides the *Æneid*, another important source for the "world-soul" concept is the philosophy of Giordano Bruno.

Wordsworth's attempted rapprochement between the human and the natural, by explicitly humanizing nature as well as by naturalizing the poetic voice, reveals the contradictions in classical mythology and in the eighteenth-century version of it. In "Home at Grasmere," the tradition of the world soul confronts the conception of the world as text, an alternative book of revelation, supplementary to the revealed Word of the Bible: Nature made available only through culture. The first raises questions of *communion* and of *inspiration;* the second, questions of *interpretation,* of *hermeneutics.* In the first, the present self's inadequacy and distance from the source are forgotten; in the second, the commonalty of origin. As in *The Prelude,* there is reference to reading nature as a printed book (a book "impressed" with "characters"), so in "Home at Grasmere" nature is treated more than once as textual. Recalling something like the youth's appetite and passion for nature evoked in "Tintern Abbey," Wordsworth writes of the pools, trees, chasms, and crags,

> I loved to look in them, to stand and read
> Their looks forbidding, read and disobey,
> Sometimes in act, and evermore in thought.
> (*WHG,* MS B, lines 919–21)

The rocks, pools, and trees are a book of laws, which can be disobeyed—we might think of the episode narrated in "Nutting"—and from which the boy was apparently an apostate, at least "in thought." This self-realization by apostasy from a written code is egotistical, potentially destructive. Nature, it is implied, is a quieting, taming, civilizing presence, rather than an inspiring, empowering, invigorating one; its ministry is the ministry of fear. But what is at work here, it is important to realize, is nature interpreted, and the very act of seeing nature as textual and as amenable to interpretation is part of that process of civilizing, of accommodating and harnessing ourselves to community instead of self, to an ideology instead of to instinct. The Wanderer's (in the early version, Pedlar's) ability to see nature as textual marks him as already subdued to human purposes, and the explicit connection with Christian discipline only highlights the extent of this process:

> Oh! then, how beautiful, how bright appear'd
> The written promise! He had early learn'd

> To reverence the Volume which displays
> The mystery, the life which cannot die:
> But in the mountains did he *feel* his faith:
> There did he see the writing.[25]

To apply a comment of Kenneth Johnston's, I find that eventually language alone reestablishes the connection with nature: "Mind does not lodge in 'poor earthly casket[s] of immortal Verse' but in language, and therefore in nature."[26] It is also important to notice that the Vale of Grasmere is not pristine wilderness (any more than Thoreau's Walden Pond was). This "abiding-place of many men" has for centuries been written over and charted by human beings. The widower's daughters, for example, have the right to cultivate their allotted spaces of ground "by sacred charter" (MS B, line 582). The fir grove planted by the widow and her late husband has a "human history" (MS B, line 635; MS D, line 416). Everything visible within the Vale is invested with human history, in fact. In this respect the "solitude" the poet enjoys turns out to be the solitariness of literary convention rather than an existential solitariness. He is not Beattie's Minstrel, standing sublime amid uncharted mountains and forests, but a reader of a text, in fact of a palimpsest bearing many layers of human overwriting.

This clearly puts "Nature's invitation" in a different light. It also might explain the change from "one Life" in manuscript B to "law supreme" in manuscript D:

> Of joy in widest commonalty spread,
> Of the individual mind that keeps its own
> Inviolate retirement, and consists
> With being limitless the one great Life—
> I sing.   (*WHG*, MS B, lines 968–72)

> Of joy in widest commonalty spread,
> Of the individual Mind that keeps her own
> Inviolate retirement, subject there
> To Conscience only, and the law supreme
> Of that Intelligence which governs all—
> I sing.   (*WHG*, MS D, lines 771–76)

25. Wordsworth, *The Ruined Cottage and The Pedlar*, 400 (MS E of *The Pedlar*). Compare *Excursion*, 1.222–27, (*WPW* 5:15).
26. Johnston, *Wordsworth and* The Recluse, 145.

Law is what appears to subsist in nature, to a mind habituated to imagining nature as textual—seeing nature as *écriture*. It will not do to dismiss this change as bad poetry or as a mere concession to Christian orthodoxy, because such a dismissal camouflages an even more profound change than that from a somewhat unorthodox theology to a more orthodox one. What happens here is a recognition of the cognitive problem ignored or postponed by the neoclassical trope of inspiration we noted in other parts of "Home at Grasmere." As Blake realized, and Rousseau did not, we cannot know or deal with "nature" except through the human, through myth or some other form of preunderstanding, a structure of laws, significances, "history." (The same perception can be found in Thoreau, for whom the experience of a completely unmitigated wilderness, in "Ktaadn," is shattering.)

In this context, too, the humanizing of the prophetic soul of the wide world appears as a "natural" extension of the rhetoric of earlier passages that project the human community of the Vale, its "peopled solitude" (the phrase is from the Alfoxden Notebook, *WPW*, 5:341), on to the Vale, describing the Vale as happy in itself, as smiling, and so on. And it is a most necessary move if there is to be communication between them.

This is why "Home at Grasmere" contains in miniature the sketch of personal development, from the fairy tales of boyhood with their Fays, Genii, and Sylphs, through the youth's interrogation of pools, chasms, trees, and crags, to the adult's self-limiting choice of Grasmere as home and as defining community, for reasons that have as much to do with human continuity as with "natural" beauty. The nature that invites must *already* be one with, or at least informed by, the reason that sanctions the invitation. The Vale of Grasmere is not untouched, undespoiled nature: it has been from time immemorial mastered, tilled, *owned*:

> so here abides
> A power and a protection for the mind,
> Dispensed indeed to other Solitudes
> Favored by noble privilege like this,
> Where kindred independence of estate
> Is prevalent where he who tills the field,
> He, happy Man! is Master of the field
> And treads the mountains which his Fathers trod.
> (*WHG*, MS D, lines 376–83)

The trope of reading nature's text, and the associated idea of nature as embodying law, appears to have forced Wordsworth to bring into greater prominence what could be called the "Michael" theme, the idea that spiritual strength and moral virtues such as fortitude and perseverance stem from, not "nature" per se, but nature interpreted, charted, and owned over several generations, the patrimonial fields. The nature/culture dichotomy is in this way undercut, rendered vacuous. There is nothing that is not culture. The original "nature," the landscape as it was before human understanding placed its mark on it, charted and interpreted it, has long since disappeared. The invocation to nature is therefore a call to the absent origin, the origin it has been essential to *forget* in order to "know" what is "known" of nature's laws.

Wordsworth's hesitation between two tropes and two traditions— the classical trope of invoking the "voice of life" itself, and the eighteenth-century Christian humanist trope of an appeal to the appearances of nature as to a text—is not, I think, a mere failure of poetic nerve, or a symptom of the onset of religious orthodoxy. It precisely dramatizes the situation confronting the modern poet. Knowledge can be grounded on past desires, fears, appetencies, memory, imaginings, and this knowledge has the strength of harmonizing suitably with the chosen pastoral mode of utterance, seeming to be the very voice of Nature itself, but risks naïveté, solipsism, the inability to encompass meaningful choice, human tragedy, contradiction, or irony. That this was a real fear is apparent from those lines in *The Prelude* in which Wordsworth refers to his certainty that even the sight of guilt, vice, and misery *could not*

> induce belief
> That I was ignorant, had been falsely taught,
> A Solitary, who with vain conceits
> Had been inspired, and walk'd about in dreams.
> (*WPrelude* [1805] 8.807–10)

Or knowledge can be grounded on the developed, moral being, able to read the "law supreme" inscribed in Nature. This necessitates the *distancing* of the self from past desires and the willingness to be "rational and suffering," perhaps even suffering the fate that Nietzsche suggests will overtake those burdened by a sense of history—an inability to act at all. In *The Prelude,* the relation between the two is developmental: the second comes from the first. Here, in "Home at Grasmere," the cost of exchanging the first for the second can no longer be ignored. "Home at Grasmere" is meant to confirm and announce the person, the self, that the speaker *has become.* The problem is how to do this without introducing a crippling dishar-mony into that self—without, that is, repudiating the very origins of that selfhood's power.

Between the first sketches for "Home at Grasmere" and the spate of revisions that resulted in what we know as manuscript D came, among other relevant works, "Elegiac Stanzas Suggested by a Picture of Peele Castle," with its eloquent repudiation of "Elysian quiet, without toil or strife" and its farewell to the "blind" happiness of "the heart that lives alone, / Housed in a dream, at distance from the Kind" (*WPW*, 4:257–58). At the personal level the poem is a response to the tragic death of the poet's brother, John. But the problem Wordsworth confronts is not personal tragedy alone; it is intrinsic to the poet's task, his enforced choice between two poetic tropes, one forgetting present pain in order to invoke "the voice of life," the other giving priority to language and so to Nature interpreted, Nature read as Law.

The marriage metaphor, the climactic trope of "Home at Gras-mere," attempts to resolve this apparently insoluble problem, to heal the division of mind from itself which we have traced in Wordsworth's narrative. Having to choose between the self-abnegation of speaking for Nature, being Nature's ventriloquist, and the closed, sterile des-tiny of reading in Nature only what humankind has already "written" there, Wordsworth selects a third way that is unrecognized by both, the visionary transformation of the world through the wedding of the human mind to Nature.[27] "Marriage" with Nature is impossible, taboo—as marriage with Dorothy would have been—yet it is the only way to reaffirm commonalty of origin while preserving (on the biblical model) different roles for the two partners. "Marriage requires that Husband and Wife be of the same Nature," wrote William Sherlock (one of Coleridge's favorite divines), referring to

27. Coleridge's "Reflections" may be the text that "Home at Grasmere" is in dialogue with, as Paul Magnuson suggests (*Coleridge and Wordsworth*, 20), but there is an important difference in the kinds of "marriage" the two poems depend on.

Christ's marriage to His church (*CN*, 3871n). *Affiliation* to Nature would be tantamount to self-abnegation, and to proclaim an absolute human superiority to nature, and ability to read it, would be merely to exchange one form of solipsism for another. Hence, both the "discerning intellect of Man" and the "goodly universe" that is to be its spouse must be equally reaffirmed, even though the two partners are not to be equal. We have only to remember the prophetic tradition of describing God's covenant with Israel as a marriage to see that there cannot be equality in such a match, so understood. Yet if the union is to transform Nature, it is also to heal the mind, which surely means that the new consciousness is not to be achieved at the cost of forgetting. The future Elysium will be "the simple produce of the common day," implying that the poet does not have to drink Lethe to get there, but, rather, has to remember who and what he is. This consciousness is undeniably a tragic consciousness, as the lines referring to the "solitary anguish" of humanity make clear; and the question that is left unresolved, in both "Home at Grasmere" and *The Recluse* itself, is whether *any* form of Elysium can be reconciled with such knowledge.

Wordsworth returns to the matter of myth in *The Excursion*, book 4, in the famous description of Apollo manifesting himself to the lonely Greek herdsman. Yet the myth has become associated with a barely audible voice, a "distant strain," even if also artfully presented as a psychological curiosity that suggests the naïve but fertile inventiveness of the primitive mind:

> —In that fair clime, the lonely herdsman, stretched
> On the soft grass through half a summer's day,
> With music lulled his indolent repose:
> And, in some fit of weariness, if he,
> When his own breath was silent, chanced to hear
> A distant strain, far sweeter than the sounds
> Which his poor skill could make, his fancy fetched,
> Even from the blazing chariot of the sun,
> A beardless Youth, who touched a golden lute,
> And filled the illumined groves with ravishment.
> (*Excursion*, 4.851–60; *WPW*, 5:136)

These lines impressed Hazlitt and Keats with their beauty, and beautiful they certainly are, but they do not constitute work on myth in Blumenberg's or any other sense. The matter of the Apollo myth is carefully held at a distance, as if for the reader's admiration. The moment has the same general narrative pattern as the "Boy of Winandermere" episode in book 5 of *The Prelude*: a lonely youth singing to the emptiness out in the hills at last falls silent and is rewarded by hearing an unearthly music. But there the similarity ends. For a description of the appearance of a god, the Apollo passage is notably lacking in that second essential ingredient of Wordsworthian experience besides beauty: fear. The passage is classicizing, in an almost sentimental manner, and while the Victorians from Browning to Oscar Wilde learned to imbue their classicizing with ironic distance, there is no such saving irony here. Nevertheless, the passage transmitted to Keats a sense of the possibilities of a new way of receiving myth, one in which the distance—and the way it lends enchantment—is exactly the point.

Five

Mythopoeic Elements in "Christabel"

" 'Christabel,' " as Walter H. Evert wrote in 1977, has "eluded critical consensus" and, despite a steady flow of commentary, continues to baffle interpretation.[1] The poem evidently owes something to the Gothic romance, and many critics, including Evert himself, have pointed out the affinities between the figure of Christabel and the Gothic heroine—young, dutiful, innocent, and terribly vulnerable. These affinities can be overemphasized, however, and on their own they do not provide a sufficient basis for understanding the poem. Its remoteness from novelistic narrative is apparent in many of its most important episodes, not the least of which is the frightening metamorphosis of Christabel (in Part II) into a stumbling, hissing double of Geraldine. No one expects a Gothic tale to obey canons of literary realism, but something is happening here that refuses to be confined even within the rather extravagant parameters of credibility that apply to the Gothic prose tales Coleridge could have known. Both events and characters are polysemous in the way we usually expect myth to be polysemous. Some of the conflicting critical accounts of the poem that now puzzle us by their inconsistency may turn out to be harmonious after all, if we take slightly higher ground and examine the poem's mythopoeic elements.

In particular I would argue that it is a mistake to see Christabel as a character in a versified novel, a "heroine," and therefore to be in any sense "on her side," whether we welcome or abhor the intrusion

1. Walter H. Evert, "Coadjutors of Oppression: A Romantic and Modern Theory of Evil," 37.

142

of Geraldine into her mother-blessed world. For all the "Gothicism" of her surroundings, the title "heroine" is as wrong for Christabel as it would be for Wordsworth's Lucy. As Jean-Pierre Mileur observes, "The attempt to create a narrative romance out of the situation at the poem's center is thwarted by the inaccessibility of a causal center or source of motive."[2] Attempts at reading the poem as a tale of sexual initiation, or of the transition from "innocence" to "experience" in some related sense, simply do not explain enough, because they provide no adequate explanation of the particular form Christabel's transformation takes.

I wish to treat "Christabel" as an instance not of novelistic narrative, nor yet of parable or allegory, but of Romantic mythopoesis. That is, I wish to draw the poem closer to Blake's *Visions of the Daughters of Albion,* Wordsworth's Lucy poems, and Shelley's *Prometheus Unbound,* and proportionately to distance it from Lewis's *The Monk* and Radcliffe's *The Mysteries of Udolpho,* analyzing Coleridge's poem as if it were written according to Shelley's dictum that a poem (as distinct from a "story") is "the creation of actions according to the unchangeable forms of human nature, as existing in the mind of the creator, which is itself the image of all other minds" (*SP&P,* 485).[3] The myth that is being "worked on" in "Christabel" is the Genesis myth, as transmitted through both the Authorized Version and Milton's dramatic treatment of the Temptation in *Paradise Lost.* The poem is richer in significance if read as a reinterpretation of this myth than if treated as Gothic romance or, psychoanalytically, as the self-revelation of the poet's sexual anxieties. My argument also suggests that the poem exposes, through the figures of Christabel and Geraldine, some of the latent misogyny of the Miltonic account, in the way it associates the feminine with weakness and with carnality.

Perhaps I should add some clarification here. By saying that the poem exposes "latent misogyny," I do not mean to extrapolate

2. Jean-Pierre Mileur, *Vision and Revision: Coleridge's Art of Immanence,* 63.

3. Richard Harter Fogle has suggested comparing "Christabel" to Blake's *Book of Thel,* but on thematic grounds: both poems describe "the first encounter of innocence with a fallen world" (*The Idea of Coleridge's Criticism,* 150).

from a reading of the poem to conclusions about Coleridge's opin-ions or ideology regarding women—either to allege that he was in any sense a "feminist" or to say that he was not. By focusing on what happens to the Genesis myth in "Christabel," I am agreeing, in general terms, with the conclusions of feminist critics regarding the poem's portrayal of female figures, but arguing that, since the poem is mythopoeic rather than a "tale" with "characters," these conclusions are relevant to a wider (and more interesting) subject, the history of reappropriations of the Genesis myth, rather than to the issue of Coleridge's opinions as such.

First, however, we must consider briefly the question of the unity of the poem. To claim that "Christabel" is a unified poem is to run counter to the aims of orthodox deconstructive criticism, as well as to dispute the mainstream critical consensus about the poem. It has seemed obvious to most traditional critics that the main problems in reading "Christabel" have to do with the relatedness or unrelatedness of the poem's two parts, and the completeness or incompleteness of the diptych, if we envisage it as a diptych. For deconstructive critics, these are not problems at all, since the mixing of genres, the wild variations of tone, as well as the poem's unfinished state, make it an obvious target for deconstructive analysis. The history of criticism of the poem, however, has until quite recently been the history of attempts to complete it, or at least to suggest how its disunity could be repaired. Assuming that Coleridge's own remarks (as reported by James Gillman and Derwent Coleridge) establish the poet's unfulfilled plans for the poem, critics have dutifully searched for proleptic evidence that the completed poem would have been a parable showing how "the virtuous of this world save the wicked" or how "the holy and innocent do often suffer for the faults of those they love." Sometimes this leads them to read back into the Geraldine of Part I the characteristics of the shapeshifter demanded by the improbable series of events Gillman gives as a summary of the projected Parts III and IV.[4] Christabel's hissing, her loss of human speech, is given a motive (she is deprived of speech so she cannot tell others what has been done to her), but there is no particular *poetic* logic in the form her transformation takes.

4. Gillman and Derwent Coleridge's reports can conveniently be con-sulted in Humphry House, *Coleridge: The Clark Lectures 1951–52*, 126–27.

H. W. Piper, in "The Disunity of *Christabel* and the Fall of Nature," is more respectful of the poem as it stands now, but Piper has to sacrifice narrative cohesion by treating Part II as a failed attempt to resume in 1799 and 1800 the interests and themes of 1797. To Piper, Geraldine's ambiguity in Part I reflects Coleridge's incipient unhappiness with the view of nature canonized in *Lyrical Ballads*: that the natural order is benevolent even when it for the moment appears evil. In support of this interpretation, he cites "Kubla Khan" and "The Ancient Mariner" as two nearly contemporary poems in which "the setting plays a vital part in the working out of the poem," though he apparently feels that the "setting" of "Christabel," Part I, is much more ambiguous than the settings of the other two poems. Both the setting and Geraldine's duplicitous character "call into question the moral purposes of the natural order."[5]

It is misleading, however, to speak of the "settings" of "Kubla Khan" and "The Ancient Mariner" as if they laid claim to the same independence from the speaker's consciousness, the same kind of "outness," as the pastoral farms of "Tintern Abbey" or the hazel trees of "Nutting." Even in his conversation poems Coleridge's language is far more concerned with nature internalized, or nature as a divinely symbolic language ("Frost at Midnight"), than with nature as "independent" entity. Coleridge himself, on his voyage to Malta in April and May 1804 (during which he had several unpleasant dreams) saw that poetry may be (in Alethea Hayter's phrase) a "rationalized dream."[6] Geraldine is surely an embodiment of mental not of "outward" forms, a figure more like Blake's "visionary forms dramatic" than like an eighteenth-century personification of nature. It is instructive that Piper has some difficulty in transferring his argument about Geraldine-as-nature to the second part of the poem. His solution—to treat the second part as less skillful than the first, indicating that Coleridge had lost sight of the fruitful ambiguities

5. H. W. Piper, "The Disunity of *Christabel* and the Fall of Nature," 217. Robert Schwartz also emphasizes the "disunity" of the poem: "the narrative, while promising the unity of a continuous and discernible meaning, rarely does more than . . . inform us of a second level of experience"—that is, the supernatural one ("Speaking the Unspeakable: The Meaning of Form in *Christabel*," 34).
6. Alethea Hayter, *A Voyage in Vain*, 50.

of Part I—imposes a further unnecessary penalty on the search for thematic and narrative unity in the poem.

Yet the unfinished state of the poem and its division into two parts are not the only features that stand in the way of a consistent parabolic interpretation. Unlike, say, Spenser, who keeps the momentum of events going by constantly reminding us (not least through the steady onward-pacing rhythm of his nine-line stanza) that each scene is but part of a larger unfolding pattern, Coleridge allows and encourages us to "freeze" the action, by having the narrator break into his own narrative:

> A sight to dream of, not to tell!
> 　　　　　(line 253; *CPW*, 1:224)
> 　Can this be she,
> The lady, who knelt at the old oak tree?
> 　　　　　(lines 296–97; *CPW*, 1:225)
> Why is thy cheek so wan and wild,
> Sir Leoline? (lines 621–22; *CPW*, 1:234)

These interruptions almost too strenuously underline the fact that the hold the poem exerts on a reader derives in large part not from expectation ("How will she get out of this one?") but from the intrinsic power of a central, heartstopping image. Even in some prose romances, such images fail to be neutralized by subsequent rescues or escapes, and therefore interrupt the narrative rhythm of the tale. For reasons I shall suggest, they impinge on the proper territory of myth and thus break the pattern of expectation that is conventional in the prose romance. Readers of Lewis's *The Monk*, for instance, surely remember the image of Agnes imprisoned in the vault and clasping to her breast the decaying body of her child, long after they have forgotten how she came to be there or how she was rescued. In Mary Shelley's *Frankenstein*, a similarly awful moment occurs when Frankenstein awakens from sleep to find the creature, which he put together from parts of human cadavers, standing over him and stretching out a yellow hand toward him. (As is well known, Mary Shelley claimed that this one scene was taken from a dream she had well before she thought out the rest of the story.) So in Part I of "Christabel" the image of Geraldine, with corpselike bosom and side, holding Christabel "As a mother with her child" (line 301; *CPW*, 1:226) is frozen for us by the narrator. It too parodies *storgè*, or mother love, as well as erotic love, and anticipates the world of "The Pains of Sleep" in its psychosexual ambiguity:

> Desire with loathing strangely mixed
> On wild or hateful objects fixed.
> Fantastic passions! maddening brawl!
> And shame and terror over all!
> Deeds to be hid which were not hid,
> Which all confused I could not know
> Whether I suffered, or I did.   (CPW, 1:390)

The impact of such images can only partly be explained through the usual kinds of interpretation—that they are emblems of life-in-death, or a horrible parody of mother love, here given connotations of necrophilia. Through such commentary, we try to express our sense that these images violate some of the most profound taboos in our culture, primarily the distinction we make between birth event and death event. The middle ground, as Jane A. Nelson points out (citing Edmund Leach), is the focus of taboo. Mythical thought, aware of such opposition, works toward a resolution, which comes about with the introduction of a third, anomalous category: the *revenant*, the incarnate god, the virgin mother. (The story of the serpent tempting Eve is at one level an attempt to explain the contradiction between a present state dominated by sorrow, toil, and division, and the recollection of earlier wholeness and happiness.) As Nelson shows, the narrativity of "Christabel" is closer to nonliterary myth than to literary narrative proper— which is not necessarily to say that it is artless. The poem poses a problem in poetic and mythopoeic logic, *"the re-union of what in this world is divided"*; and the sense of division and opposition that pervades the poem is embodied chiefly in "familial and sexual" relationships—Leoline and Christabel, Geraldine and Christabel, Christabel and her absent mother, Leoline and Geraldine.[7] (It was a problem that haunted Coleridge for many years if not to the end of his life; one of the Malta notebooks contains the entry "Mem. To examine whether Dreams of Terror & obscure Forms, ugly or not,

7. Jane A. Nelson, "Entelechy and Structure in 'Christabel,'" 385–87. See also Jonas Spatz, "The Mystery of Eros: Sexual Initiation in Coleridge's *Christabel*," 113.

be commonly preceded by Forms of Awe & Admiration with distant Love"—*CN*, 1998.)

It is notable, however, that in Coleridge's *poetry* the perception of division or opposition very often shows itself as a threat not to the stability of outward things, nor even to psychic stability as such, but to *the very possibility of poetic utterance itself.* The "Ode to the Departing Year," written at the close of 1796, which "prophesies, in anguish of spirit, the downfall of this country," ends:

> I unpartaking of the evil thing,
>> With daily prayer and daily toil
>> Soliciting for food my scanty soil,
> Have wail'd my country with a loud Lament.
> Now I recentre my immortal mind
>> In the deep Sabbath of meek self-content;
> Cleans'd from the vaporous passions that bedim
> God's Image, sister of the Seraphim.   (*CPW*, 1:168)

The phrase "I unpartaking of the evil thing" should not be read as the poet's claim to moral superiority. It is spoken in the character of national prophet, and is a recognition of the fact that in order to utter prophetic words at all, the poet must be blessed with unity of being. Biblical thought constantly images evil as "double-mindedness" (Psalms 12:2, 51:6, 119:113), while the forked tongue or sharp-edged (cutting, splitting) tongue is the dominant metaphor for false or deceitful utterance (Psalms 52:2, 57:4, 140:3). Coleridge himself uses the image of the forked tongue in the late poem "Alice du Clos," in which he quotes a proverb about the slit tongue being the badge of the traitor (*CPW*, 1:469). More important, the inability to speak one's thought because of disunity in the inward being is a theme common to several of Coleridge's poems that abjure the prophetic stance. In the 1796 sonnet "When they did greet me father," for instance, the poet's attempt at prayer is frustrated by "Th'unquiet silence of confused thought / And shapeless feelings" (*CPW*, 1:153), where the apparent self-contradiction of "unquiet silence" focuses the speaker's dilemma, inner turmoil preventing the prayerful response demanded by the occasion. A different kind of inner disharmony prevents the Ancient Mariner from voicing the prayer he knows he should speak: as he longs for death, for self-annihilation, he cannot at the same time affirm his being (or the being of Being) through prayer.

In "The Pains of Sleep," too, the first thing in the speaker's mind is the possibility of utterance itself and the intimate connections among poetic utterance, love, and prayer. The attempt to pray, like the initiation into love, presupposes and requires wholeness in the self.

When the prayer state is successfully achieved in Coleridge's poetry, there is usually a corresponding emphasis on unity of being, as at the conclusion of the 1807 poem "To William Wordsworth," written after Coleridge heard Wordsworth read *The Prelude* (then known, of course, simply as "the poem to Coleridge") at Coleorton:

> Scarce conscious, and yet conscious of its close
> I sate, my being blended in one thought
> (Thought was it? or aspiration? or resolve?)
> Absorbed, yet hanging still upon the sound—
> And when I rose, I found myself in prayer.   (CPW, 1:408)

Silent prayer, presumably, just as Christabel's prayer on behalf of her lover is silent, indicating perfect community between the person praying and the one prayed to—no need for the intervention of speech. The language of familial and sexual relationship which Coleridge adopts in "Christabel" should not blind us to the fact that the primary "division and opposition" the poem is concerned with is not in nature, nor even in sexual or familial "identity," but in the profoundest reaches of the self: an experience corresponding to Wordsworth's sense of "treachery and desertion in the place / The holiest that I knew of" (*WPrelude* [1805], 10.80–381). In "Christabel," as in "The Pains of Sleep," the victim is also the doer of evil ("Sure I have sinn'd") while the agent, Geraldine, the "worker of these harms," looks more like a victim, "still and mild" (lines 381, 298, 300; CPW, 1:228, 226). More to the point, in Part II the moment that dominates the narrative, the moment for which everything else seems only a preparation, is the moment when Christabel's power of speech is paralyzed:

> Christabel in dizzy trance
> Stumbling on the unsteady ground
> Shuddered aloud, with a hissing sound.
>   (lines 589–91; CPW, 1:233)

Here the narrative comes to a final halt, save for the "Conclusion to Part II," which is really a second way of describing the same condition, the same discovery of treachery and desertion within the self. The loving father, compelled to utter his "love's excess" by sheer pressure of emotion, finds that his words slip, slide, and perish, betraying an unsuspected rage and pain alongside the love. If the father's words, as suggested here, are "wild," like a monster that, once set free, exhibits destructive powers his maker never intended him to have, then the bitterness they express is nevertheless *there*, part of their content, whether "unmeant" or not. From this perspective the "Conclusion to Part II" appears to be a commentary not on a moral truth, at least in the first instance, but on a truth about speech and about its frightening disconnectedness from willed thought and meaning. The fathers Leoline and Coleridge are their own victims in the sense that each is "responsible for" the utterance, even though the bitterness it expressed was unwilled or unmeant (just as Coleridge feared at times that he may have been in some obscure way "responsible for" the loathsome images summoned up in his dreams):[8]

> pleasures flow in so thick and fast
> Upon his heart, that he at last
> Must needs express his love's excess
> With words of unmeant bitterness.
> Perhaps 'tis pretty to force together
> Thoughts so all unlike each other;
> To mutter and mock a broken charm,
> To dally with wrong that does no harm.
> Perhaps 'tis tender too and pretty
> At each wild word to feel within
> A sweet recoil of love and pity.
> (lines 662–72; *CPW,* 1:235–36)

In this wildly associative, dreamlike, and amoral moment, parallel not only to Leoline's rage but also to Christabel's dizzy trance, human relationship is turned to "sorrow and shame," love to "rage and pain," and prayer to "a broken charm." Coleridge has perhaps recognized in this image the horror of his own state—the paralysis of poetic and prayerful utterance. Hazlitt—if it was Hazlitt who wrote the review of the "Christabel" volume in the *Examiner,* June 2, 1816—was quite

8. See David S. Miall, "The Meaning of Dreams: Coleridge's Ambivalence," 69.

right to say of Coleridge that "he comes to no conclusion."[9] There is no "conclusion" because the real subject of "Christabel" is not a story but a state. In that respect "Christabel" shows affinity not so much with traditional narrative poetry as with Blakean mythopoesis. Like *Visions of the Daughters of Albion*, Coleridge's poem depicts a strangeness in human existence; and instead of moving forward to a specious resolution, it ends with the dominant image of a human soul in its temporally divided and speechless state, as if recognizing that a miraculous hairbreadth escape would be at best a weak palliative. Each part of "Christabel" focuses on a distinct moment of horror arising from some profound division and havoc in the self: the first part, on the displacement of Christabel's mother's spirit by the sinister Geraldine; the second part, on the desperate situation of Christabel struggling to speak her peril but unable to do so, "O'ermastered by the mighty spell" (line 620; *CPW*, 1:234). Both moments exist outside the normal moral cause-and-effect paradigms of the day world: both are "dark sayings" unfolding the "disquietness of heart" that emerges unsummoned from a prayerful moment of "Deep inward stillness & a bowed Soul" (*CN*, 259).

These biblical phrases (from Psalm 49:4, Psalm 43:5, and Psalm 44:25) come from an entry in the Gutch memorandum book, possibly a list of references to be used in a projected Essay on Prayer. The phrases group themselves around an experience similar to the ones adumbrated in an outline of the prayer experience (*CN*, 257). In "Christabel" and "The Pains of Sleep," however, the preparation for prayer and the gradual composing of the mind to a state of contemplation are followed by the terrible irruption of loathsome phantoms, the sense of evils done and suffered, which contaminates the still mind of the worshiper and taints the prayers he or she is struggling to utter. With her mother's spirit near, or at least not banished, Christabel prays in "gentle vows," pious tears just beginning in her eyes—"both blue eyes more bright than clear, / Each about to have a tear," another image of motherhood (lines 285, 290–91; *CPW*, 1:225). After her mother's spirit is banished and replaced by Geraldine, the desire to pray remains but there is a change—"tears she sheds— / Large tears that leave the lashes bright"—and she moves now

9. J. R. de J. Jackson, ed., *Coleridge: The Critical Heritage*, 205.

"unquietly" (lines 315–16, 323; *CPW*, 1:226). In Christabel's troubled sleep we confront the third stage of prayer as Coleridge described it: "Repentance & Regret—& self-inquietude" (*CN*, 257).

Some psychoanalytical criticism of Coleridge has perhaps tended to obscure an important aspect of the "absent mother" motif in "Christabel": for Coleridge, the idea of mother love is closely associated with prayer and the ability to pray. Coleridge's memories of childhood prayer, as Kathleen M. Schwartz points out, always involved his mother—never his father—and the outline of the Essay on Prayer associates prayer closely with mother love (*CN*, 263; and cf. *CN*, 750).[10] Sir Leoline's kind of piety seems by contrast distinctly patriarchal, or Urizenic: "Each matin bell, the Baron saith, / Knells us back to a world of death" (lines 332–33; *CPW*, 1:227).

Part I of "Christabel," then, speaks of a Christabel element in the human spirit which is openhearted, generous, prayerful, and attuned to nature's gentler aspects. In the language of the Gutch memorandum book (based on Psalm 22:3), the Christabel-in-us "inhabit[s] God's praises" (*CN*, 259). She is orphaned, however, after the departure of a certain kind of spirituality that is associated in the poem with womanhood and motherhood. This deprivation leaves her vulnerable to the irruption of the tyrannous Geraldine. In mythopoeic terms it is entirely credible that the "unchangeable form," Christabel, should accept as well-intentioned and even pitiable the Geraldine element, which presents itself as an emissary of higher powers or as descended from "a noble line" (lines 227–28, 79; *CPW*, 1:223, 218).

That-which-is-Geraldine is, however, specious, deceitful, potent, and capable of imposing its will on "Christabel," as shown by its deformed shape underneath the "silken robe" (line 250; *CPW*, 1:224). "Geraldine" may here be glossed not merely as nature (Piper's view) but the natural man, existence-in-the-flesh, Blake's Rahab. She belongs to a long and dishonorable tradition of succubae and tempt-

---

10. Kathleen M. Schwartz, "Prayer in the Poetry of S.T.C.," 23. Rhonda Johnson Ray develops the idea that Christabel is a St. Teresa figure who also symbolizes Coleridge's idea of a true Christian Church ("Geraldine as Usurper of Christ: An Un-mystical Union," 513, 518). While the line comparing Christabel to a hermitess does reinforce Christabel's similarity to St. Teresa, I differ from Ray in seeing Christabel's piety as directed at nature (in its gentler aspects), rather than at mystical union with Christ.

resses, including most notably Spenser's Duessa, in whom the double aspect of the flesh—beautiful to view, but subject to corruption and exercising a tyrannical power over the soul—is imaged (*The Faerie Queene*, 1.8.47).[11] Christabel's innocent adoration of nature has no defense against the unredeemed carnality that Geraldine represents. The result of this psychomachy is the transformation of unaffected piety, and the holy sleep of a calm soul (*CN*, 191), to a state of "self-inquietude." Geraldine's oldest ancestors are Eve and the serpent; she is woman as patriarchal religion sees her: duplicitous, seductive, a snare, and a delusion, identified with the flesh, an embodiment of "lower powers." The words of the seventeenth-century moralist Joseph Glanvill may be taken as typical of this tradition: "Now this is the present unhappy state of Man; our *lower* powers are gotten uppermost. . . . The *Woman* in us still prosecutes a deceipt like *that* begun in the Garden; and we are wedded to an *Eve*, as fatal as the Mother of our Miseries."[12] The image of the woman-serpent, borrowed from classical tradition by Christian writers to represent this misrule of man by fleshly appetites, reaches its nadir in the representation of Sin, in Milton's *Paradise Lost*, as "Woman to the waste, and fair," but in her lower part "a Serpent arm'd / With mortal sting"(2.650, 652–53).[13] Stuart Peterfreund, noting the serpentine qualities of Geraldine, further suggests that the deformity of her bosom and side may be a link with Milton's Satan, who "first knew pain" when the spear of the archangel Michael wounded him in the side. This wound, Peterfreund points out, does not diminish Satan's power to work spells.[14]

Despite the persuasiveness of some recent feminist readings of "Christabel," it seems to me possible for a feminist critic to recognize this deceitfulness and carnality in Geraldine and still not necessarily

11. Fogle suggests the comparison of Geraldine to Duessa (*Idea of Coleridge's Criticism*, 133) and observes: "There may be evil for us in mother, friend, or lover, ambiguous but real, unwilled but inherent in being itself" (132).

12. Joseph Glanvill, "Against Confidence in Philosophy and Matters of Speculation" (1676), quoted in Donald Greene, "Latitudinarianism and Sensibility: The Genealogy of the 'Man of Feeling' Reconsidered," 169–70.

13. Milton, *Works*, 2, Part 1:61.

14. Stuart Peterfreund, "The Way of Immanence, Coleridge, and the Problem of Evil," referring to *Paradise Lost*, 6.327.

interpret the poem itself as misogynist, as overtly endorsing the patriarchal view of women as "fatal," their sexuality as a ploy by which Satan drags men down. Indeed, the point about Geraldine-as-Duessa is that she is not woman, but monster, a mythic embodiment in female form of deceitfulness and carnality—the monster that patriarchal religion imposed on woman by identifying her with the evil that there is in being itself. (Christabel is not a "woman," in the sense of a woman *character*, either, and reading the poem as myth rather than as novelistic narrative helps us to see this.) However, Karen Swann argues that those who see Geraldine as a Duessa figure are themselves "ruffians" who either refuse to hear Geraldine's story of her abduction or treat it as a "come-on." To Swann, Geraldine is at first a figure conjured up by Christabel herself "to get around patriarchal law, which legislates desire." Swann later suggests that Geraldine's "origins are as much in literature as in Christabel"; for Swann, the whole Geraldine-Christabel relationship exposes the conspiracy of male authorities to project their *own* hysterical fear of desire on to the female.[15] I think the poem does do this, but by working at a level deeper than that of literary or romance convention. The poem rereads myth, or, rather, it rereads the Christian reading of the serpent-woman myth. If Geraldine is seen as a mere projection from Christabel's own psyche, this transmutation loses its power. There are also good reasons why Christabel's mother is absent, which go beyond Swann's suggestion that the phrase "wandering mother" is a reference to the malady of hysteria (549). Christabel's mother, if alive, would presumably have been able to teach Christabel to love nature without being swallowed up in it. As it is, caught between a father who is alien, authoritative, and life hating, and a mother substitute who is a patriarchal caricature of womanhood, Christabel cannot protect her own vulnerable kind of innocent spirituality; she is helpless to stop herself falling prey to the speciously beautiful representative of the flesh.[16]

15. Karen Swann, "'Christabel': The Wandering Mother and the Enigma of Form," 534, 538, 540.
16. Swann's reading also depends on a rapid switching of points of view, so that Geraldine is first a Gothic heroine whose story deserves a "fair hearing," then a figment of Christabel's overheated brain, then a literary convention. This turns the poem into a sort of farrago. And, given the

The worst consequences are saved for the second part of the poem, however, as Christabel finds herself unable to enlist the help of her father, whose piety is of the morbid, death-obsessed kind, in contrast to the fresh-air-and-wildflower piety of Christabel's absent mother. Instead, Sir Leoline seems strangely attracted to Geraldine's specious grandeur, as a pharisaical religiosity is often pruriently attracted to what it affects to despise. Worse still, Christabel is shown "passively" imitating the serpentine look of "dull and treacherous hate" thrown in her direction by Geraldine (lines 605–6; *CPW*, 1:234), and in the midst of her trance she is unable to make any sound other than a serpent's hiss. As in the night world of "The Pains of Sleep" the evildoer has all along enjoyed the appearance of virtue while the victim is shown guilty of complicity in her own downfall. Interpretations that view Christabel's downfall as purely or primarily sexual in nature surely narrow the significance of most of Part I of the poem. Christabel fails to read the warning signs—Geraldine's refusal to pray, the tongue of light in the dying fire (lines 142, 159; *CPW*, 1:221)—with the result that Christabel, the embodiment of spiritual wholeness, quickly permits herself to accept Geraldine, the embodiment of carnality, existence-in-the-flesh, as what she appears to be, a lady of "noble line." Christabel has sinned, and she is punished by being turned into another Geraldine. This is the justice of the imagination, the same justice that is properly meted out to Milton's Satan:

> a greater power
> Now rul'd him, punisht in the shape he sin'd,
> According to his doom: he would have spoke,
> But hiss for hiss returnd with forked tongue
> To forked tongue, for now were all transform'd
> Alike.   (*Paradise Lost*, 10.515–20)[17]

The forked tongue is no more than a recognition, a rendering into physical terms, of the fact that Satan and the rebel angels have deceived themselves as well as their victims Eve and Adam. Christabel,

---

premises of Swann's reading, is it simply too literal-minded to ask why, if Geraldine is a figment of Christabel's mind, she appears so convincingly before Sir Leoline?

17. Milton, *Works*, 2, part 2:323.

too, has become divided in nature. She is at least partly subject to the tyranny of Geraldine, and of those Geraldine serves, the ambivalent powers of "the upper sky." The spell is "lord of [her] utterance" to such an extent that she cannot explain the danger to her father but can only blurt out a desperate entreaty that he send the deceiver away.

A close connection is assumed here between speech, especially prayerful utterance, and wholeness. Christabel appeals to Sir Leoline by her mother's soul (line 616; *CPW*, 1:234), a reminder that prayer grows from the unity of being suggested in the image of mother and child, rather than from the relationship of father to child; compare the narrator's repeated prayer "Jesu, Maria, shield her well!" (lines 54, 582; *CPW*, 1:217, 233). There is even a hope that the undeceived and single-natured poet Bracy may be able to banish the evil "With music strong and saintly song" (line 561; *CPW*, 1:232). As far as this narrative is concerned, however, that-which-is-Christabel is deeply compromised by its contact with that-which-is-Geraldine, and the consequences are fatal to poetry itself: to be forced into silence, robbed of the power of utterance, is equivalent to the complete loss of "poetic space," the power of projecting from the self an answering and reciprocally self-confirming otherness, the power to affirm Being as the ground of self.

Paul H. Fry has argued that Wordsworth and Coleridge rejected the older identification of "poetic space," or the system of relationships that gives meaning to poetry, with the order of genres. In the new Romantic poetic, Fry suggests, "poetic space is what we half perceive and half create on the basis of an ad hoc symbiosis of mind with nature." The function of symbolism within this poetic is "the making-present of some universal power that is universally absent until by magic the *nomen* grows numinous. . . . Were it not . . . defiant of determinism by externally given origins, this faith would attach itself to the office of prayer."[18] If "Christabel" is essentially, as I have proposed, a poem about poetic utterance, depicting a state in which the inward stillness necessary for such utterance, as it is for prayer, is destroyed by disquietness of heart and self-deception, then Coleridge seems to have rejected any "ad hoc symbiosis of mind with nature" almost before it produced any results, suspecting, with Blake, that nature and the natural man are not only ambiguous

18. Paul H. Fry, *The Poet's Calling in the English Ode*, 134–35.

but tyrannous, deceitful usurpers claiming descent from the "noble line" of Being itself. The substitution of the fleshly Geraldine for the absent mother-spirit is a horrible actualization of the way in which that-which-is-Christabel, in its orphaned loneliness, makes the natural man its adoptive parent (an anticipation of Stanza 6 of Wordsworth's "Intimations" Ode), and in Part II of the poem the stultifying of prayerful utterance is the inevitable consequence. If Christabel had been able to speak to Geraldine, she might have said something like this:

> Thou Mother of my Mortal part.
> With cruelty didst mould my Heart.
> And with false self-decieving tears,
> Didst bind my Nostrils Eyes & Ears.
>
> Didst close my Tongue in senseless clay
> And me to Mortal Life betray.[19]

For the prophetic poet, poetic speech must assert itself in absolute freedom from the mortal part, the "evil thing," and to allow the lower powers of mortal life to close around the mind is to resign oneself to tongue-tied silence.

19. William Blake, "To Tirzah" (*Complete Poetry and Prose*, 30).

Six

Refiguring Myth

Queen Mab, "Hymn to Intellectual Beauty," and "Mont Blanc"

Shelley's *Queen Mab,* written between spring 1812 and February 1813—that is, soon after Shelley had committed himself to a determined fight against Christian orthodoxy—contains in its passionate attack on the consequences of religious dogma a powerful restatement of d'Holbach's materialist-necessitarian account of the origins of religion. It was this materialist account that was the basis of Dupuis' *Origine de tous les cultes* and other late-Enlightenment theories of the beginnings of religion, already discussed in Chapter 1. Shelley is therefore going back more than forty years for this theory, but this testifies to d'Holbach's lasting power over radical young minds. Shelley not only gives that theory a key place in his first major poem, he also quotes d'Holbach extensively in his annotations to the poem, beginning with the argument that "God" is simply an abstraction, a name for the unknowable cause of causes:

> Man's earliest theology made him, firstly, fear and worship the elements themselves, things that were material and crude; then he bestowed his adoration on the powers that controlled the elements, on inferior spirits, on heroes, or on men gifted with extraordinary qualities. Having considered more deeply, he believed he could simplify things by placing all of nature under a single agent, a spirit, a universal soul, who set nature itself and all its parts in motion.[1]

1. "La première théologie de l'homme lui fit d'abord craindre et adorer les éléments même, des objets matériels et grossiers; il rendit ensuite des

Despite the shortcomings of *Queen Mab,* soon recognized by Shelley himself, the passage from canto 6 in which he summarizes d'Holbach's theory of early religious beliefs evidently struck him as having intrinsic importance—he published it separately in 1816, under the title "Superstition." Religion itself in this passage is personified first as a deluded infant, then as a superstitious youth, then as a power-hungry, crazed adult:

"Thou taintest all thou lookest upon!—the stars,
Which on thy cradle beamed so brightly sweet,
Were gods to the distempered playfulness
Of thy untutored infancy: the trees,
The grass, the clouds, the mountains, and the sea,
All living things that walk, swim, creep, or fly,
Were gods: the sun had homage, and the moon
Her worshipper. Then thou becamest, a boy,
More daring in thy frenzies: every shape,
Monstrous or vast, or beautifully wild,
Which, from sensation's relics, fancy culls;
The spirits of the air, the shuddering ghost,
The genii of the elements, the powers
That give a shape to nature's varied works,
Had life and place in the corrupt belief
Of thy blind heart: yet still thy youthful hands
Were pure of human blood. Then manhood gave
Its strength and ardour to thy frenzied brain;
Thine eager gaze scanned the stupendous scene,
Whose wonders mocked the knowledge of thy pride;
Their everlasting and unchanging laws
Reproached thine ignorance. Awhile thou stoodst
Baffled and gloomy; then thou didst sum up
The elements of all that thou didst know;
The changing seasons, winter's leafless reign,
The budding of the heaven-breathing trees,
The eternal orbs that beautify the night,

---

hommages à des agents présidents aux éléments, à des génies inférieurs, à des héros, ou à des hommes doués de grandes qualités. A force de réfléchir, il crut simplifier des choses en soumettant la nature entière à un seul agent, à un esprit, à une âme universelle, qui mettoit cette nature et ses parties en mouvement" (*Système de la nature* [1781], quoted in *SCW*, 1:148). Wherever possible, I cite the Reiman-Powers text of Shelley (*SP&P*). Prose works not in Reiman-Powers, including the notes to *Queen Mab,* are cited from *SCW*.

> The sun-rise, and the setting of the moon,
> Earthquakes and wars, and poisons and disease,
> And all their causes, to an abstract point
> Converging, thou didst bend, and called it GOD!"
> (6.72–102; SP&P, 47–48)[2]

The continuation of the passage depicts religion, after a bloodthirsty career in the name of the "abstract point" called God, now declining into imbecility and exhaustion; for the Shelley of 1812–1813 evidently believed that religion had almost run its course, despite its feeble, vengeful persistence. The poem assumes the temporal, transient nature of all religious systems, as does the "Letter to Lord Ellenborough" (printed in June 1812 and therefore contemporaneous with *Queen Mab*). The "Letter" makes the case that Christianity is no different from other religions and may be rather worse in its use of violence to enforce belief. "Does not analogy favour the opinion, that as like other systems it has arisen and augmented, so like them it will decay and perish . . . [?]" (*SCW*, 5:290). The "Letter" continues by arguing that the very origin of Christianity is owing to historical accident. Were it not for the peculiar combination of circumstances created by Jewish "fanaticism" and the failure of Roman authority, "the christian religion never could have prevailed, it could not even have existed" (291). Intelligent readers, this argument implies, will from now on understand the world in materialist-necessitarian terms, realizing that what really keeps the universe going is not God but a "universal Spirit" or world soul:

> Even the minutest molecule of light,
> That in an April sunbeam's fleeting glow
> Fulfils its destined, though invisible work,
> The universal Spirit guides.
> (6.174–77; SP&P, 49)

Like Dupuis and Volney, Shelley anticipates a future age when humankind will permit itself to be governed only by "reason's voice,"

2. In the 1816 version the last two lines here quoted were altered, softening the "atheism" of the passage, if only slightly: "And all their causes, to an abstract point / Converging, thou didst give it name, and form, / Intelligence, and unity, and power." For information about the 1816 version of these lines, I am indebted to *The Poems of Shelley*, ed. Geoffrey Matthews and Kelvin Everest, *1804–1817*, 1, 323–24.

more or less identified with the voice of nature itself. From the Voltairean motto "Ecrasez l'infame!" to the trust in nature's higher wisdom which informs the poem's conclusion, *Queen Mab* draws heavily on the thinking of the French Enlightenment.[3]

With Volney and Dupuis, Shelley traces mythological beliefs to their superstitious origins in the tendency of primitive men to ascribe godlike attributes to sun, moon, stars, and other natural phenomena. The denunciation of religion is so thoroughgoing that myth, even in the most general sense of human beings' fictive attempts to explain the world, seems to have no value left at all except as a telling symptom of the "corrupt heart" of primitive religion. By virtually identifying "primitive" thought with religion itself, and attacking its imaginative constructions so vigorously (implying that they were historically bound to lead to the horrors of religious wars), Shelley seems to place imaginative narratives *of all kinds* under suspicion—a mistake that Blake avoided even in his most "naturalistic" work, *The Marriage of Heaven and Hell*. Even the point Shelley makes in addressing the Catholics of Ireland in "An Address to the Irish People" (January 1812)—that religious beliefs should be judged by how far they "make men good" (*SCW*, 5:216)—hardly enters into consideration in *Queen Mab*. That these beliefs might possibly have value to the artist other than as examples of pitiable superstition—poetic value, that is—does not seem to have occurred to Shelley until after the completion of *Queen Mab*, unless we except the narrative of Ahasuerus in canto 7, which anticipates in its dramatic content the conversation between Asia and Demogorgon in *Prometheus Unbound*.

Ahasuerus seems to say, in answer to Ianthe's question "Is there a God?," that the vengeful Jehovah of the Old Testament indeed exists as long as human beings continue to worship him: Moses heard this God speak, Jesus gave him a superficially less terrible aspect, but he still tyrannizes over humankind, and Ahasuerus, like

3. That Shelley took Voltaire's motto as a personal axiom is shown by his quoting it in a letter to Thomas Jefferson Hogg, January 6, 1811 (Kenneth Neill Cameron et al., eds., *Shelley and His Circle*, 2:688). He later was more critical of what he came to see as the oversimplified and dogmatic materialism of the French ideologues, but blamed their narrowness on the institutions that produced them rather than on the men themselves. See Terence Allan Hoagwood, *Skepticism and Ideology: Shelley's Political Prose and Its Philosophical Context from Bacon to Marx*, 145, 180.

a parody of Prometheus defying Jupiter, resolves to "hurl / Defiance at his impotence to harm / Beyond the curse I bore" (7.199–201; *SP&P*, 56). Ahasuerus is trapped in his despair—*his* false belief, unlike Prometheus', holds no prospect of a liberalizing dialectic—but in his speech to Ianthe, there is the germ of a different and more poetically creative way of articulating beliefs whose veracity the poet still wishes to put in question.[4]

In the fall of 1812, Shelley made the acquaintance of Thomas Love Peacock, and at least partly through this new friendship Shelley's knowledge of myth took a new turn. Peacock was something of an amateur orientalist, having as a young man studied classical and Near Eastern art at the British Museum, as well as some of the rapidly increasing number of available works on Near Eastern beliefs. By October 1812, he had probably already begun work on what was intended to be a narrative epic in twelve books, based on Zoroastrian beliefs and entitled *Ahrimanes*.[5] The sources Peacock cites in the longer extant version of the work, which was never completed, include "the astronomical mythologists," Volney, Dupuis, Bryant, and Hyde, as well as the *Prometheus* of Æschylus, the *Zendavesta*, and Virgil. Peacock's enthusiasm for Zoroastrianism, along with the "zodiacal philosophy" of the vegetarian John Frank Newton (also a Zoroastrian), helped to induce Shelley to change his attitude toward myth, abandoning the sterile skepticism of d'Holbach in favor of a view that accepted mythology as a manifestation of what human beings were *capable of imagining*, and as embodying, in imaginative form, certain powers and qualities, both good and evil, that it projects as universal. The germ of this view, I have suggested, is implicit in Ahasuerus' answer to Ianthe's question: Jehovah is a real voice to Moses and to his later worshipers, including Ahasuerus himself, even though the poet (and Ianthe) think Ahasuerus is still deluded in allowing this false deity such power over him.

4. Stuart Curran discusses the figure of Ahasuerus at some length, seeing him as an "icon of sublime futility" (*Shelley's Annus Mirabilis: The Maturing of an Epic Vision*, 21). I agree with this description, but I nevertheless argue that dramatic possibilities are at least glimpsed here. This part of *Queen Mab* may have been written *after* Shelley first met Peacock, however. See Cameron et al., eds., *Shelley and His Circle*, 3:236.

5. See Cameron et al., eds., *Shelley and His Circle*, 1:94–95, 3:236.

At any rate, after *Queen Mab*, Shelley—without being any less committed to what a recent critic calls "the moral poet's obligation not only to respond but to respond truthfully to mankind's needs"[6]—develops a more creative and still more subversive way of using myths. But he does not give them more than a circumscribed, conditional authority, as poetic creations of the human spirit to be valued only so far as they are liberating and not constraining. In this way, mythology, when revisioned as borrowing its authority from the human imagination itself, can subvert the complacent acceptance of orthodox religious belief. Mythology becomes an important part of the armory of the skeptical poet who, seeing the present corrupt state of society, determines to use his poetry to show humankind the possibility that a new age may be imminent. In the hands of a skeptical writer, mythology can do this work precisely because it lacks higher authority: to those in the know, a mythological treatment advertises itself as both artful and politically engaged, and through a parallel kind of innuendo it points to the ephemerality of all belief systems.

Shelley is hesitant to claim that there is a one-way, causal connection between writing and social progress, however—that radical writing brings about social change. In "Proposals for an Association of . . . Philanthropists" (March 1812), he speculates that there might be such a connection between the writings of the Encyclopedists and the French Revolution; but he immediately qualifies this by saying that it might be a mistaken assumption that an earlier event caused a later one: "We have no other idea of cause and effect, but that which arises from necessary connection; it is therefore, still doubtful whether D'Alembert, Boulanger, Condorcet, and other celebrated characters, were the causes of the overthrow of the ancient monarchy of France" (*SCW*, 5:264). If the Encyclopedists contributed to the spread of knowledge (and therefore to the democratization of France), it is equally true that the terrible material conditions of the French people made the country ripe for revolution.

Yet there remains the problem of how one uses myth for its potentially liberating function without once more giving it the power to enslave human beings to a single dogma. There is in humans a hunger for belief that can betray all but the most scientifically minded into

6. Mary A. Quinn, "The *Daemon of the World*: Shelley's Antidote to the Skepticism of *Alastor*," 758.

putting trust in harmful superstitions. As the deist Theosophus says in Shelley's dialogue "A Refutation of Deism," "There is a tendency to devotion, a thirst for reliance on supernatural aid inherent in the human mind" (*SCW*, 6:45). Theosophus is naïvely adopting this argument as a way of proving the existence of God, but for Shelley, as Roland A. Duerksen argues, and for those other "critical Romantics" Blake and Keats, the task of the imagination is to cleanse the mind of "the accrued encumbrances of social conditioning" that make true self-awareness impossible.[7] The authority of myth, and of theology, is one feature of this "conditioning" that Shelley has his reader cast off. To use myth *at all,* as a poet, Shelley first has to revision it into something that is not sanctioned by a transcendent order, nor even by the human validation of many centuries of tradition. Shelley realizes after "Queen Mab" that for a poet to use any traditionally authoritative discourse—that of Christianity or Islam, for instance, or of pagan antiquity—is to risk implicating his own discourse even if the poet wishes merely to employ the authoritative discourse "dramatically," without committing himself to it.[8]

The characteristic way in which Shelley deals with this crucial problem for the remaking of myth can be illustrated with a striking example. In a passage that first appeared in the notes to *Queen Mab* and was later incorporated in *A Vindication of Natural Diet,* his essay urging the merits of vegetarian food and abstention from alcoholic liquor, Shelley produces what may be one of the most interesting reasons ever given for becoming a vegetarian, drawing on what was a commonplace of skeptical argument in the classical era. Our gods, Shelley argues, are projections of our own natures, so if we are vegetarians we are not likely to believe in a god who can be propitiated by cruel treatment of his creatures. Our god will, rather, be a deity who rejoices in his creatures' happiness:

> [The vegetarian] will escape the epidemic madness, that broods over its own injurious notions of the Deity, and "realizes the hell that priests and beldams feign." Every man forms as it were his god from his own

7. Roland A. Duerksen, "The Critical Mode in British Romanticism," 9. See also Paul Hamilton, "Romantic Irony and English Literary History," 30: "With the second generation of the English romantics comes a kind of poetry visibly worried about which reading it invites."
8. This point is made very well by John Archer, "Authority in Shelley."

character; to the divinity of one of simple habits, no offering would be more acceptable than the happiness of his creatures. He would be incapable of hating or persecuting others for the love of God. (*SCW*, 6:16; cf. 1:163)

This remark provides insight into more than just Shelley's personal commitment to vegetarianism and his admiration for the family of John Frank Newton. Though introduced with a light touch (like several of the better-known remarks in "A Defence of Poetry"), the passage has behind it the weight of a mind well informed about mythology, religion, and human psychology. It may suggest that Shelley's interest in Orphism—documented by Ross Woodman[9]— was more than just a way for him to think about the writing of poetry. It suggests that Shelley sought a psychological, human-centred theory of myth. Shelley's "Every man forms . . . his god from his own character" reminds us how radical Shelley's own handling of myth really was. For Shelley is not saying, as the traditional sort of apologist for a religion generally does, "Believe in my god, and you will be saved." He says, rather, "Change your way of life first, and you will inevitably remake your god in a different and more benign image." In other words, a given way of life is not to be thought good because a god has willed it so; rather, a way of life creates the consciousness in which supernatural sanction for it is to be found.

It is as well to remind ourselves that there is nothing in Coleridge or Wordsworth quite comparable to this. With Shelley, we have entered a different realm of discourse, and this difference is most marked in his handling of myth. It is not simply that, in Shelley's thought, gods—"pagan" or otherwise—are a register of human character, of human aspirations, passions, and fears. When a writer consistently holds to the principle that consciousness is bound up with a chosen way of life, and that consciousness can be altered— not by crude dogmatizing, still less by punishing people for believing the "wrong" thing, but by placing before them those forms and ideas that are conducive to a happier life—then the revisioning of a myth, even when the myth is as "timeless" as Pan, Apollo, or Prometheus, becomes a means of changing the world by first changing the human

9. See Ross G. Woodman, *The Apocalyptic Vision in the Poetry of Shelley*, 32: "Orphism was to Shelley what the Bible was to Blake: the great code of art."

imagination. Shelley fully recognizes that one of the historical functions of myth has been as a means of social control, and that the
creation of a new mythopoeic work or the reinterpretation of an
old one can be directly relevant to the contemporary political and
social situation. He recognizes the possibility of, in Marilyn Butler's
phrase, "using myth as a purveyor of belief to the contemporary
world" even while he consistently denies—as David Hume also did—
that "belief" is a matter of the will. Hence the description of poetry,
in A *Philosophical View of Reform*, as "the most unfailing herald, or
companion, or follower, of a universal employment of the sentiments
of a nation to the production of beneficial change" (*SCW*, 7:19).
It would be inconsistent with the skepticism that is the basis of
Shelley's mature thought to assert bluntly that poetry changes the
world; yet good poetry regularly seems to accompany social progress,
and in some way not subject to human investigation it may display
the same beneficial forces at work and even help them.[10] This is
also the argument of the Preface to *Prometheus Unbound*, yet until
fairly recently it was common for critics to divide Shelley into the
"political" writer and the "poet" or "idealist," relegating either half to
secondary importance depending on the critic's own taste.[11]

The manner in which Shelley's poetry works to cleanse the
reader's mind of permanent or so-called innate forms is most clearly
evident in "Hymn to Intellectual Beauty" (*SP&P*, 93–95). The anti-
Christian thrust of stanzas 3 and 5 is immediately obvious. God,
ghosts, and Heaven are dismissed as "poisonous names." In *Queen
Mab* they were included implicitly in the "specious names, / Learnt

10. Butler, "Myth and Mythmaking in the Shelley Circle," 67. For a
brief criticism of the kind of approach that obscures the social functions of
myth, see ibid., 51–52. For Shelley's eventual rejection of the determinism
of such thinkers as d'Holbach, Voltaire, and Condorcet, see the discussion
in Hoagwood, *Skepticism and Ideology*, 180–82.

11. Hoagwood astutely points out that on the same page of the *Examiner* in which "Hymn to Intellectual Beauty" first appeared (January 19,
1817), immediately following the poem, appeared an announcement about
a meeting of "friends of economy, public order, and reform." He comments,
"[Shelley] could not and did not overlook the fact that his own verses on
Intellectual Beauty were appearing in a context (literally on the page) of the
political problems" (*Skepticism and Ideology*, 157).

in soft childhood's unsuspecting hour" (*SP&P*, 36).[12] This can be
seen as a strategy of displacement; these names are overthrown, like
Jupiter, to be replaced by a new Shelleyan trinity—"Love, Hope, and
Self-esteem," corresponding to the Pauline "Faith, Hope, Charity."
(No religion, Shelley writes in "A Defence of Poetry," "can supersede
any other without incorporating into itself a portion of that which
it supersedes" [*SP&P*, 496].) But I think such a reading stops short
of registering the full, subversive turn of the poem. Mere displacement of one deity or virtue by another is not its method. "Hymn to
Intellectual Beauty" tricks the complacent reader, anyone who looks
to poetry for the uncomplicated affirmation of transcendent values,
by using the disguise of a traditional genre and the poetic device of
apostrophe to a Spirit, into expecting that the divine being it addresses will be elevated into rivalry with the Christian God. Instead,
the poem does something much more revolutionary: it subverts
our habitual ways of thinking about *naming,* and hence questions
the possibility of even conceiving of a divine being, since we can
conceive of no being that does not have a name.

The possibility of an Apollonian mastery of language is present
in the poem, but only by way of a negation:

> Man were immortal, and omnipotent,
> Didst thou, unknown and awful as thou art,
> Keep with thy glorious train firm state within his heart.
> (lines 39–41)

The only philosophy that can be extracted from these lines is that it
is a human characteristic to feel that some power unknown denies
us immortality and omnipotence. The further hint that this power
is "awful" and has a "glorious train" plays off the rest of the sentence
in intriguing ways. Logic finds an immediate contradiction in the

---

12. The Silsbee Notebook at Harvard University contains a copy of the
poem cut from the *Examiner* of January 19, 1817. It is dated in Shelley's
hand "Switzerland: June—1816." The printed text of line 27, "Therefore the
names of Demon, Ghost, and Heaven," is emended to read "Therefore the
name of God & ghosts and Heaven," which shows that Shelley wanted the
attack on the orthodox conception of the Deity to be quite explicit. See
Stuart Curran, "Shelley's Emendations to the *Hymn to Intellectual Beauty.*"

granting of any attributes whatever to a being who is unknowable. Myth, perhaps, does not. But by juxtaposing its myths so closely with this outright denial of the logic of traditional metaphysics, the poem forces a revaluation of the very nature of the language of myth. The reader is forced to look beyond the negations—since everything in the poem is named or introduced within a context of negation—to find meaning in the process of negation itself. In Shelley's myths of power, as Spencer Hall has said, there is "a deep-seated skepticism about all such pretensions to know what cannot, on principle, be known."[13] In "The Triumph of Life," Shelley was to mythologize this tendency of mortal existence to obliterate and extinguish everything we hold on to, including thought itself, as the "shape all light" whose feet

> seemed as they moved, to blot
> The thoughts of him who gazed on them, and soon
> All that was seemed as if it had been not.
>   (*SP&P*, 466)

In "Hymn to Intellectual Beauty," the first thing said about Love, Hope, and Self-esteem is that they *depart*. Even the Being to whom the poem pretends to be addressed is not a firmly established presence, but the shadow of an absence: "The awful shadow of some unseen Power / Floats though unseen amongst us" (lines 1–2). The Power is unseen; its shadow floats among us; but the shadow is itself unseen. It is a black hole of knowledge, something that can be thought about, if at all, only by imagining the minute vacillation made in our thoughts by its absence-presence. It is the wholly submerged rock in the stream, the presence of which can be detected only by the slight deflection of the current as the stream flows around it. To name it is impossible, since names are purely human creations that exist at several removes even from thought, and cannot encompass the shadow of the unseen.

> No voice from some sublimer world hath ever
>   To sage or poet these responses given—

13. Spencer Hall, "Power and the Poet: Religious Mythmaking in Shelley's 'Hymn to Intellectual Beauty,'" 124.

> Therefore the name of God and ghosts and Heaven,
> Remain the record of their vain endeavour.
>
> (lines 25–28)

Carefully read, then, the poem does not erect a new moral or religious *code*, nor a pagan *mythology*, nor a *doctrine* such as "atheism," though all these things may be extrapolated from the poem by readers whose preoccupations steer them in the appropriate direction. (As Hall wisely observes, "Skepticism is less a philosophical concept for Shelley than a highly subjective complex of attitudes, feelings and methodologies through which he orients himself to experience and to the making of poetry.")[14] My own preoccupation with the possibility of a new myth criticism prompts me to find in the poem some glimpses of a historical change in the interpretation of myth, the beginning of a new line of analysis that assumes the human, social origins of myth and their function as encoding a particular social order. (This makes it possible to ask whose interests they serve, for example.) "Intellectual Beauty" suggests that myths signify not by naming, nor even by the process of *changing* names; rather, they signify by constantly displacing each other and so making the inadequacy of language and therefore of thought apparent to us. "Work on myth" is a process of constant demythologization. This is evidently far removed from the sentimentalizing of myth that readers such as Maurois, in the earlier part of this century, found in Shelley. Wordsworth's "Intimations" Ode pursues the phantom of permanence and finds "the fountain light of all our day," the "master light of all our seeing" in "those first affections, / Those shadowy recollections" (*WPW*, 4:283), but Shelley's poem explores the way of negation, and paradoxically finds light in the shadow of his "unseen Power."

> Thy light alone—like mist o'er mountains driven,
> Or music by the night wind sent

14. Spencer Hall, "Shelley, Skepticism(s), and Critical Discourse—A Review Essay," 74. I also agree with Lloyd Abbey's view that Shelley is first of all a humanitarian who on humanitarian grounds denies the *philosophical* validity even of his own poetic visions (*Destroyer and Preserver: Shelley's Poetic Skepticism*, 9).

> Through strings of some still instrument,
> Gives grace and truth to life's unquiet dream.
>   (lines 32–36)

This apostrophe to the "unseen Power" works to demythologize itself in the very act of pretending to create a myth, as can best be elucidated by comparing it with Shelley's interpretation of Jesus' teachings, in the fragmentary "Essay on Christianity" (probably written between 1815 and 1817 and so approximately contemporary with the poem). Having argued that Jesus sanctioned none of the dogmatic and superstitious abstractions of Christian theology, Shelley credits him with an elevated, poetico-philosophic conception of the Deity as an invisible, freely moving Power that cannot be confined within human conceptualizations. It is hardly necessary to point out that the metaphor used here, of the lyre awakened into sound by the wind, is identical with that in "Intellectual Beauty":

> We live and move and think, but we are not the creators of our own origin and existence, we are not the arbiters of every motion of our own complicated nature; we are not the masters of our own imaginations and moods of mental being. There is a Power by which we are surrounded, like the atmosphere in which some motionless lyre is suspended, which visits with its breath our silent chords, at will. (SCW, 6:231)

This line of argument, with a metaphor like that employed in "Intellectual Beauty" and phraseology strongly resembling that of "Mutability," is to deny that Jesus could have had any special insight into the purposes of the Creator, at least no more than any other gifted individual. The argument is also to suggest that it is wrong to try to police people's spiritual beliefs, to impose uniformity on the ever-changing currents of life ("we are not the masters of our own imaginations"). The result is to make eternal flux a good, and to imply the need for a new poet of eternal change who like Jesus will overturn established dogmas. The absence at the heart of "Hymn to Intellectual Beauty" prefigures the immense gloom of Demogorgon at the heart of the action of *Prometheus Unbound*. It also prefigures the victory of Pan; the ceremony of quasi-Orphic dedication with which the poem ends is an opting for change, a dedication of the poet's own self to the god of change—natural and social. The "vow" of stanza 6 cannot, I think, be read as a conventional dedication to the god apostrophized in the poem. The transient, unknowable nature of Intellectual Beauty has already been sufficiently illustrated for us so we do not make the mistake of crediting it with absolute existence independent of mind. It makes more sense to say that the speaker dedicates himself to a phenomenology—a distrust of absolutes, a recognition of the fallibility of human language. The worship of any given deity is mistaken as long as the name is taken for the thing. Shelley's "Hymn" is ironically named, for it puts an end to the genre of the hymn. It suggests that worship, and the whole structure of cult and theology that surrounds any act or stance of worship, depends on the concealment of a mistake.[15] The speaker of the "Hymn" continues to worship, but his act is not predicated on a humanistic rehabilitation of myth as expressing profound human feelings—a Joseph Campbell style reaffirmation of the "eternal" validity of myth—but an embracing of the way of negation comparable to Nietzsche's. The speaker of the "Hymn" can "worship" Intellectual Beauty only because, though a name, it names nothing more than a way of perceiving.

In the "Essay on Christianity," Shelley finds this same refusal to *name* characteristic of Jesus:

> According to Jesus Christ, God is neither the Jupiter who sends rain upon the earth, nor the Venus thro whom all living things are produced, nor the Vulcan who presides over the terrestrial element of fire, nor the Vesta that preserves the light which is inshrined in the sun and moon and stars. He is neither the Proteus or the Pan of the material world. But the word God, according to the acceptation of Jesus Christ, unites all the attributes which these denominations contain, and is the interfused and overruling Spirit of all the energy and wisdom included within the circle of existing things. It is important to observe that the author of the Christian system had a conception widely differing from the gross

15. As John W. Wright paraphrases Shelley's position: "Man . . . should recognize . . . that all his learning and all that he calls desirable depend directly on the activity of his own imagination" (*Shelley's Myth of Metaphor,* 35). See also Jean Hall, *The Transforming Image: A Study of Shelley's Major Poetry,* 45. Spencer Hall argues that the "Hymn" "confers a religious valuation on the secular state of consciousness I have referred to as psychological transcendence" ("Power and the Poet," 133). But here Wright and Jean Hall seem to me nearer the mark.

imaginations of the vulgar relatively to the ruling Power of the universe. He every where represents this power as something mysteriously and illimitably pervading the frame of things. (*SCW*, 6:229–30)

The irony is, for Shelley, that the name of Jesus itself became the instrument by which the Church enslaved millions.

If the "Hymn to Intellectual Beauty" works through the impossibility of naming, and undermines all worship except of the name of a way of perceiving, "Mont Blanc" carries still further the subversion of the mythmaking power as a source of objects of worship. "There are no mythological presences in 'Mont Blanc,' " a recent critic points out, "no gods either of good or evil."[16]

Shelley's earth in "Mont Blanc" (*SP&P*, 89–93) is a flowing, unstable, Heraclitean one: "dædal earth" is the term used here, as it is in "Song of Pan." The nurturing permanence that Wordsworth sought in nature, in the "Intimations" Ode, is not here.[17] Although the word "dædal" can be glossed as "cleverly fashioned" (Reiman and Powers so gloss it), in this context it can also carry some of the implications of tricksterism that it has in the "Song of Pan." It was Icarus, Dædalus' son, who was the aspiring, sun-worshiping overreacher. Dædalus was chiefly the craftsman, partly the deceiver, helping Pasiphaë to couple with the white bull of Poseidon and, in his most famous exploit, taking the form of a bird to overfly the walls of his prison. "Dædal" means partly that every form on the earth, the rocks, mountains, and glaciers no less than the growing plants, is or has been in movement.

> The fields, the lakes, the forests, and the streams,
> Ocean, and all the living things that dwell
> Within the dædal earth; lightning, and rain,

16. Angela Leighton, *Shelley and the Sublime: An Interpretation of the Major Poems*, 61. Spencer Hall, in "Shelley's 'Mont Blanc,' " 200–201, warns against mistaking the "Power" addressed in the poem for an entity independent of the poet's imagining: "The Power in 'Mont Blanc' cannot be separated as if it were an antecedent ontological principle, from the process of symbol-making dramatized in the work." However, I do not agree with Hall that the climax of the poem is "an affirmation of, and commitment to" the creative power of imagination (203). Such an interpretation seems inconsistent with the questioning of human powers, and of the very boundaries of the self, that runs throughout the poem.

17. For a persuasive account of Shelley's relationship to Wordsworth, see Donald Reiman, "Wordsworth, Shelley, and the Romantic Inheritance."

Earthquake, and fiery flood, and hurricane,
The torpor of the year when feeble dreams
Visit the hidden buds, or dreamless sleep
Holds every future leaf and flower;—the bound
With which from that detested trance they leap;
The works and ways of man, their death and birth,
And that of him and all that his may be;
All things that move and breathe with toil and sound
Are born and die; revolve, subside and swell.

(lines 84–95)

The irregularly rhyming pentameter lines reinforce the reader's sense that nothing in this world is stable, nothing lasts for long. (The rhymes "streams . . . dreams," "rain . . . hurricane," "dwell . . . swell" in the first twelve lines of verse paragraph 4 are not repeated within that verse paragraph.) What is more, the human mind is not set up as a rock of permanence in contradistinction to this fluid, ever-changing world of impressions, but participates in its change-ableness. The poem subverts, indeed, the boundary line between "outward" and "inward" which we tend to take for granted, and the reality of personal identity.[18] Words conventionally associated with our impressions of nature, such as "waves," are applied to mental states; words for mental states and concepts are applied to an "external" world, as in the exclamation "Dizzy Ravine!" The technique is not always artfully concealed: the lines "Power *in likeness of the Arve* comes down / From the ice gulphs" (lines 16–17, emphasis added) show how the mental abstraction, "Power," is projected on to a sense perception, the torrent. Through this bewildering, flowing chaos of impressions and thoughts, it is clear only that mind and nature exist in an "unremitting interchange" in which the life of each feeds the life of the other. The phantoms and ghosts that visit the speaker's mind, the "still cave of the witch Poesy" (line 44), seem generated from a power as mysterious and dark as the shadowy, shapeless form of Death, in Book 2 of *Paradise Lost*, which in an incestuous coupling begets monsters on its own mother, Sin.

In *Queen Mab*, Shelley had personified nature as "all-sufficing Power, / . . . Thou mother of the world!" (*SP&P*, 50). Whether Shelley abandoned Necessitarianism because it held too much "gloom,"

---

18. John Rieder, "Shelley's 'Mont Blanc': Landscape and the Ideology of the Sacred Text," 790. See also Jean Hall, *The Transforming Image*, 46–47.

as Neville Rogers suggests, is probably impossible to establish for certain.[19] "Mont Blanc" shows, rather, that if there is an all-sufficing Power in the universe, the human mind cannot grasp it. In ascribing to the mountain a "voice" that can "repeal / Large codes of fraud and woe" (lines 80–81), Shelley again follows the way of negation: the codes are *repealed,* not replaced by a better, more libertarian one. John Rieder is wrong, I think, to argue that Shelley turns Mont Blanc, the mountain, into a "sacred text," of which he, Shelley, is to be the priestly or aristocratic mediator to humankind. Still less does Shelley claim for himself the serenity of the mountain.[20] The speaker's quest for some image or metaphor by which the Universal Mind might be made accessible to thought seems vitiated by the very intensity and the perpetual-motion flow of surrounding impressions, so that it is difficult to tell for certain whether "thou art there" (line 48) refers to the Mind or to the actual Ravine.[21]

There are, of course, echoes of Wordsworth's tribute to "the mighty world / Of eye, and ear,—both what they half create, / And what perceive" (WPW, 2:262) in these lines:

> Thou art pervaded with that ceaseless motion,
> Thou art the path of that unresting sound—
> Dizzy Ravine! and when I gaze on thee
> I seem as in a trance sublime and strange
> To muse on my own separate phantasy,
> My own, my human mind, which passively
> Now renders and receives fast influencings,
> Holding an unremitting interchange
> With the clear universe of things around.
> (lines 32–40)

Shelley challenges the Wordsworthian sublime, however, by his insistence on the *unknowability* of the Power, and the complete importation of the external world's mutability into the mind of the speaker. The speaker does *not* find a symbol of permanence among the changing faces of nature, or in the repetition of sense experience,

19. Neville Rogers, *Shelley at Work: A Critical Inquiry,* 29.
20. Rieder, "Shelley's 'Mont Blanc,'" 780, 795.
21. On the relation between words and things in "Mont Blanc," see Leighton, *Shelley and the Sublime,* 66.

as the speaker in "Tintern Abbey" does. Rather, he is "Driven like a homeless cloud from steep to steep" (line 58). Nor can the poet have easy recourse to an internal surrogate for the permanence he cannot find in the external. Apollonian, overreaching genius is impossible, because this world lacks a stable point of reference. Human language, constantly influenced and modified by the "unremitting interchange" between mind and world, is a fluid, ever-changing medium that can never achieve a steady correspondence with the world it pretends to describe. What is "on high" (line 52) is not an eye with which the Universe beholds itself and knows itself divine, but the bleak, still, white form of the mountain, which emerges by glimpses as a symbol of indifferent Power, dwelling apart in its tranquillity. In a letter to Thomas Love Peacock, Shelley described Mont Blanc as the throne of the terrible destructive Persian god Ahriman, but the very lack of overt reference to Ahriman in the poem indicates that no human imaginings, not even Ahriman, are sufficiently destructive to embody the absolute negation around which the poem circles as if flirting with its own collapse.[22]

Paul de Man, in a critique of Wordsworth that in some ways is strikingly parallel to Shelley's in "Mont Blanc," argues that it is better to pass beyond the Wordsworthian concept of correspondence between nature and consciousness, because only a consciousness independent of nature is able to interpret the world. (This, I think, is the point of the rhetorical question with which the poem ends.)[23] But Shelley's poem also warns us that to be independent of nature is not to be *superior* to it, and that, indeed, the natural world continues to flow in on the senses and press on the mind, making impossible the Apollonian, "solar" stance as a way of "interpreting" the world, however expressive of a human craving for harmony and order.

There is another sense in which "Mont Blanc" denies the Apollonian vision, in the lines describing the glaciers with their towers, domes, and caves of ice. The sun-reflecting dome and the caves of ice also exist side by side in Coleridge's "Kubla Khan," establishing the dynamic polarity between which Kubla, the type of mortal genius,

22. See Shelley's letter of July 22–August 2, 1816, in *The Letters of Percy Bysshe Shelley,* ed. Frederick L. Jones, 1:499. See also Judith Chernaik, *The Lyrics of Shelley,* 51.

23. De Man, *Rhetoric of Romanticism,* 59–60.

has attempted to create his artificial paradise.[24] Mary Robinson, one of the first people to quote Coleridge's poem in print (in the *Morning Post*, October 17, 1800), indeed seized on the line "A sunny pleasure-dome with caves of ice!" as the central image. It seems that Shelley, too, was sufficiently impressed to adopt some of Coleridge's imagery in the poem he had in hand:

> there, many a precipice,
> Frost and the Sun in scorn of mortal power
> Have piled: dome, pyramid, and pinnacle,
> A city of death, distinct with many a tower
> And wall impregnable of beaming ice.
> . . . Below, vast caves
> Shine in the rushing torrents' restless gleam,
> Which from those secret chasms in tumult welling
> Meet in the vale, and one majestic River,
> The breath and blood of distant lands, for ever
> Rolls its loud waters to the ocean waves.
>   (lines 102–6, 120–25)

If the imagery is from "Kubla Khan," however, it is starkly changed: this is not a hymn to the power of mortal genius to create even a temporary garden of delights in the face of approaching decay and dissolution. Despite the suggestion of temple and imperial palace in "dome, pyramid, and pinnacle," no sun god rules here, certainly not Apollo. Those extreme elements of nature, Frost and the Sun, scorn mortal power, and they have no face to turn toward humankind.

24. Coleridge's poem was first printed, along with "Christabel" and "The Pains of Sleep," in a pamphlet that appeared on May 25, 1816, when Shelley was already in Switzerland. But Byron (at whose urging, in fact, "Christabel" appeared) had almost certainly heard Coleridge recite "Kubla Khan" when the older man visited him in London toward the end of April 1816. It is well known that Byron had seen "Christabel" in manuscript and partly memorized it, and that he repeated some lines of it to Shelley, Mary Shelley, and Polidori in June of that year. Though Byron had no copy of "Kubla Khan," then, and Shelley apparently did not see a printed copy of the poem while he was in Switzerland and writing *Mont Blanc*, Byron may have repeated at least some lines of the poem to his friend. See Cameron et al., eds., *Shelley and His Circle*, 4:646n, 800–801n. For evidence that Byron could "spout" "Kubla Khan" by heart, see Thomas Medwin, *Journal of the Conversations of Lord Byron* (London: Henry Colburn, 1824), 174.

The pinnacles and domes that they form are a "city of death," and the glacier itself (the Mer de Glace) is a "flood of ruin" (line 107), the word "ruin" picking up the earlier reference to the ruin the Earthquake-dæmon wrought (line 73). This "flood of ruin" is a metamorphosis of the city in line 105. An ice city, even a city of death, is at least partly reduced to human terms: the imagination feels at home in it. But no sooner is this ice city imagined than—like the spirit of Intellectual Beauty—it departs or, rather, is transmuted into the glacier, the "flood of ruin." The displacement of one metaphor, "city" (so obviously a metaphor), by another, "flood," enacts the recoiling of the mind from the knowledge of its own death, perhaps of its own futility. Nothing stands in the way of the glacier:

> vast pines are strewing
> Its destined path, or in the mangled soil
> Branchless and shattered stand: the rocks, drawn down
> From yon remotest waste, have overthrown
> The limits of the dead and living world,
> Never to be reclaimed.   (lines 109–14)

Where the limits of the dead and living world have been overthrown, it is deceptive to speak of apocalypse, since the very notion occurs in a human teleology in which natural catastrophe somehow reflects human corruption. In true apocalypse, some god, wishing to cleanse the world of human misrule, creates a new heaven and a new earth. In this world of life-in-death, even this negative, eschatological comfort is impossible. Those serpentine messengers of the great mountain, the glaciers, are supremely indifferent not only to human anxieties but to "The limits of the dead and living world." By casually importing into this world ("our" world) ageless fragments of rock from the formations it has destroyed, the glacier demonstrates the entire indifference of natural powers to human beliefs about where life comes from or what is "alive" and what is "dead." The torrents, welling from their "secret chasms" (line 122), have, then, none of the erotic aura they have possessed for most readers of "Kubla Khan." In the context of this dehumanized world, from which "the race / Of man" has fled, the idea of seeing erotic pleasure in the energy of the torrent seems absurd. Shelley has troped "Kubla Khan" in such a way as to make garden *and* chasm, Coleridge's demonic, energetic wilderness as well as his paradisal garden, look parochially humanized and domesticated. In "Mont Blanc," it is not Apollo and Dionysus that confront each other; the aspiring imagination of the onlooker is not challenged by a riotous eroticism but by something much closer to panic terror. If we look for literary analogues to the experience evoked by "Mont Blanc," I suggest that Thoreau's shattering wilderness experience on Mt. Ktaadn, or the dreadful echo that drives Adela Quested from the Marabar Caves in Forster's *Passage to India*, are much closer than Dionysian ecstasy.

One recent reading of the poem proposes that "to create a mythology is to assert that nature and the mind of man may be fitted to one another, as Wordsworth writes, 'In love and holy passion,' in order to confirm man's ability to transform the silence of the objective world into a meaningful voice which converses with the human intellect." This is too narrow a definition of mythology, I believe. It may define the particular, Wordsworthian kind of mythologizing Shelley puts in question here, but it hardly embraces all mythologizing. (We need only remember how vehemently Blake rejected Wordsworth's claim that the external world was fitted to the mind.) The essay continues: "'Mont Blanc,' however, only gestures toward this possibility, for Shelley's skepticism would not allow him to degrade mythological speculation into dogma."[25] If "Mont Blanc" only "gestures" toward the possibility of hearing a meaningful voice in nature, I would argue that in doing so it exhausts that particular kind of mythologizing as a poetic possibility for Shelley. However, a new and more human-centered kind of mythologizing was thereby created (see Chapter 7).

The much-debated lines that end verse paragraph 3, then, can be interpreted as a key to all mythologies or, more precisely, as a key to undo all mythologies.

> The wilderness has a mysterious tongue
> Which teaches awful doubt, or faith so mild,
> So solemn, so serene, that man may be,
> But for such faith with nature reconciled,
> Thou hast a voice, great Mountain, to repeal
> Large codes of fraud and woe; not understood
> By all, but which the wise, and great, and good
> Interpret, or make felt, or deeply feel.
> (lines 76–83)

25. John B. Pierce, "'Mont Blanc' and *Prometheus Unbound*: Shelley's Use of the Rhetoric of Silence," 113.

Because of the habit of reading "Mont Blanc" as a response to and misprision of Wordsworth, we have come to interpret the "faith so mild" (line 77) as a Shelleyan adaptation of Wordsworthian "wise passiveness," or perhaps—if "adaptation" is too conciliatory a word for what is really a heresy within Wordsworth's nature creed—an atheist's attempt to displace Wordsworthian assurance with a new faith, disabused of any lingering trust in benevolent nature. Plainly, if reconciling man and nature is the aim, it cannot be done in "Mont Blanc" on the basis of the benevolence of nature, nor indeed on the basis of its apocalyptic destructiveness, since both of these are obvious human attempts to impose pattern on arbitrary events. The large codes of fraud and woe that the mountain's voice repeals are, in the first instance, religion, which springs from a false reading of our place in the world. Second, I think, the codes include all other mythologies, insofar as they are received as anything more than poetic inventions. Reconciliation with nature must mean being reconciled to the perpetual mutability of nature, and its counterpart in our *own* mutability, the perpetual flux and reflux of human feelings and language.

This is what the poem "Mutability" (which first appeared along with "Alastor" in 1816) unsuccessfully tries to delineate. In this poem, Shelley is constrained by the conventions: the language of Renaissance elegy bears down too hard on the verse.

> We are as clouds that veil the midnight moon;
>> How restlessly they speed, and gleam, and quiver,
> Streaking the darkness radiantly!—yet soon
>> Night closes round, and they are lost for ever:
>
> Or like forgotten lyres, whose dissonant strings
>> Give various response to each varying blast,
> To whose frail frame no second motion brings
>> One mood or modulation like the last. (*SP&P*, 88)

The *abab* rhyme scheme and regular stanza form belie the Humean message: selfhood is an illusion, we are bundles of fast-arriving, fast-departing impressions. Shelley's imagery, drawing on moon, cloud, and Eolian lyre, is almost comforting in its familiarity. There is no panic terror in "Mutability." In "Mont Blanc," on the other hand, language is strained, catachresis and outrageous forms of prosopopoeia are brought into play, and (not least) the irregular, even chaotic rhyme scheme suggests the lurking fear that there is *no* pattern, *no* meaning, in the manifestations of nature, not even the vaguely cyclical one hinted at in "Mutability." Thought is governed not by some ultimately comprehensible deity, nor by godless natural cycles, but by "The secret strength of things" (line 139).

"Mont Blanc" is, therefore, in one sense, a complete leveling of the mythological ground. Future mythopoesis must start from this zero point: nothing in nature authorizes or guarantees any human narrative, myth, or personification. Science shows that in actuality things do not repeat themselves, and the myth of eternal recurrence that has provided writers as recent as Lawrence and Graves an escape from history is already, in Shelley, showing its inadequacy.[26] Faced with the white emptiness of the mountain, the imagination simply collapses in exhaustion:

> the very spirit fails
> Driven like a homeless cloud from steep to steep
> That vanishes among the viewless gales!
> (lines 57–59)

The poem, as has often been pointed out, concludes with the unanswered question,

> And what were thou, and earth, and stars, and sea,
> If to the human mind's imaginings
> Silence and solitude were vacancy?
> (lines 142–44)

The reader's imagination, prompted to formulate an answer to this question, finds itself gazing into nothingness; without the human mind's imaginings, plainly, the mountain would be inconceivable. The entire poem we have just read belongs to the realm of "imaginings"—that is clear from the interflowing of ravine and mind, universe and mind, enacted in lines 1–11. But as the poem thus turns back on itself, undermines its own coherence, it frees the reader from any myth, doctrine, or system it may temporarily have invoked. It does this more completely, perhaps, than any later poem of Shelley's, with the exception of "The Triumph of Life."

26. See on this subject Walter J. Ong, S.J., "Evolution, Myth, and Poetic Vision," 4–7.

In such occasional poems as the "Dedication" to *Laon and Cythna,* Shelley does continue to employ the traditional poetic device of identifying events and emotions of his own life with the phenomena of nature, the round of the seasons, as in the lines, addressed to Mary, "Thou Friend, whose presence on my wintry heart / Fell, like bright Spring upon some herbless plain" (*SP&P,* 97). But the absolutist Apollonian perspective, in which the human consciousness dominates and surveys all of nature, saying to itself like Ted Hughes's roosting hawk, "My eye has permitted no change," is untenable except as it may be temporarily adopted by one or other of Shelley's personae or dramatic characters, or absorbed as one function of language itself.

Seven

The Contest of Apollo and Pan in Shelley's Later Poetry

In 1820, urged by her husband to further develop those literary talents that he expected her to display, Mary Shelley composed two "mythological dramas," one based on the Persephone myth and the other on the story of King Midas.[1] Though interest in Mary Shelley's work has increased enormously in the past decade, it remains true that the only parts of these dramas commonly read today are the lyrics Percy Shelley contributed to them, most particularly the "Song of Apollo" and "Song of Pan," which he wrote for the play *Midas*. Since Mary Shelley herself published these lyrics as separate pieces when she came to edit her husband's work, a plausible case could be made for continuing to treat them as separate compositions, as independent studies of a well-known mythological *topos*, the contest of Apollo and Pan. The effect of such an approach, in one sense, privileges Mary Shelley's role as editor: her intervention "rescued" the songs from the inferior context to which they would otherwise be consigned, her own play. However, quite apart from the premature dismissal of the play itself, which this approach implies, my

1. Bodleian Library, Oxford, MS Shelley d.2. The dramas were published in 1922 and are presently being reedited according to present-day standards of scholarship. See Mary Shelley, *Proserpine and Midas: Two Unpublished Mythological Dramas*. I follow the manuscript readings. On Percy Shelley's assumption of the role of "mentor-teacher to his young student-mistress" Mary Godwin, a role that continued after their marriage, see Mellor, *Mary Shelley*, 23, 28.

purpose throughout the present study has been to demonstrate the importance of the contemporary contexts that are most relevant to particular reinterpretations of traditionary myths. In these chapters, my concern is what we can learn about the "reception of myth" in Percy Shelley's work, using the evidence available. Mary Shelley's play—more particularly, the way she presents and reworks the Midas story—is a crucial part of the evidence for that reception, a contemporary retelling of the Midas story which Percy Shelley was obviously aware of in writing the two songs. These lyrics develop and interact with the context Mary Shelley provided for them, and some of their significance is lost if that context is ignored. In order to appreciate the ways in which "Song of Apollo" and "Song of Pan" reinterpret the myths they are based on, we have to examine the treatment of the Midas story in Mary Shelley's play. Further, as I hope to show, it has a bearing on the specific kind of conflict that the two poems represent as arising between Apollo and Pan, figures that continue to resonate in Shelley's later work as personifications of two rival language-myths.

The Midas story is well known from Ovid's *Metamorphoses*, book 11. Midas was a Phrygian king who had been taught the mysteries of Bacchus by Orpheus himself. After acquiring from Bacchus the gift of turning whatever he touched to gold, a gift that made life intolerable, he preferred to live in the woods and worship Pan. Pan was the most rural and uncultivated of the gods, but he once boasted that the music of his pipes surpassed that of Apollo himself, and he even dared to enter into a competition with the sun god, the result to be adjudicated by Tmolus, the resident deity of the mountain where the contest was to take place. Midas happened to be wandering there and, entranced by Pan's music, stopped to listen. When Pan's song ended, Apollo took up his lyre and played so sweetly that everyone except Midas agreed Apollo had won the contest. Midas, for his foolishness in preferring the uncultivated song of Pan to the music of the Patron of musicians, was disfigured with ass's ears.[2]

2. For discussion of the Ovidian source of this story, see Patricia Merivale, *Pan the Goat-God: His Myth in Modern Times*, 6. On Pan in Arcadia and the differing traditions of Arcadia in Greek and Latin literature, see Erwin Panofsky, "*Et in Arcadia ego*: Poussin and the Elegiac Tradition," 297–303. One Orphic hymn praises Pan as supreme among the gods and lord of all

Renaissance writers, as Patricia Merivale shows, read this story as an unequivocal demonstration of the foolishness of preferring "illiterate rusticity" to the high culture personified by Apollo and the Nine. But Mary Shelley makes a number of changes in her dramatization of the story. She places the song contest before the gift of the golden touch (in Ovid, the contest is narrated second). She also changes the order of the songs. In her version, Apollo sings first, followed by Pan, although Tmolus still pronounces Apollo the winner:

> Phoebus, the palm is thine. The Fauns may dance
> To the blithe tune of ever merry Pan;
> But wisdom, beauty, & the power divine
> Of highest poesy lives within thy strain.
> Named by the Gods the King of Melody,
> Receive from my weak hands a second crown.
> (fol. 23ᵛ)

Mary Shelley's play does alter the result slightly in favor of Pan, however, since in her version it is Pan himself who appeals to Midas, pointing out that Tmolus is not a disinterested judge. (Tmolus needs Apollo's warmth to thaw the snow on the mountain and to foster the growth of trees and plants.) Midas, the one representative of the human race present at this contest, pronounces judgment in favor of Pan:

> Immortal Pan, to my poor, mortal ears,
> Your sprightly song in melody outweighs
> His drowsy tune; he put me fast asleep. . . .
> (fol. 23ᵛ)

Apollo's punishment of Midas, in the circumstances, is made to look like the result of pique or jealousy, rather than an authoritative judgment by the god of music on a foolish mortal's error. There is also an interesting hint, in Midas' remark about the sprightliness of Pan's performance, that Apollo's song was too solemn, serene, and high-minded for mortal ears.

---

the elements. See Jacob Bryant, A *New System*, 1:311. On "Universal Pan," who in English poetry first appears in Milton's "On the Morning of Christ's Nativity," stanza 8, see Merivale, *Pan the Goat-God*, 27, 61.

Percy Shelley contributed the two songs of the rival gods to this mythological drama, and since 1824, when Mary Shelley printed them as "Hymn of Apollo" and "Hymn of Pan," they have been read as a pair of contrasting lyrics, independently of the play. Milton Wilson, in his study of Shelley's later poetry, demonstrates Shelley's subtle and adventurous use of anapaestic rhythms in "Song of Pan" and points out that Pan's song has a "rapid, darting movement" that gains by comparison with Apollo's more solemn rhythms. This contrast in rhythms, Wilson suggests, signifies more than merely a contrast in poetic taste between the sun god and the forest god. "We need to relate the pipe and the lyre": neither Apollo nor Pan is a complete poet (just as neither the idealist nor the realist is a complete individual).[3]

More usually, the lyrics have been evaluated merely as, to adapt Wordsworth's phrase about Keats, pretty pieces of paganism. Merivale, for example, rather dismissively judges "Song of Pan" as "a pleasant nature lyric with intermittent mythical evocations." Judith Chernaik, in a more positive and still valuable reading, rates the poems more highly, seeing them as attempting "the intensely sympathetic realization of a natural and mythological world existing entirely apart from human life." Chernaik ignores the obvious difficulty of conceiving a Shelleyan "natural and mythological world" that would exist independently of "the human." But she is right to suggest that the poems should be recognized as much more than *jeux d'esprit*.[4] Though the drama for which they were intended is lighthearted and burlesque in spirit, the contest of the two gods dramatizes a debate about the nature of poetry that has relevance to Shelley's major work. Because he wrote them for a *play*—that is, they are not definitive, impartial portraits of the two gods but are spoken by dramatic characters who interact with each other—we should recognize that the two songs are rich in contextual significance. "Song of Apollo" and "Song of Pan" can be read the way we read Blake's contrasting pairs of songs. Each lyric is ironic with respect to the other; each hypostatizes

3. Milton Wilson, *Shelley's Later Poetry: A Study of His Prophetic Imagination*, 31. On the matter of Shelley's ability to entertain two apparently conflicting philosophies simultaneously, see also Ronald Tetreault, *The Poetry of Life: Shelley and Literary Form*, 103–4.

4. Merivale, *Pan the Goat-God*, 60; Chernaik, *Lyrics of Shelley*, 135.

a rival phenomenology, a rival attitude toward nature, humanity, and human perception. Like Blake's Innocence and Experience, each implies a commitment to a certain view of what poetry is "for." Most of all, the contrast between them is the kind of binary opposition that several of the Romantics (Coleridge, Schelling, Emerson) struggled to take into a higher synthesis but that in our own age it no longer seems possible or even salutary to synthesize. In the remainder of this chapter, I hope to justify my assertion that each song constructs its own poetics and to show that the Pan-Apollo conflict, so read, is implicitly present in Shelley's major work.[5]

Apollo, in Shelley's poem, is self-portrayed as the bright light of truth itself, *lumen siccum*, the enemy of deceit and evil, triumphant over "Dreams" and over the moon (his sister deity):

> The sleepless Hours who watch me as I lie
>   Curtained with star-enwoven tapestries
> From the broad moonlight of the open sky;
>   Fanning the busy dreams from my dim eyes,
> Waken me when their mother, the grey Dawn,
> Tells them that Dreams and that the moon is gone.
>   * * *
>   . . . Whatever lamps on Earth or Heaven may shine
> Are portions of one spirit; which is mine.
>   (lines 1–6, 23–24; *SP&P*, 367)

It is a majestic conception: Apollo as the source of all light, possessor of the one spirit of truth and right action ("from the glory of my ray / Good minds, and open actions take new might"). His language aspires to be what Paul de Man calls "the solar language of cognition that makes the unknown accessible to the mind and to the senses."[6] Apollo has the serenity of pure intelligence admiring its own lucidity.

---

5. Patricia Merivale cites evidence of a cheerful "Pan cult" among members of Shelley's circle, the more serious side of this cult testifying to their "esteem for paganism and the values imputed to it" (*Pan the Goat-God*, 64). I hope I do not imply that Shelley's interest in Pan was humorless; on the contrary, I want to argue that Pan's playfulness is part of the attitude to language that Shelley embodies in him. And Pan's ambivalence—his tricksterism has both a light and a dark side—is amply demonstrated by Merivale herself.

6. De Man, *Rhetoric of Romanticism*, 80.

His attendants, the Hours, diligently shoo away the dreams that might disturb his sleep, so that he is not troubled by any doubt-casting visitations from the night world as he prepares for his daily tour of the globe turned upward for his inspection. "I am the eye with which the Universe / Beholds itself, and knows it is divine" (lines 31–32; *SP&P*, 368). Despite the cyclical movement of the poem—from dawn to evening—it is very clear, as Milton Wilson points out, that Apollo prefers noon to any other time. Moreover, unlike Pan, who realizes that his song is not winning his audience's sympathy, Apollo cannot imagine any disjunction between himself and his audience.[7] There is no wavering, no hint of doubt that the world exists in order to be brought to the consciousness of its own divinity in Apollonian splendor. This is "the grandeur of enthusiastic imagination," to quote Shelley's description of a statue of Apollo seen at the Capitol in Rome (*SCW*, 6:231). These lines are an excellent summary of the transcendentalist tenets that the whole purpose of Nature is to develop consciousness and that this purpose is best fulfilled when the poet, the highest type of mind, expresses the divine harmony of the world he perceives. At such a moment the poet identifies with the sun itself, outshining his own human imperfections, as Shelley prophesied for John Keats: "Keats, I hope, is going to show himself a great poet; like the sun, to burst through the clouds, which, though dyed in the finest colours of the air, obscured his rising."[8]

That Shelley could see the poet as a supreme witness to the divine harmony, the "Sun-treader" of Browning's youthful adoration, perhaps does not need to be demonstrated, but there is a further connection, between the sun and the written word. This is suggested by some lines from Shelley's notebook, which Neville Rogers cites: "Wilt thou offend the Sun thou emblemest / By blotting out the light of written thought."[9] Language is like the sun, throwing light on what is obscure and unreasonable. In Apollo's world, or the world as seen from the Apollonian point of view, there is no questioning the supremacy of light over darkness, mind over matter, right over wrong, reason over emotion. Apollo's eye puts the universe in order

7. Wilson, *Shelley's Later Poetry*, 36–37.
8. Shelley to Charles Ollier, May 14, 1820, in *Letters*, 2:197.
9. Shelley's notebook, in the Huntington Library, San Marino, Calif., quoted by Neville Rogers, *Shelley at Work*, 218.

and brings it to knowledge. The rather chilling possessiveness with which Apollo regards his empire ("All harmony of instrument and verse, / All prophecy and medicine are mine") follows perfectly from the logic of the supremacy of intellect. The even, six-line stanza and the generally perfect rhymes of the lyric ("lie . . . sky", "waves . . . caves", "air . . . bare", "kill . . . ill", "might . . . night") suggest the apparently effortless supremacy of Apollo's reign. The song perfectly dramatizes the "Apollonian hypothesis," as Walter Evert usefully summarizes it:

> The complete spiritual cycle of individual human life and growth is comparable to the annual cycle of physical life and growth in external nature. These cycles are not only comparable by developmental analogy but are harmonious with each other because identically subject to the influence of a single beneficent power, or law, which manifests itself in and through them. This power is the law of universal harmony . . . best exemplified concretely in the late-Greek conception of Apollo.[10]

Our age has learned from Nietzsche to regard this "orthodox" conception of Apollo as fragile and detached from reality: at best, a tenuous protection against the knowledge of suffering that Greek culture expressed in the cruelest rites of the god Dionysos; at worst, a representation of the hegemony of pure reason, which is derided in *The Genealogy of Morals* as an impossibility, a contradiction. To Nietzsche, Apollo represents music employed in the service of calm, noble images; music, the vehicle of Dionysian frenzy and self-forgetfulness, brought under the contemplative, controlling power of the "principium individuationis," of self-possession:

> Moved by the urge to talk of music in Apollonian similitudes, [the lyric poet] must first comprehend the whole range of nature, including himself, as the eternal source of volition, desire, appetite. But to the extent that he interprets music through images he is dwelling on the still sea of Apollonian contemplation, no matter how turbulently all that he beholds through the musical medium may surge about him. . . . Being an Apollonian genius, he interprets music through the image of the will, while he is himself turned into the pure, unshadowed eye of the sun, utterly detached from the will and its greed.[11]

10. Walter H. Evert, *Aesthetic and Myth in the Poetry of Keats*, 30–31.
11. Nietzsche, *The Birth of Tragedy*, 45–46.

Part of the tension in the contest of Apollo and Pan, we may feel, is exactly that Pan represents "the whole range of nature," but a nature that *resists* interpretation by human motives and that is perpetually disruptive of the Apollonian characteristics, self-possession, control, and pure reason.

The "Song of Pan" is different not only in style and imagery, but also in its handling the myth on which it "works." Unlike Apollo, whose sphere is the sun's orbit, his chief attributes those of constancy and harmony, Pan is a god of the earth and its processes, his chief attributes those of perpetual change and division. Andrew Tooke's *Pantheon*, for instance, read Pan as "a Symbol of the Universal World" and interpreted his divided nature in this way:

> In his upper part he resembles a Man, in his lower part a Beast; because the superior and celestial part of the World is beautified, radiant, and glorious. . . . In his lower parts he is shagged and deform'd, which represents the Shrubs and wild Beasts, and Trees of the Earth below. His Goat's Feet signifie the Solidity of the Earth; and his Pipe of seven Reeds, that Celestial Harmony, which is made by the seven *Planets*. (226–27)

Less moralistic commentators emphasized not so much the low carnality of Pan as his association with an idealized, Virgilian rather than Ovidian Arcadia. Shelley's poem owes much to the Renaissance vision of Arcadia as a haven from the contentiousness of a Christianized but divided Europe with its burdensome sense of history. Pan was also credited with creative powers, even with being an embodiment of the animating power of the Divine Spirit spoken of in the Orphic hymns, as Richard Payne Knight emphasizes in his summary of "the true Orphic system" in *An Account of the Remains of the Worship of Priapus*: "PAN is addressed in the Orphic Litanies, as the first-begotten Love, or Creator incorporated in universal matter, and so forming the world. The heavens, the earth, water, and fire, are said to be members of him; and he is described as the origin and source of all things . . . as representing matter animated by the Divine Spirit"(60).[12]

12. See also Knight, *Worship of Priapus*, 121: "The Goat . . . represented the creative Attribute, and the Lyre, Harmony and Order."

In Shelley's poem, too, Pan claims some of the attributes of Orpheus, being able to still the sounds of the waves, the wind, the birds, bees, and cicadas.

> The wind in the reeds and the rushes,
> The bees on the bells of thyme,
> The birds in the myrtle bushes,
> The cicadæ above in the lime,
>   And the lizards below in the grass,
> Were silent as even old Tmolus was,
>   Listening my sweet pipings.
>   (lines 6–12; *SP&P*, 368)

This is a clever ploy, since Orpheus, who could also pacify wild beasts with his music, was Apollo's disciple and, like Apollo, carried a lyre; Pan suggests that he knew how to charm the beasts and still the wind even before Orpheus did. But Pan also celebrates change: from day to night, the "dancing stars" and the "dædal Earth," human love, death, and birth, and the overthrow of the Titans by the Gods (lines 25–28). The earth is not governed by *one* light, *one* spirit, but by a multitude of processes, which are also the processes of thought. Pan is the trickster, joker, and mischief maker, even suggesting slyly a reason for Apollo's silence:

> And all that did then attend and follow
> Were as silent for love, as you now, Apollo,
>   For envy of my sweet pipings.
>   (lines 22–24; *SP&P*, 368)

This is dramatically effective, but it also suggests the trickster's skill at creatively "misreading" his opponent's attitude. We cannot imagine Apollo stooping to such sly use of a debater's tactics, but we might also smile at Pan's agility, realizing that Apollo does not have a monopoly on intelligence.

Apollo is very much a god, principally in his abhorrence of change and of things not being what they seem, but Pan, in a reference to the story of his pursuit of Syrinx, seems to make the inevitable deception and disappointment in love a kind of bridge between the divine and the human. Pan, much more than Apollo, is a god for human beings in their confusion, doubt, fickleness, and awareness of change. Contrary to Chernaik's argument that Pan is pure nature, "entirely apart" from the human, Pan embodies a Shelleyan version of the common human fear that, as it is expressed in the "Essay on Christianity," "we are not the creators of our own origin and existence . . . we are not the masters of our own imaginations and moods of mental being" (SCW, 6:231). Perhaps this, too, helps to account for Midas's preference for the song of Pan:

> And then I changed my pipings,
> Singing how, down the vales of Mænalus
> I pursued a maiden and clasped a reed.
> Gods and men, we are all deluded thus!—
> It breaks in our bosom and then we bleed.
> (lines 29–33; SP&P, 369)

Apollo had his own delusive loves (of Daphne, for example; see *Metamorphoses*, 1), but we can hardly imagine him speaking of his romantic adventures in this tone.

Pan's song is, as we would expect, more "wild," more inconclusive and fugitive than Apollo's. Moreover, Apollo's depicts a highly ordered, well-governed, dream-free world, whereas Pan's stresses the complexity and deceptiveness of nature ("the dædal Earth"), of love ("we are all deluded thus!"), and of perception. Pan's song is a warning against the overreaching hunger for the absolute that haunts the Romantic. Pan is a more useful god than Apollo because Pan's deceptive ephemerality best reflects human experience and language. Pan, whose name could mean "all," has never been linked to one immutable meaning.[13] But human consciousness must be consciousness *of* something, so Pan, even in his perpetual ephemerality as the changing material world, represents the possibility of consciousness though not of totality, transcendence, or the Absolute.

The dramatic context for which they were written may explain some of the characterization Shelley puts into each of these poems, but I think that the pursuit of dramatic realism is not the whole story. Shelley crystallizes in these songs two different poetics, two ways of looking at poetic language.

13. See Merivale, *Pan the Goat-God*, 9.

One clue to the nature of this opposition is to be found in Emerson's essay on Plato. There, Emerson suggests that Pan may be understood as "speech, or manifestation."[14] Emerson himself had lived through the conflict between the desire to idealize, to be uplifted into the divine nature (expressed with startling intensity in the famous "transparent eyeball" passage in *Nature*), and the mischievous, doubt-making promptings of a more skeptical turn (his "Montaigne"). Language, as most critics now recognize, was one of his primary interests. To see Pan as "speech, or manifestation" suggests a new way of understanding Shelley's work, not in the well-worn terms "Platonism" and "skepticism," but in terms of rival language-myths.[15] Language is Apollo: lucid, orderly, medicinal, interpreter of the world's intelligence to itself. Or language is Pan: a representation (Emerson's "manifestation"), something that displaces, a deception, a seductive "piping," quieting the bees and the cicadas and leading one into the ever-shifting labyrinth of a fugitive reality, the "dædal Earth." These two language-myths, though focused for us in the "Song of Apollo" and "Song of Pan," are present in Shelley's poetry, from 1816 on, as he questions his own heritage of myth and seeks the new kind of mythopoesis he was to formulate in the Preface to *Prometheus Unbound*. The Apollonian stance, far from being Shelley's characteristic poetic mode, is found only where it is one function of language itself, in contexts where the discourse is clearly subject to the "critique of authority."[16]

A good example of this dramatically placed or "self-critiquing" use of the Apollonian function of language occurs in act 4 of *Prometheus Unbound*:

14. Ralph Waldo Emerson, *Representative Men*, 84. Proteus is also associated with the ability of speech to deceive and to evade definition. See Theresa M. Kelley, "Proteus and Romantic Allegory," 630.

15. Studies that emphasize the "Platonic" strain in Shelley include Carlos Baker, *Shelley's Major Poetry: The Fabric of a Vision*; Rogers, *Shelley at Work*; and Woodman, *Apocalyptic Vision*. Studies that emphasize his skepticism include C. E. Pulos, *The Deep Truth: A Study of Shelley's Skepticism*; Wright, *Shelley's Myth of Metaphor*; Abbey, *Destroyer and Preserver*; Jean Hall, *The Transforming Image*; Archer, "Authority in Shelley"; and Hoagwood, *Skepticism and Ideology*.

16. Archer, "Authority in Shelley," 260.

Language is a perpetual Orphic song,
Which rules with Dædal harmony a throng
Of thoughts and forms, which else senseless and shapeless were.
(4.415–17)

The newly liberated Earth here affirms the Apollonian myth of language as governing, guiding, and harmonizing the shapeless plethora of forms, but it is Apollonianism reconciled with the regenerative power of Pan, an "Orphic song." In dramatic terms, this fourth act of the drama represents a move from the single, heroic, but agonistic stance of the Prometheus (act 1) to a reveling in the multiplicity, flux, and change of the natural world, permeated and animated by Love. It is a move from "Thought's stagnant chaos" (4.380) to the erotic dance of a self-sustaining cosmos. Politically it prophesies a move from a rigidly absolutist system to a successful, peaceful revolution.[17] Apollonian transcendence is reenvisioned as the rule of love, creating out of the Prometheus-Asia relationship a new, androgynous universal being, binding humankind to each other with stronger links than Jupiter's tyranny ever could and governing the universe in a benign way rather than punitively, as the sun guides the planets:

a chain of linked thought,
Of love and night to be divided not,
Compelling the elements with adamantine stress—
As the Sun rules, even with a tyrant's gaze,
The unquiet Republic of the maze
Of Planets, struggling fierce towards Heaven's free wilderness.
(lines 394–99)[18]

But this benign Apollonianism is achieved only at the end of the play. In act 1, Prometheus is Apollonian not in a medicinal, harmonizing,

17. With "Thought's stagnant chaos" compare "the stagnant ocean / Of human thoughts" in *The Revolt of Islam* (canto 1, stanza 38, lines 467–68), a more explicitly political context. Abbey interprets this "stagnant ocean" as "the dogmatic stupor which, before the French Revolution, had frozen European society into tyrannical hierarchies" (*Destroyer and Preserver*, 46).

18. On the "androgynous" universe in act 4, see Ross G. Woodman, "The Androgyne in *Prometheus Unbound*," 247. See also Jean Hall, "The Socialized Imagination: Shelley's *The Cenci* and *Prometheus Unbound*," 350.

"Orphic" way but only in the absolutism of his stance, the "calm, fixed mind" that his heroic defiance of Jupiter necessitates.

> Pity the self-despising slaves of Heaven,
> Not me, within whose mind sits peace serene
> As light in the sun, throned.
>
> (lines 429–31)

This is a god speaking, and he exhibits the serenity we would expect of a god—to that extent, the speech is "in character." But it soon becomes apparent that Prometheus' unmoving defiance of Jupiter is matched by Jupiter's hatred of him. Indeed, Jupiter is made in Prometheus' own image, maintained in his tyranny by Prometheus' defiance, and no resolution of the standoff is possible until Prometheus relaxes his stance and repents of his curse. Highlighting the paradoxical similarity between Prometheus and Jupiter is the repetition by the Phantasm of Jupiter of Prometheus' original curse. Most significant, however, is Prometheus' admission that his curse was impulsive—"words are quick and vain" (1.303)—and so may, presumably, later be retracted. That is, though a god, he admits to having changed his mind, and he reinterprets the text of the curse that the Phantasm of Jupiter has just recited for him to hear: "Grief for awhile is blind, and so was mine" (1.304). It is not often noticed how human this makes Prometheus. Æschylus' Prometheus is heroic and unbending, so that we admire him but hardly like him. Shelley's Prometheus is still heroic, but not in a wholly inhuman way; the "elements" are "mix'd" in him, as Shakespeare's Mark Antony says of another defier of tyranny, Brutus. Once Prometheus has retracted his curse, he still has to purge himself of latent hostility toward Jupiter, the particular kind of hostility that expresses itself as pity. The remaking, rebirth, or Orphic transformation of Prometheus is not completed until he can love, which does not happen until act 3.

Prometheus' ability to accept and embrace change in himself as well as in the world around him is not only a reinterpretation of Æschylus' portrayal; it also provides Shelley with the main line of development of his play, which is from stasis to change and movement. Toward the end of act 1, the spirits of the earth appear, called up by Earth herself; they represent the powers that (like Pan) are bound to no law and do not inhabit fixed forms, but by their very mobility and protean nature provide the opportunity for growth and renewal. It could be said that acts 3 and 4 of the play exist to explore the "happy changes" (2.4.84) that ensue after Hercules arrives to unbind Prometheus from the rock. In lines that recall Lear's invitation to Cordelia—"Come, let's away to prison / . . . And take upon's the mystery of things / As if we were God's spies"[19]—Prometheus invites Asia and her sister nymphs to contemplate the mutability of things from the cool shade of a cave:

> A simple dwelling, which shall be our own,
> Where we will sit and talk of time and change
> As the world ebbs and flows, ourselves unchanged—
> What can hide man from Mutability?—
> . . . And we will search, with looks and words of love
> For hidden thoughts each lovelier than the last,
> Our unexhausted spirits, and like lutes
> Touched by the skill of the enamoured wind,
> Weave harmonies divine, yet ever new,
> From difference sweet where discord cannot be.
>   (3.3.22–25, 34–39)

Prometheus, having initiated and accepted change in himself, is supposed to appear here not as an exhausted, spent hero, like Lear or Milton's Samson, but one with "unexhausted spirit" now capable of infinite variations on his theme, "harmonies divine, yet ever new." According to one recent critic, act 3 is also meant to be a vision of a future in which male and female will be more nearly equal.[20] But in this, unfortunately, it has only limited success. Prometheus can retire from confrontation because, like Lear, he has already undergone all the changes he needs to. Here Prometheus' humanness goes perhaps too far: the spectacle of the determined, wise, and brave benefactor of humankind turning into a lute that the cosmic wind plays on has too much tragic pathos, of a kind appropriate to a human subject—the poet of "Ode to the West Wind," for instance— but not to a god. Further, Prometheus' statement that he and Asia will be "unchanged" seems immediately contradicted by the lines

19. *King Lear*, 5.3.8, 16–17.
20. Nathaniel Brown, *Sexuality and Feminism in Shelley*, 180. For a more critical view of act 3, see Jean Hall, *The Transforming Image*, 91.

comparing them to wind-played lutes. Too conditioned, perhaps, by masculinist views of struggle as significant only when it is combat between heroic male figures, we may still see the moment as one of Rousseauean languor and dissipation, rather than one of titans appropriately enjoying well-earned rest after victorious struggle. If change is to be celebrated, it must be in a different key from the action of the play so far.

The most important change to be celebrated is in perception, a fact demonstrated by the experience of the "Spirit of the Earth" who appears in act 3, scene 4. From seeing the world as filled with ugly creatures—"toads and snakes and loathly worms"—angry and ill-tempered people and poisonous plants, the Spirit of the Earth (like Coleridge's Mariner) has undergone a change of heart, participating in the new, musical sense of delight released by Prometheus' unbinding. Now the toads and snakes appear to her beautiful, the plants are no longer poisonous, and human beings become "mild and lovely forms" (3.4.69). It is a "Pan" vision of nature. This act of seeing afresh, this magical change in perspective, mirrors Prometheus' own change, when he looked again at the curse that had kept him chained to the precipice and realized that it was not irrevocable, or at least that its significance had changed. As critics have begun to recognize, if Jupiter's apparatus of tyranny had been overthrown by force, Shelley would simply have been dramatizing a male power struggle. Instead, Jupiter and his swords, chains, and thrones are *thought* out of existence, changed to "ghosts."[21]

It is not only Prometheus' championing of humankind against religious and political tyranny that makes him humanly attractive, then: it is that he accepts and embraces change, unlike Jupiter, who would prefer that his iron law endure forever. Shelley transforms and renews the Prometheus myth by showing Prometheus as actually coming closer to the human race he heroically defended, by giving up his single-minded defiance of Jupiter. In the words of his mother, the Earth, he is "more than God, / Being wise and kind" (1.144–45).

21. Woodman points out the far-reaching implications: "By releasing the 'one great mind' from the limited male image of it, Shelley through the androgyne felt he had released the 'great poem' from the burden of its essentially patriarchal past by unveiling in Asia an image of its feminine origins or source" ("The Androgyne in *Prometheus Unbound*," 239).

The power that brings about this massive change, a "secret strength of things" that does not abide Asia's question, is Demogorgon. According to the mythological researches of Shelley's friend, Thomas Love Peacock, Demogorgon was the father of Pan, as well as of the Fates. Demogorgon's throne, situated among volcanic mountains, exemplifies the more terrifying aspect of the power that can change the face of the earth, the "Earthquake-dæmon" of "Mont Blanc."

Demogorgon's throne is associated with another, even more terrifying power, however. The vapor the volcano disgorges has mind-altering properties, and Asia's sister Panthea explicitly compares this place to the ancient Delphic oracle and other sites where men and women breathed intoxicating fumes and found themselves endowed with visionary and quasi-shamanic powers. It is another image in which the natural processes of the earth are treated as interwoven with thought processes.[22] Asia and Panthea both suffer the effects of the volcanic vapors, so that their confrontation with the "mighty Darkness" that is the visible form of Demogorgon takes place in the visionary state, a state of altered consciousness. This is important, because Demogorgon is not an instructor or an "authority," in the usual sense of the word. He does not teach Asia a doctrine or enlighten her. Rather, like a guru or Socratic teacher, he speaks as she does, enabling her own visionary intuition, stimulated by the fumes that fill the volcanic cave, to provide her with the knowledge she seeks from him. Demogorgon speaks:

> —If the Abysm
> Could vomit forth its secrets:—but a voice
> Is wanting, the deep truth is imageless;
> For what would it avail to bid thee gaze
> On the revolving world? what to bid speak
> Fate, Time, Occasion, Chance and Change? To these
> All things are subject but eternal Love.
>> ASIA
> So much I asked before, and my heart gave

22. See G. M. Matthews, "A Volcano's Voice in Shelley," 172–73, 178–79. The Delphic oracle was not strictly a shamanic oracle, according to Mircea Eliade, since it was part of a highly developed cult, and shamanism as he defines it is a mysticism, not a religion or cult. However, there are certainly similarities. See *Shamanism: Archaic Techniques of Ecstasy*, 8, 387–88.

The response thou hast given; and of such truths
Each to itself must be the oracle.

(2.4.114–23)

Demogorgon's point can only be that Asia herself is subject to Fate, Time, Occasion, Chance, and Change; and no answer can be given to a being whose very nature is subject to all these things. What language can one use to speak to a being whose language, along with her other attributes, is in constant flux? The confrontation of Asia with Demogorgon poses the central problem of Shelleyan mythmaking: how to find a language to speak of the One, the Unchanging, when all available languages (mythical and otherwise) are human products, subject to "Fate, Time, Occasion, Chance and Change."[23] Asia's experience in the cave of Demogorgon parallels those of the poet in "Hymn to Intellectual Beauty" and "Mont Blanc." There is no voice that gives final answers to such questions as who made the world and why human feelings and beauty are transient. We ourselves provide, through mythology and poetry, the answers. These are valid only as long as they do not become dogmas and enthroned as omnipotent godhead, the process of turning metaphor into transcendence that Nietzsche critiqued. When a myth becomes totalitarian, as happened to Jupiter, the world is enslaved. Visionary experience and the mythmaking that proceeds from it are meant to have a healing power, like the dance of the shaman. As soon as it becomes rigidified into an instrument of political and religious oppression, it loses its only justification, its connection with the intuitive resources of the human mind, represented in this drama by Asia.

Asia's interview with Demogorgon perfectly illustrates Shelley's way with myth. Her ability to question Demogorgon, and the innate ability to create imaginative responses to her own questions, proceed from the mind-altered state that she entered by breathing the volcanic vapors from Demogorgon's cave. She is in a special relation with the powers of earth; she hears "the ghostly language of the ancient earth" (in Wordsworth's phrase), more intimately than a normal state of consciousness permits. Shelley's reading of ecstatic experiences—those of the Mænads of Dionysos, the priestesses who

23. See Tilottama Rajan, *Dark Interpreter: The Discourse of Romanticism*, 90; and Leighton, *Shelley and the Sublime*, 96.

uttered oracles at Delphi, and perhaps the poet of "Hymn to Intellectual Beauty"—is not that they remove the ecstatic to a transcendent
realm, but that they put the ecstatic in closer touch with the living
processes of the earth.

In the poems of the year following the completion of *Prometheus
Unbound,* however, change or mutability remains a disturbing issue. At the level of myth, the liberating possibilities of change in
consciousness and in the interpretation of language have been revealed in Asia's entranced interview with Demogorgon, Pan's sire,
in Prometheus' reunification with Asia, and in the linguistic revelry
of the fourth act of the play. In the human realm, however, Apollonian myths of permanence are constantly being projected as the
mind rebels against the distress that the world's instability brings—
the bright masks that Nietzsche describes, like "luminous spots . . .
designed to cure an eye hurt by the ghastly night."[24] "The Sensitive-
Plant" (*SP&P,* 210–19), written in the spring of 1820, is perhaps
the most poignant cry against the devastation of human hopes by
death, and opens up themes that receive more mature treatment in
"Adonais." The plant of the title grows in a beautiful garden, tended
by a Lady. Because the sensitive plant (*Mimosa pudica*) reproduces
without a mate, it is represented in the poem as yearning more than
other plants toward "what it has not—the beautiful!" (1.77).[25] After
the Lady's death, noxious weeds and fungi invade the garden and
the plants deteriorate. Eventually, after a cold winter, the Sensitive-
Plant stands a "leafless wreck" (3.115). Curiously, the cyclic pattern
of nature, which helps to sustain a mood of hope in "Hymn to
Intellectual Beauty" and "Ode to the West Wind," is absent from "The
Sensitive-Plant." Spring does not return for the lilies and hyacinths,
nor for the Sensitive-Plant itself. But to this apparently mournful
narrative Shelley characteristically adds an *envoi* or "Conclusion"
that radically reinterprets the first three parts of the poem as a
description of the death of the garden merely as it appeared to a
human observer lacking the visionary gift. The speaker wonders
whether death itself is not an illusion, created by the limitations
of our human senses:

24. Nietzsche, *The Birth of Tragedy,* 60.
25. For a possible source for Shelley's knowledge of *Mimosa pudica,* see
Patricia Hodgart, *A Preface to Shelley,* 120–22.

> Whether the Sensitive-Plant, or that
> Which within its boughs like a spirit sat
> Ere its outward form had known decay,
> Now felt this change,—I cannot say.
> ("Conclusion," lines 1–4)

The idea that the "outward form" of the plant may not be all of the plant that exists, that perhaps the plant has a permanent form, which like the Lady and the garden itself still exists in some transcendent realm, connects the poem to Shelley's Neoplatonic interests, which become still more evident in "Adonais"; but it is important to note that Shelley's "Platonism" is used here not in a doctrinal manner but rather to express a saving skepticism about human limits. "'Tis we, 'tis ours, are changed—not they" (line 20). The theme of change or mutability undergoes a paradoxical transformation here. Observing mutability in the natural world and in the death of those we love should not lead us to despair, because it is after all quite possible that a change in *ourselves,* in our murky and obscure perceptions, not in the things we mourn, has brought about our loss. In "The Sensitive-Plant," much of the poignancy comes from the fact that the plant itself (perhaps a figure for the poet, in his spiritually unmated loneliness) has an unsatisfied yearning for "the beautiful." This characteristic associates it with the Platonic interpretation of Eros, or Desire, as the power that influences humankind to adore the Good, the True, and the Beautiful. Without committing itself to Platonic doctrine, the poem suggests that the intense desire that something *should* be so may in some mysterious way prove that it *is* so.

This breakthrough is important because it marks a new way for Shelley to question and transform the myth of eternal return. Change, in the form of the ever-renewing cycle of the seasons, the Great Year *(Magnus Annus)* of classical myth, and the Zoroastrian twelve-thousand-year cycle, is liberating, at one level, and this liberating impulse is given full play in "Ode to the West Wind" and in the final chorus of *Hellas* (SP&P, 438–40):

> The world's great age begins anew,
>   The golden years return,
> The earth doth like a snake renew
>   Her winter weeds outworn.
> (lines 1060–63)

But at the end of *Hellas* is a very human expression of weariness with the cyclic patterns, a weariness that projects itself as the desperate cry,

> O cease! must hate and death return?
> .Cease! must men kill and die?
> Cease! drain not to its dregs the urn
>   Of bitter prophecy.
> The world is weary of the past,
> Oh might it die or rest at last!
>   (lines 1096–101)

Like the goddess Urania in *Adonais*, the poet of *Hellas* is tormented by two opposing forces. One is the impulse to admire and adore whatever manifestation of the Beautiful appears from time to time in the course of human life—whether it is in Keats's poetry, or in the birth of a new and more liberal civilization. But this impulse must eventually lead toward death, since poets are ephemeral and even civilizations die, and those who would continue to love them must pursue them into another world. Thus it conflicts with the knowledge that goddess and poet are "chained to Time" (*Adonais*, line 234). Like the speaker in Keats's "Ode to a Nightingale," Urania cannot choose to follow her symbol of poetic creation, John Keats, into eternity, because she would then abandon her own function.

This intense and potentially paralyzing conflict lends great force and tragic power to those poems in which it is successfully overcome. "Ode to the West Wind" (*SP&P*, 221–23) is one of them. First, it is important to note what is perhaps sufficiently obvious: that this is not a "loco-descriptive" poem, despite its origin in a woodland walk near Florence and the elegiac Wordsworthianism of some of the early sketches.[26] The "point of view" is not confined to any part of Italy nor indeed to any place on, above, or below the earth. Rather, the action, so to speak, takes place simultaneously on three levels of reality: the natural world, the individual mental processes of the poet, and the level of the Great Year, of those major cycles in the life of the human race that for Shelley's generation were heralded by the French Revolution. In consequence, Shelley forces us to consider what mode of consciousness must be necessary in order to conceive

---

26. See Rogers, *Shelley at Work*, 220–22.

the poem. The very act of conceiving the poem, that is, frees the reader from the conventions of the observer describing a landscape or the lyric poet invoking a natural force such as a wind or storm. Time, in its normal daily cycles, has become dispiriting, "A heavy weight of hours." The wind is invoked as an agent not merely of seasonal change, but of apocalyptic change, the herald of a new Great Year. Though the poem is wildly syncretic, with indirect references to the lyre of Apollo, the breath of Pan, and the coils of Neptune, the dominant image in the first two stanzas is that of the bacchanal. The imagery evidently owes something to a bas-relief that Shelley saw on a plinth in Florence, which represented "Mænads under the inspiration of the God [Bacchus]." Though it actually supported a statue of Minerva when he saw it, Shelley speculated that it must originally have been an altar to Bacchus, since the scenes depicted were utterly inappropriate to Minerva. His description emphasizes the way the Mænads embody the constantly changing appearances of nature:

> The tremendous spirit of superstition aided by drunkenness and producing something beyond insanity, seems to have caught them in its whirlwinds, and to bear them over the earth as the rapid volutions of a tempest bear the ever-changing trunk of a water-spout, as the torrent of a river whirls the leaves in its full eddies. Their hair loose and floating seems caught in the tempest of their own tumultuous motion, their heads are thrown back leaning with a strange inanity upon their necks, and looking up to Heaven, while they totter and stumble even in the energy of their tempestuous dance. (SCW, 6:323)

The slight note of disapproval apparent in this description—for superstition and drunkenness were not things that Shelley habitually admired—gives way in the poem to a succession of images that mirror the bacchanal's ability to overwhelm all distinctions between physical and spiritual, human and natural. It is as if the visits of the unseen Power in "Hymn to Intellectual Beauty," having become dulled over time, must be ecstatically reinvoked, and since the context of the poem is political or world-historical as well as personal, the ode reaffirms the revolutionary creed of the earlier poem, that change in itself is good.

The boundaries of the human and natural are broken down, but so are the boundaries of the common human faculties. A good illustration of this is stanza 3:

Thou who didst waken from his summer dreams
The blue Mediterranean, where he lay,
Lulled by the coil of his chrystalline streams,

Beside a pumice isle in Baiæ's bay,
And saw in sleep old palaces and towers
Quivering within the wave's intenser day,

All overgrown with azure moss and flowers
So sweet, the sense faints picturing them!
                    (lines 29–36)

The sea is "dreaming" the "old palaces and towers," a good instance of the transference of human mental processes to the natural world that plays such a large role in this poem. But then the flowers growing on the submerged buildings are described as "So sweet, the sense faints picturing them!" This use of a Keatsian swoon in such a context is remarkable, because it envisages the mind creating images of such beauty that the mind itself "faints." A promise of beauty is made, but then immediately retracted (the sense cannot bear to imagine such beauty), and we must turn back to the secondary meaning evoked by the word "faints"—the sense "feints" picturing them. Such images are transferred from the outward world to the mind, but the mind itself knows them to be self-created—something the mind "feints."

The most often quoted instance of this breaking of barriers between external and internal, world process and thought process, is probably the appeal to the wind to "Make me thy lyre, even as the forest is." But this very obvious combination of a kind of reversed metaphor (the poet will be to the wind as the lyre is to its human player) with simile ("even as the forest is") depends for its effectiveness on two allusions to myth, both used in an extraordinarily subtle way. One is the oblique reference to the Apollo myth. The lyre is Apollo's instrument; so here, if the poet becomes the instrument, the player—the West Wind—is meant for Apollo. The poet will not himself be the healer, but he will be the instrument of healing. Apollo also presented Orpheus with a lyre, so there are Orphic echoes in the stanza too. But the lyre image is also the occasion for a reconciliation between Apollo and Pan, for the old rivalry between the *stringed* instrument (Apollo's lyre) and the *wind* instrument (Pan's pipes) is transcended in a new synthesis: the breath of the West Wind itself becomes the player of the lyre.[27] The human poet, instrument of the wind, combines Pan's power to generate new growth and Apollo's visionary command and healing powers.

The momentary reconciliation of Apollo and Pan is achieved one more time in Shelley's late poetry, in the entertaining, erotic, and playful "The Witch of Atlas" (*SP&P*, 348–67). The first stanza sets the tone of half-mocking nostalgia for a world in which poetic imaginings had not yet been driven from the earth by Error and Truth (presumably, religious Error and scientific Truth):

> Before those cruel Twins, whom at one birth
>   Incestuous Change bore to her father Time,
> Error and Truth, had hunted from the earth
>   All those bright natures which adorned its prime,
> And left us nothing to believe in, worth
>   The pains of putting into learned rhyme,
> A lady-witch there lived on Atlas' mountain
> Within a cavern, by a secret fountain.
>   (lines 49–56)

This tone is sustained throughout the poem by the *ottava rima* stanza form, most familiar to us now as the medium of Byron's *Don Juan*. But rather than biting satire Shelley's poem offers a sort of holiday tour of Mediterranean mythology, or an animated and more colorful Lemprière.

The Witch is daughter of Apollo and one of the Atlantides (stanza 2), so she inherits the Apollonian characteristics of beauty and brightness: "garmented in light / From her own beauty" (lines 81–82). She has the Apollonian and Orphic power to pacify beasts and draw them to her: "all gaunt / And sanguine beasts her gentle looks made tame" (lines 92–93). She also draws to her throne in the Atlas Mountains of North Africa some of the wilder and more mischievous gods, demigods, nymphs, and dryads of the Greek pantheon: Silenus, Dryope, Faunus, Priapus, and Universal Pan. Pan does not here have the attributes of satyr's legs and cloven hooves, and is not pictured as primarily sexual or priapic. Nevertheless his meeting with the Witch is charged with erotic tension. He is *Universal* Pan, the mysterious,

27. Theresa M. Kelley suggests that the lyre and the conch-trumpet are fused into one instrument in *Prometheus Unbound*, 3.3.64–83 ("Proteus and Romantic Allegory," 636).

omnipresent power of nature that fills the world and its creatures with the desire to thrive and multiply—not the leering goat-god of popular tradition and of horror stories.

> And Universal Pan, 'tis said, was there,
>   And though none saw him,—through the adamant
> Of the deep mountains, through the trackless air,
>   And through those living spirits, like a want
> He past out of his everlasting lair
>   Where the quick heart of the great world doth pant—
> And felt that wondrous lady all alone—
> And she felt him upon her emerald throne.
>   (lines 113–20)

The Witch responds to this unseen god, evidently, because she has something in common with him; she is not a member of the upstart Olympian pantheon, but has an ancestry reaching back to the older, cruder, Arcadian traditions of Greece with which Pan himself is associated. She knows the secrets of the Golden Age (stanza 18), and her poetry is a poetry realized in nature. Shelley in this way invokes (without committing himself to) the optimism identified by Hans Blumenberg as characterizing the Romantic attitude to myth, the hope that behind the frivolous surface of classical mythology was concealed "the unrecognized, smuggled contents of an earlier revelation to mankind, perhaps the recollection of Paradise, which was so nicely interchangeable with Platonic anamnesis."[28] The Witch represents the possibility of a life without guilt, dogma, false piety, and "cant," and her tricks always aim at releasing the true beauty of the soul from the pain, guilt, and dogmatism in which it has become encased:

> She, all those human figures breathing there
>   Beheld as living spirits—to her eyes
> The naked beauty of the soul lay bare,
>   And often through a rude and worn disguise
> She saw the inner form most bright and fair—
>   And then, she had a charm of strange device,
> Which murmured on mute lips with tender tone,
> Could make that Spirit mingle with her own.
>   (lines 569–76)

28. Blumenberg, *Work on Myth*, 48; see also 273.

In the magic of the Witch's perception, Apollonian serenity and wisdom are united with Pan's knowledge and acceptance of life and mutability. Like all Shelley's more serious efforts at mythopoesis, the Witch of Atlas derives validity not from the myths themselves that constitute his raw material, but from the interpretive spin he gives them. After the devastating analysis of human limitations carried out in "Mont Blanc," a direct confrontation with the emptiness of received doctrine (whether in the form of theology, philosophy, or myth), Shelley shows his command of mythological material by starting again from the very source of myth—human experience and its realization in language.

Eight

Myth and the Enabling of Poetic Utterance

John Keats

Keats's sonnet "On Seeing the Elgin Marbles" presents an early version of a frequent topos in Keats's poetry. The poet, or poet-surrogate, stands before a representation of a human figure or figures, and hesitantly, anxiously, almost overwhelmed by the grandeur of the object before him, he interrogates it, searching for some clue to the hidden knowledge that the figure seems to embody.

> My spirit is too weak—mortality
>   Weighs heavily on me like unwilling sleep,
>   And each imagined pinnacle and steep
> Of godlike hardship tells me I must die
>   Like a sick eagle looking at the sky.
> $\qquad\qquad\qquad$ (*KP*, 93)[1]

The parallels that come to mind include the poet's wondering interrogation of the human forms that surround the Grecian urn, the narrator's awed questioning of Moneta's statuesque form in *The Fall of Hyperion*, and the climactic meeting between Mnemosyne and Apollo in *Hyperion: A Fragment*: "And there was purport in her

---

1. In arguing that "the speaker's activity is emphatically up for inspection" in the "Elgin Marbles" sonnet, William Crisman similarly reads the poem as primarily about the interpreter's lack of privilege, even seeing him as "a figure on whom unfair sentence has been passed, a persecuted god" ("A Dramatic Voice in Keats's Elgin Marbles Sonnet," 50, 55).

207

looks for him, / Which he with eager guess began to read / Perplex'd"
(3.47–49; *KP*, 353), when Apollo's "reading" of Mnemosyne's mysterious form precipitates his apotheosis. What is dramatized in all these
instances is a productive moment, full of anticipated possibility and
a sense of high destiny, but also of fear, difficulty, and puzzlement.
We can recognize it, I think, as the very moment of the modern
reception of myth.

What at first seems dominant in "On Seeing the Elgin Marbles"
and in Apollo's meeting with Mnemosyne is what we have been
taught is the poet's anxiety as he becomes aware of the oppressive
presence of tradition. "On Seeing the Elgin Marbles" seems a classic
statement of this feeling of paralysis and powerlessness. The poet
desires the immortality granted by the creative gift, but the poem
opposes to this desire an apparently overwhelming sense of mortality.
Even in this sonnet, however, in which the sense of mortality that
the sight of the marble figures instills seems to have all but negated
the immortal longings essential to a poet, there is a hint that the
onlooker's silence before a tremendous and "godlike" work of art is a
sign that he does indeed possess the poetic gift, not that he lacks it.
For the poet to assert his right to speak in the presence of the marble
figures would be a kind of sacrilege. It is precisely his awed silence
that testifies to the genuineness of his poetic vocation. Many other
"dim-conceived glories of the brain," the poem continues, "Bring
round the heart an undescribable feud; / So do these wonders a
most dizzy pain," (lines 9–11). The capacity to feel such pain, to
absorb something of the still-potent grandeur along with a sense of
the "rude / Wasting of old time" (lines 12–13), is surely the mark
of a nascent poet just like the torments Apollo feels before his
deification in *Hyperion*, 3. Keats seems to suggest, then, that the
confrontation with an "older" knowledge can be an empowering as
well as a humbling experience.

The topos also demands to be included in any discussion of
myth in the Romantic period because it is in this form that Keats
most often structures the goddess myths he appropriates. That is,
Keats frequently represents the topos of confrontation with an older
knowledge as a young male speaker (Endymion, Apollo, Lycius, the
knight at arms, the poet in *The Fall of Hyperion*) addressing a goddess
or other supernatural female figure (the moon goddess, Mnemosyne,
Lamia, the Belle Dame, Moneta). The moment of recognition is

often linked with the strict observance of a taboo against premature speech, as if, like Madeline retiring to her bedchamber on St. Agnes' Eve hoping for a vision of her lover, the poet must keep silent so that invisible agencies may do their work. The power of poetic utterance is granted simultaneously, or nearly so, with the moment of recall, just as Madeline breaks the folkloric taboo against speech when the living but deathly pale Porphyro becomes visible to her in place of her warm dream of him. At this moment the poet experiences not a defeat, but a liberation, or even an apotheosis—"Knowledge enormous makes a God of me" (*Hyperion*, 3.113; *KP*, 355).

In Platonic terms, this recall or recognition can be identified with anamnesis, the moment when the truth that we know already, but have not been permitted to recall, floods into the mind and transforms us. Plotinus, in the Fourth Ennead, went so far as to claim that memory attests to the permanence and stability of the soul, while the world that appears to the senses and the very human body itself are in constant flux and so impede memory. The more we attend to the body and the visible world, the more we must forget; remembering, on the other hand, is a guarantee of the soul's immortality.[2] Even in our own century, some poets—among them, Marianne Moore—continue to affirm the truth of anamnesis, but in psychological rather than metaphysical terms. In "The Mind Is an Enchanting Thing," Moore notes how deceptive is the apparent powerlessness of the mind: "It has memory's ear / that can hear without / having to hear."[3] Some knowledge that lies outside the mind, or at least beyond the control of the conscious mind, brings creative power out of seeming passivity.

In pointing to the frequency with which Keats returns to this topos, I am not trying to argue that we should re-Platonize Keats, however. My purpose in this chapter is, rather, to argue that Keats's modernity is most clearly apparent in his use of the figure of the self-doubting interpreter. The sense of poetic empowerment and of exciting possibility is balanced by a sense of loss, a fear that

2. "Memory, in point of fact, is impeded by the body. . . . The Soul is a stability; the shifting and fleeting thing which body is can be a cause only of its forgetting, not of its remembering—Lethe stream may be understood in this sense—and memory is a fact of the Soul" (*The Enneads*, 283 [4.3]).

3. Marianne Moore, *Complete Poems*, 134.

figurative language may express only absence, never presence. It is true that, in a well-known letter of February 27, 1818, to the publisher John Taylor, Keats wrote that poetry "should strike the Reader as a wording of his own highest thoughts, and appear almost a Remembrance."[4] Keats offers this to Taylor, however, as one of those "axioms" that his poetry cannot live up to. Poetry "should . . . appear almost a Remembrance": it is an effect that poetry should have on its readers, not a given, necessary characteristic. For a modern, ironic consciousness, the act of understanding implied by anamnesis reaches no metaphysical certainties. The sense of recognition is a quality of the moment, an epiphany created by the temporary alignment of the poetic figure with the linguistic order present in the reader's mind. From this perspective, as Geoffrey Hartman says, "symbols or figures point to a lack: to something used up or not sufficiently 'present.'" Interpretation then becomes the attempt to recover and impersonate that presence. And interpretation, as the recovery of at least the illusion of "presence," must always appear to reveal what is already there, not to erect the new in its place. The aim of the interpreter is to *recognize*, rather than to create ex nihilo; or, as Hartman has it (quoting Freud), to "refind" an object that corresponds to the one presented in the poetic figure.[5]

We can distinguish in Keats's poetry certain moments of recognition and ecstatic insight, often leading to poetic utterance, and moments when the onlooker fails to make the object he or she is interrogating "speak," so that silence (or death, poetically its equivalent) supervenes. The onlooker's speech may be associated with the imperfect, the rudely human, and even with sacrilege. The dreamer-narrator of *The Fall of Hyperion* fears that since he is no poet, his utterance may be sacrilegious in the temple of Moneta (1.140; *KP*, 481). In such instances, silence is associated with renewal, with possibility,

4. John Keats, *Letters*, 1:238.
5. Geoffrey H. Hartman, *The Fate of Reading*, 38. The idea that the spoken word betokens "presence" will be familiar to readers of Walter Ong. Ong holds that the very ephemerality of the spoken word is part of its special power, and reminds us of the traditional association between the divine creative word and poetic utterance (*The Presence of the Word*, 111–12). I am concerned here, however, not with the truth or untruth of the idea that speech connotes "presence" but with Keats's use of it as a poetic figure.

even with godlike creativity and the poetic vocation. The spoken word is limited, finite; the unspoken word is powerful, infinite, an ideal "poetry." Yet silence may also be deathly, cold, a *memento mori*, and speech godlike, life giving, even erotic: the first part of "Isabella" is a case in point.

Many of Keats's most subtle poems, however, seem to project both patterns simultaneously, making us aware that each metaphoric structure is constantly qualified by the presence of the other. So, in "Ode on a Grecian Urn," there is a subtle movement between the speaker's sense of his mortality, and therefore of the sacrilegious nature of his speech, and his ability to transcend that mortality and make the urn "speak." The silence of the urn is partly a deathly one, since in several ways the urn signifies mortality, a sleep and a forgetting, but it is also a silence of potential creation, since it enables the poet to create or recreate the moment of life pictured on the urn. The poet makes the urn "speak," interpreting its concealed knowledge for us through an extraordinary use of prosopopoeia. In "The Eve of St. Agnes," as Porphyro gazes upon the silent form of Madeline, his speech—the song he sings to the accompaniment of Madeline's lute—is sacrilegious, but at the same time it awakens her to the forgotten or unadmitted knowledge of erotic fulfillment; and Madeline breaks her own self-imposed taboo on speech in order to rouse Porphyro from his deathlike state.

It would be an oversimplification, then, to argue that the second of these two overlapping metaphorical structures, identifying speech with life, came to prevail over the first in Keats's mature poetry. Keats's use of the prophetic and "Apollonian" view of speech as life-giving and creative in the first *Hyperion* suggests that for this work Keats had to overcome the traditional association of silence with the sacred and of speech with sacrilege. As doubt is said to be the necessary accompaniment to faith, however, so the alternative view, that silence is sacred, speech sacrilegious, accompanies the human poet's re-articulation of the Apollonian faith in the dream prologue to *The Fall of Hyperion*.

These metaphorical patterns grow out of a long struggle with the poetic problem of absence, the sense of "something used up or not sufficiently 'present,' " in Hartman's phrase, and the related need to reinterpret and revitalize the forms that symbolize such absent powers.[6] One famous passage in *Endymion*, after satirizing the empty clangor of earthly empires, their deafening trumpets, drums, and shoutings, describes the silence of the divine powers and the divinity of silence:

> Are then regalities all gilded masks?
> No, there are throned seats unscalable
> But by a patient wing, a constant spell,
> Or by ethereal things that, unconfin'd,
> Can make a ladder of the eternal wind,
> And poise about in cloudy thunder-tents
> To watch the abysm-birth of elements.
> Aye, 'bove the withering of old-lipp'd Fate
> A thousand Powers keep religious state,
> In water, fiery realm, and airy bourne;
> And, silent as a consecrated urn,
> Hold sphery sessions for a season due.
> (1.22–33; *KP*, 164)

The moon goddess invoked in the rest of this passage as one of the few "Powers" or "far majesties" who have condescended to reveal themselves to humankind is powerful precisely because her influence is silent: at sunset, when Apollo's "gold breath is misting in the west" (line 44), Diana "unobserved steals unto her throne" (line 45) and sheds blessings over the wren and the humble oyster as well as mountains and ancient trees, "with silver lip / Kissing dead things to life" (lines 56–57; *KP*, 165). Even the "monstrous sea" obeys her powerful but always silent commands (lines 69–71). In this context, the "high Poet" mentioned in line 48 is, strangely, a silent poet, and his first response to the moon goddess is a silent homage:

> She unobserved steals unto her throne,
> And there she sits most meek and most alone;
> As if she had not pomp subservient;

6. See in particular Lawrence Kramer, "The Return of the Gods: Keats to Rilke," for a consideration of this question as it affects Keats's "theophanies." Robert M. Ryan suggests that the influence of Benjamin Bailey, who was a candidate for ordination, led Keats to become interested in the question of interpretation—including problems of translation (*Keats: The Religious Sense*, 119).

As if thine eye, high Poet! was not bent
Towards her with the Muses in thine heart.
(lines 45–49)

To speak at such a time would indicate, paradoxically, the absence of
the poetic gift, an inability to give Diana the silent homage that she
rightly demands of men. Much as Aphrodite is represented as having
a servant and messenger (Eros) who is himself incapable of love,
the patroness of poets is not only silent herself but demands silent
worship. While Diana's silent influence pervades the human and
animal worlds, Apollo, patron of music and poetry, whose cult affirms
an identification of speech and song with the godlike, is appropriately
invisible beneath the horizon. The two moments—when speech
is sacrilegious, and when it is erotically and poetically potent—are
separated as night is from day. In his conversations with Peona, too,
Endymion learns to doubt his vision. Peona, as Stuart Sperry points
out, is a voice of skepticism, actually challenging Endymion's "faith
in the truth of his visionary pursuit" and warning him against the
power of fancy.[7]

This is not to deny that in other poems (most clearly in the
"Ode to Apollo," written in February 1815) Keats had already invoked
Apollo as the god "functionally representative of his own experience
and reflection," as Walter H. Evert argues. Rather, the emphasis in
Endymion on silent adoration of Diana demonstrates how Keats
would eventually have to approach Apollo and his cult again, and
more subtly, as an enabling metaphor of poetic creation, a means of
overcoming the self-imposed sacred silence of the onlooker. In arguing that in *Endymion*, Diana/Cynthia "merges" with Apollo (her twin
brother) and "becomes his alter ego," making Diana and Apollo more
or less interchangeable as sources of both heavenly radiance and
poetic inspiration, Evert glosses over a significant problem in Keats's
poetic thought, ignoring as well the differences in poetic tone between invocations of the moon goddess in *Endymion* and invocations
of the sun god elsewhere.[8] Endymion's Muse, like the Muse invoked
in "Sleep and Poetry," governs mildly, subtly, wordlessly—"The very
archings of her eyelids charm / A thousand willing agents to obey"—

7. Stuart Sperry, *Keats the Poet*, 100.
8. Evert, *Aesthetic and Myth*, 38, 105.

and for that very reason her rule is "the supreme of power" ("Sleep and Poetry," lines 238–39, 236; *KP*, 74–75). But the enlargement of Endymion's human senses has not brought the power to articulate his visionary experience, has not metamorphosed Endymion into a speaking *poet*.

Such distrust of the "roughness of mortal speech" (*Endymion*, 2.818; *KP*, 157) is the basis for many later versions of the interpreter figure as mortal, limited, and thus unfit to speak of things celestial. Many passages in Keats's work speak of the need for the true interpreter of beauty to keep silence before the face or object that, silent itself, calls for interpretation. In the "Vistas of solemn beauty" that the poet's imagination anticipates in "Sleep and Poetry," he will imitate the sacred silent language of earth and "wander / In happy silence, like the clear Meander / Through its lone vales" (lines 73–75; *KP*, 70–71). Speech is too definite, limiting, and human to have a place in this paradise. It is silence that speaks of enrichment and possibility—so also most notably in the sonnet "On First Looking into Chapman's Homer." In one obvious sense the poem is about interpretation, which can initiate us into new realms of experience. Martin Aske emphasizes this aspect and takes the optimistic view that the speaker's reading of Chapman is an "originatory" action: "The poet's experience is privileged because of its sense of 'firstness.' . . . Keats' epiphanic encounter with Homer seems to promise a transcendence of temporal difference, and history forgotten, as the modern poet comes face to face with his ancient muse."[9] Yet equally striking is a failure of interpretation, the recognition that the poet does not know where to seek what he would know. Homer's epic is of a godlike vastness, its very atmosphere intoxicating, like the clear air laden with scent of bay trees in "Sleep and Poetry." Chapman's version has none of the secondariness usually associated with a translation: its air is the same "pure serene" as Homer's. The listener is caught up by a greater power. The phrase "watcher of the skies" subtly suggests one who inhabits the skies as well as one who observes them, I think, and "stout Cortez . . . with eagle eyes" is the soaring genius looking down at our earth as well as the heroic but earthbound traveler. Yet the exhilaration of lines 7–13 ends not with a cry or song but with silence and a "wild surmise." The cult of Apollo does not extend as far as the Pacific. The "firstness" of "On

9. Martin Aske, *Keats and Hellenism*, 42.

First Looking into Chapman's Homer" is somewhat qualified by the poem's expressing the impossibility of saying anything about Homer, after Chapman. Whatever is said will inevitably be supererogatory, a translation of what is already translated. Like the poet, the reader may interrogate Chapman's text, but in the same spirit as Cortez interrogates the vast prospect before him, in silent wonder. The poem accepts its own inevitable secondariness, having graciously and even devoutly yielded the privilege of Apollonian speech to the double precursor, Homer-Chapman. Although the reader is invited to participate in the contrary privilege of ascent to a vantage point and enjoyment of a vast prospect, Homer's "world," the irony of the poem is that its praise of Cortez's *silence*, and its refusal to reutter or reinterpret the tradition, conveys the tradition's oppressiveness and inaccessibility. It is as if the poet's own language has projected out of its inadequacy and secondariness the ideal of a speech that is translucent, immediate, and primary. The poet does not choose silence because the tradition is oppressive and unknowable; rather, the tradition is awe inspiring and unknowable because the poet, emulating Cortez, chooses silence. In just the same way, in the sonnet "To Haydon, with a Sonnet Written on Seeing the Elgin Marbles," Keats creates the obscure sense of possible sublimity through the near tautology "what I want I know not where to seek."

In "Isabella," "The Eve of St. Agnes," and "La Belle Dame Sans Merci," three poems in which a lover is momentarily placed in the position of an "interpreter" of the beloved's silent form, the lover's power of utterance is in precarious balance with a reverent but poetically dangerous devotion to silent worship. In "Isabella," Lorenzo tells himself "I may not speak," and yet not to speak is synonymous with (literal) death for both lovers. Isabella falls ill, and Lorenzo resolves to risk a declaration of his love.

> So said he one fair morning, and all day
> His heart beat awfully against his side;
> And to his heart he inwardly did pray
> For power to speak; but still the ruddy tide
> Stifled his voice, and puls'd resolve away.
> (lines 41–45; *KP*, 246)

The evident irony here is that the lovers' inability to speak their passion has brought at least one of them close to death, but that proximity gives one of them courage to speak and so break the spell that binds them. The identification of poetic speech with regeneration, with eros, is explicit in stanza 9:

> "Love! thou art leading me from wintry cold,
>   Lady! thou leadest me to summer clime,
> And I must taste the blossoms that unfold
>   In its ripe warmth this gracious morning time."
> So said, his erewhile timid lips grew bold,
>   And poesied with hers in dewy rhyme:
> Great bliss was with them, and great happiness
> Grew, like a lusty flower in June's caress.
>   (lines 65–72; *KP*, 247–48)

Their silence has helped to create the aura the lovers each perceive around the other; but their silence is also death-dealing, and by a blessed circumstance (not too far removed from Madeline's retiring supperless to bed) one of them is provoked to speech before it is too late.

By the end of the poem, however, this identification of speech with life and eros has undergone a grotesque reversal. The apparition of the murdered Lorenzo that appears to Isabella parodies the lovers' erotically charged speech, revealing the unpalatable truth that ordinary, human speech does not make its author immortal. The "under-song" of Lorenzo and Isabella's loving words is death.

> It was a vision.—In the drowsy gloom,
>   The dull of midnight, at her couch's foot
> Lorenzo stood, and wept: the forest tomb
>   Had marr'd his glossy hair which once could shoot
> Lustre into the sun, and put cold doom
>   Upon his lips, and taken the soft lute
> From his lorn voice, and past his loamed ears
> Had made a miry channel for his tears.
>
> Strange sound it was, when the pale shadow spake;
>   For there was striving, in its piteous tongue,
> To speak as when on earth it was awake,
>   And Isabella on its music hung:
> Languor there was in it, and tremulous shake,
>   As in a palsied Druid's harp unstrung;
> And through it moan'd a ghostly under-song,
> Like hoarse night-gusts sepulchral briars among.
>   (lines 273–88; *KP*, 255)

The pathos of the vision described in the first of these stanzas is complicated, in the second, by numerous ironies and ambiguities. Death has robbed Lorenzo of the power to speak "as when on earth," and even the form his apparition takes is ambiguous, being partly human and partly nonhuman. The phantom appears to be a "he" in line 279 ("his . . . voice") but an "it" in line 282 ("its . . . tongue"), and the "it" in line 287 could refer either to the "shadow" or to the unmusical "music" of its speech. The awkward inversion and consonantal clusters in line 288 further increase the reader's sense of dislocation and incoherence. The earlier image of speech as erotic and life giving is here negated by a frightening image of mortality that particularly stresses the *inarticulateness* it imposes on the lovers.

As Kurt Heinzelman has shown, there is an immediately relevant economic context to Keats's confrontation with the vulnerability of poetic speech in "Isabella." Lorenzo's murderers are Isabella's ambitious brothers who think his prospects inadequate for a potential husband for her. In Keats's treatment of this theme, Heinzelman argues, an earlier "georgic" sense of the value of poetic labor combines with "another, more troubled way of understanding the literary process," the result being that the economic status of poetic speech in modern times and in the capitalist economic order is painfully foregrounded. Keats's experience of the literary world taught him that poetic speech is a commodity that can be bought and sold in the literary marketplace: "The more Keats apologizes to Boccaccio, the more he links himself implicitly to the brothers' venturing capitalism." Death, the archenemy of poetic speech in "Isabella," now connotes not just human mortality in general but, more particularly, the unavoidable material status of everything (including love and poetry) in the capitalist world where cash value is the ultimate measure. Keats "purchases his modernity by deviating from Boccaccio on the material importance to the story of the brothers' economics, only to have this deviation remind him that his art echoes more sources than one."[10]

In many respects, "The Eve of St. Agnes" describes the same death-threatened world as "Isabella": the Beadsman's breath "Seem'd taking flight for heaven," the room where Porphyro speaks to Angela

10. Kurt Heinzelman, "Self-interest and the Politics of Composition in Keats's *Isabella*," 170, 175, 176.

is "silent as a tomb" (line 113; *KP*, 303), the lovers flee toward the "southern moors" ("the bleak Dartmoor" in one variant; line 351 and note); but the overcoming of silence, both erotically and poetically, is more central. Porphyro is represented as fully aware of what is called in *Endymion* the "roughness of mortal speech" (2.818). For obvious reasons, silence is the most essential condition of his enterprise— "He ventures in: let no buzz'd whisper tell" (line 82; *KP*, 302). More important, he understands that speaking to Madeline is the second in the ascending series of erotic privileges he aspires to, after the privilege of silent "worship," as if reaffirming its connection with the sexual is a way for Keats to revalidate poetic speech and reclaim it from the dead hand of material "circumstance." Porphyro

> implores
> All saints to give him sight of Madeline,
> But for one moment in the tedious hours,
> That he might gaze and worship all unseen;
> Perchance speak, kneel, touch, kiss—in sooth such things have been.
> (lines 77–81)

Just as essential to this mutual transgression into the sacred, however, is Madeline's silence. The charm will not work unless Madeline retires to bed not only "supperless" but speechless too: "No uttered syllable, or, woe betide!" (line 203; *KP*, 308). As in the "Chapman's Homer" sonnet, silence is a ploy to invoke the power of "the sacred," and the mortal who would trespass in a consecrated realm must abjure the roughness of mortal speech. In the silence of her sleep, Madeline is "Clasp'd like a missal where swart Paynims pray" (line 241; *KP*, 310)—that is, significantly, a closed book, an unread and uncomprehended page. In the central moment of the poem (stanzas 32–36), this deathward progression to no death is arrested and reversed by what is now commonly recognized as a stratagem or deception.[11] Porphyro plays Madeline's lute, "Close to her ear touching the melody" (line 293; *KP*, 313), representing her in his song as "La belle dame sans mercy," and soon wakes her from a dream of Porphyro himself. But the dream Porphyro was transfigured with "looks immortal" (line 313; *KP*, 314), and, unlike the silent Porphyro

11. I refer to Jack Stillinger, *The Hoodwinking of Madeline and Other Essays on Keats's Poems*, 73, 77.

now kneeling by her bed, "Fearing to move or speak" (line 306), he *did* speak to her, in "complainings dear" (line 313). Madeline's dream-charged speech in effect turns the "pallid, chill, and drear" Porphyro (line 311) into the "Ethereal" lover (stanza 36), and he becomes the lover she saw in her vision. Each lover impersonates the other's image. Each makes the other's image speak, in an unusual kind of prosopopeia. By transgressing the embargo on speech Madeline (who, as Stillinger points out, is still in her trance, though now dreaming with eyes open)[12] creates for herself a mortal lover who is yet more than mortal, a lover transfigured by her own "voluptuous accents" (line 317).

Some readers see the ironies in this episode as wholly destructive and the love of Porphyro and Madeline as delusory. It is possible to argue, however, that the poem contains and controls the ironies it produces; that the scene of mutual recognition between Porphyro and Madeline is governed not by a fear of deceit, or of Dionysian violence to the integral self, but by the desire to make poetic utterance possible. Death and religious awe both threaten human speech—held sacrilegious in their presence—so that Porphyro's stratagem is not only a means of (momentarily) circumventing death and fulfilling erotic desire but also a means of overcoming the embargo imposed by folk tradition on lovers' speech. I am not denying the presence of a "ghostly under-song"; indeed, it is necessary to my point. The dutiful lover's silence enhances the beloved's radiant beauty, but such silence is inevitably death-dealing in the long run. The fond maiden's self-imposed silence under the rule of St. Agnes threatens to "stifle" her, turning her into a mutilated Philomel, a distinctly unpropitious mate for the poet-surrogate Porphyro.[13] The lovers conspire to break the spell. Porphyro's song and Madeline's voluptuous speech defy taboo, but in doing so make a regenerative union between them possible. Moreover, the "trick" through which Madeline is seduced is parallel to the "trick" (or "whim") by which poetic utterance— here, the narrative itself—is made possible. Enjoining silence on the foemen and on Madeline, the narrator breaks his own injunction in

12. Ibid., 81.
13. The threat to Madeline, as an antitype of Philomel, was pointed out by Beverly Fields, in "Keats and the Tongueless Nightingale: Some Unheard Melodies in 'The Eve of St. Agnes.'"

creating the poem. Further, as the sexual explicitness of the poem (like the "simplicity" of "Isabella") risks the hostility of the critics and the consequent failure of the work in the literary marketplace, it is evident that the taboo on erotic speech has to do with more than just folk tradition: it is a very immediate problem for the publishing poet.

As Earl Wasserman has pointed out, "La Belle Dame Sans Merci" (the last of our three poems representing the onlooker or interpreter as a lover) draws on a folk legend well known to readers of Scott's *Minstrelsy of the Scottish Border,* that of Thomas the Rhymer, or Thomas of Ercildoune.

> In the version available to Keats in Robert Jamieson's *Popular Ballads,* 1806 (the variant in Scott's *Minstrelsy* differs in a few important details) Thomas encounters a beautiful lady whom he thinks to be the Queen of Heaven, but who identifies herself as "the queen of fair Elfland." She takes him upon her milk-white steed, for he must serve her for seven years; and for forty days and nights they ride through blood while Thomas sees neither sun nor moon.[14]

One aspect of the traditional story not touched on by Wasserman is the lady's strict instruction to Thomas to keep silence, whatever he may hear or see in Elfland. There is no direct reference in Keats's poem to the elfin lady prohibiting the knight from speaking, however. The motif has been absorbed into the larger theme of the knight's inadequacy and what Wasserman calls "the absence of song" in the desolate landscape where the knight is seen loitering (65). What the poem does provide is an apparent contrast between the human speech of the knight, narrating his tale, and the potent, magical word of the elfin lady.

> I set her on my pacing steed,
>   And nothing else saw all day long,
> For sidelong would she bend, and sing
>   A fairy's song.

> She found me roots of relish sweet,
>   And honey wild, and manna dew,
> And sure in language strange she said—
>   I love thee true.
>   (lines 21–28; *KP*, 358)

14. Earl R. Wasserman, *The Finer Tone,* 68.

The contrast between the lady's magical song and the knight's regret-ful, uncreative speech seems clear. The knight is silent in Elfland, or at least he does not claim to have spoken, as if in recognition that human speech would be sacrilegious there, would break the spell. The lady's song, like Porphyro's in "The Eve of St. Agnes," is the prelude to erotic release, and the knight's silence in Elfland permits her exercise of erotic power. But in the realm of mortals, on the "cold hill's side" where the knight tells his story, speech and silence have both become deathly, a condition that affects even the knight's description of the lady. As he remembers his experience the knight's language subtly questions the elfin lady's power. Her song could not stop the knight from recalling the fact of his mortality, signified by the procession of the death-pale kings, princes, and warriors. The lady's tongue is "strange," her song a "fairy's song"; so how can we believe her protestation, "I love thee true"? "I love thee," spoken in "language strange," demands the reassuring addition of the word "true" and of "sure" in the preceding line, yet the combined effect of the two adverbs is not to validate but to undermine the surface meaning. The knight's language is a human language and cannot, it seems, translate the elfin lady's words without in some way questioning them.

Equally relevant to our topic is another of Keats's likely sources: Spenser's *Faerie Queene*, 1, canto 9, where, as Arthur lies sleeping, a "royall Mayd" appears and invites his love. The Spenserian register is one of doubt just tipping over into delight and faith:

> But whether dreames delude, or true it were,
> Was neuer hart so rauisht with delight,
> Ne liuing man like words did euer heare,
> As she to me deliuered all that night. (1.9.14)

No living man ever heard such words, but I *did* hear them, is Arthur's wondering response. In Keats's poem the balance tips toward skep-ticism—*did* I hear such words? A living, mortal man may not be able to hold commerce with such supernatural beings as the elfin queen; the only words the knight at arms understands during his ad-venture are the words of the death-pale kings, princes, and warriors: "La belle dame sans merci / Hath thee in thrall!" (lines 39–40). The knight's memory of his experience is a diminishment of it, not the empowerment that anamnesis brings.

From a human perspective, the magical quality of the elfin queen's language is in part a projection of the poet-surrogate's futile hope for a permanent and translucent language of his own. If human language is recognized as "frail," accessible but impermanent, the logic of a mythopoeic imagination would suggest that a language of stable terms, which always meant what it said, must be the exclusive privilege of the gods.

Precisely because Apollo is not a "poet-surrogate" but a god, the patron, protector, and cynosure of the poet, the very source of all human song, Keats can use him to interrogate successfully the mute image of Mnemosyne, memory, in *Hyperion*. The gap between knowledge and utterance so evident in "La Belle Dame Sans Merci" is conjured away in *Hyperion*; Apollo is not an absent god whom the poet invokes, but a present power whose words the poet speaks. As Apollo interrogates the goddess of memory, she remains silent, but her silence, instead of threatening the poet-god's utterance, here empowers him to speak, to interpret, even to impersonate her image. Wordsworth's *Excursion* (familiar to Keats) describes Apollo as seen by some Greek herdsman: "A beardless Youth, who touched a golden lute, / And filled the illumined groves with ravishment" (*Excursion*, 4.859–60; *WPW*, 5:136). In Keats's representation of Apollo, Mnemosyne holds the musical instrument, a harp, but Apollo speaks:

> "O tell me, lonely Goddess, by thy harp,
> That waileth every morn and eventide,
> Tell me why thus I rave, about these groves!
> Mute thou remainest—mute! yet I can read
> A wondrous lesson in thy silent face:
> Knowledge enormous makes a God of me."
> (3.108–13; *KP*, 355)

This unrestrained and creative intercourse between memory and poesis shows Keats assuming the power to justify his own mythopoeic act by claiming the Apollonian precedent. The paralyzing ironies of "La Belle Dame Sans Merci" are not neutralized altogether, but distanced by their projection on to the failing generation, the Titans, whose loss of divinity is signaled by their loss of the power of speech. Saturn speaks "As with a palsied tongue" (1.93; *KP*, 332); he is said to have "snatch'd" utterance, rather than claimed it (line 140; *KP*, 333);

Oceanus speaks "In murmurs" (1.171; *KP*, 346); Enceladus in "ponderous syllables, like sullen waves / In the half-glutted hollows of reef-rocks" (2.305–6; *KP*, 349). In contrast to this tortured and orotund speech, Apollo's speech is enthusiastic, life giving, and prophetic. As it takes on life-giving power, too, there is a change in the way it bodies forth knowledge. What the prophetic poet must "know" in order to speak new life is personified in the shape, in the very face, of Mnemosyne. Such knowledge, that is, must appear to the prophetic poet's consciousness not as something inquired about and discovered, but as something "remembered." As in the "Chapman's Homer" sonnet, the address to the moon goddess in *Endymion*, and the "Ode on a Grecian Urn," a mystified questioner here interrogates and attempts to interpret a silent image. The use of the trope here differs considerably, however. By a peculiar application of the technique of prosopopoeia the face (prosopon) of Memory is left silent, "mute," while the inspired poet speaks his "remembered" knowledge: " 'I can read / A wondrous lesson in thy silent face: / Knowledge enormous makes a God of me.' " Apollo's question to Mnemosyne, "Where is power?" (3.103; *KP*, 355), is rhetorical in the sense that he already possesses the answer, or, rather, will possess it when he articulates it. In this moment invention and recall (anamnesis) are represented as identical. Apollo speaks "from Memory," as it were, but the memory exists for him only at the moment when he articulates and thus discovers it. This moment in the poem counterbalances Hyperion's earlier questioning of the cold Phantoms who have begun to inhabit his solar palace. Hyperion's passing from a state of prophetic knowing to one of inarticulateness is answered and balanced by Apollo's countermovement from ignorance to prophetic knowing.

"La Belle Dame Sans Merci" cannot have been written earlier than April 21, 1819, and the writing of *Hyperion: A Fragment* was broken off some time before April 20, 1819. This seems to suggest that the "ironic" version of the interpreter motif was in no sense *replaced* by that work's prophetic stance. Indeed, *Hyperion* refers to human speech as "our feeble tongue" (1.49; *KP*, 330) and projects on to the defeated Titans the inarticulate grief and lack of prophetic knowledge ascribed in earlier poems to the mortal poet or poet-surrogate. This suggests that for Keats the metaphoric structure portraying poetic utterance as potentially godlike continued to overlap and combine with metaphors of utterance as frail and even sacrilegious. Each of these structures necessitates the other as its essential corollary.

The poet's questioning of the silent urn in "Ode on a Grecian Urn," for instance, elicits thoughts of mortality in the same way as Hyperion's questioning of the cold Phantoms that gather to warn him of his impending overthrow. The urn's stillness, its promise of semiotic permanence, are in a sense built on death—the deaths of all those generations between the creation of the urn by Keats's imaginary artist and the poet's present attempt to read or interpret the urn's images. The urn can validate the "Apollonian equation," " 'Beauty is truth, truth beauty,' " only against the mortality of "When old age shall this generation waste" (line 46; KP, 373). The urn's silence still permits the poet's speech, however. Or as Geraldine Friedman has argued, in examining the gender politics implicit in a male speaker's interrogating a female form (the urn), the poet's claiming the privilege of interpretation "is figured as a male subject's sexual pursuit of a female object of desire."[15] As in Apollo's one-sided dialogue with Mnemosyne, the prosopopoeic technique (the urn is a "historian," can "express" a tale, and so on) permits the poet to "remember" or recognize what the urn represents; his knowledge is spoken as remembered not discovered knowledge, and the ode is, therefore, to a degree, prophetic in mode, despite our awareness of a death-haunted undersong in the speaker's interrogation of the urn. The speaker's question "What leaf-fring'd legend haunts about thy shape?" (line 5; KP, 372) registers not baffled incomprehension, but expectation, the male speaker's assumption that he can know what the urn has to say. As Mnemosyne's mute face enables Apollo to remember the knowledge that makes him a god, so the urn's "silent form" (line 44) enables the speaker to "remember" the Arcadian scene which he (and not the urn) then re-creates.

A similar sense of expectation is present in the opening lines of T. S. Eliot's "Marina":

> What seas what shores what grey rocks and what islands
> What water lapping the bow
> And scent of pine and the woodthrush singing through the fog

15. Geraldine Friedman, "The Erotics of Interpretation in Keats's 'Ode on a Grecian Urn': Pursuing the Feminine," 226.

What images return
O my daughter.

Eliot's speaker, too, elects to "Resign my life for this life, my speech for that unspoken," but not before he has retrieved as from memory the knowledge essential for his initiation—"I have forgotten, / And remember."[16]

Three times, as Helen Vendler convincingly demonstrates, the speaker's awareness of the urn as medium, and of its figures as marble rather than as living men and women, breaks in upon his prosopopoeic re-creation of the urn: at lines 11, 28, and 38.[17] No sooner has the speaker begun to interpret the images on the urn by animating and impersonating them than he is confronted with a painful reminder of his own mortality, contrasted with the apparent immortality of the figures on the urn. The two kinds of response— one entering into the scene on the urn and recognizing its human- ity, its universality; the other distancing the urn and treating what it purports to represent as ultimately inaccessible and resistant to interpretation—are both as Vendler says "authentic," both equally "poetic," but they remain in tension with each other.

The two kinds of response also exploit or perhaps are generated by the two different figurative modes. The scene on the urn is distant, inaccessible, or "far above" the human realm (line 28), but the poet's speech is potentially sacrilegious and all too human; while the poet lives within the scenes on the urn and explicates them from the standpoint of a participant, his language trespasses into the realm of the erotic ("more happy, happy love!," line 25) and he becomes a kind of presiding Dionysian deity. Finally, however, Keats tries to tran- scend the two limited and limiting modes by making the urn speak for itself, forcing it to give up its "meaning" by imposing his own text on its silence. When the urn itself speaks, as it does in the closing lines, its language turns out to be alien, like the "language strange" of the elfin queen, cryptic, blank, and impenetrable. "The urn can speak of

16. T. S. Eliot, *Collected Poems 1909–1962*, 115, 116.
17. Helen Vendler, *The Odes of John Keats*, 127. Vendler argues that "the constitutive trope of the *Urn* is interrogation" (118). I suggest that the "questions" in stanza 1 of the ode, like Eliot's "What seas what shores . . . ," are not really meant as interrogative. The speaker already "knows" what the scene is, essentially; the names of the participants do not greatly matter.

nothing but itself, and its self-referentiality is nowhere clearer than in the interior completeness of its circular epigram, which encounters our ironic sense of its limitation."[18] Geraldine Friedman, who argues persuasively that the ode shows prosopopoeic speech as a kind of sexual violence, a rape of the urn's self-possessed silence, points out that at the end of the poem either there is a violation, a rape, of the previously "unravished" urn, mirroring the orgiastic scene evoked in stanza 1, or (if the last lines of the poem are considered radically indeterminate and resistant to interpretation) the urn "eludes phallic penetration by obscuring its own revelation . . . As the text voices itself," she continues, "voice also becomes text, with the result that a feminine speaking subject is effaced or killed into writing."[19]

To break out of this closed circle of the artifact's self-referentiality, to recover the human dimension by once more following the mediating role of the interpreter and the reanimation of the human figure through anamnesis, we must move on to the last great interpretation scene in the Keats canon: the prologue to *The Fall of Hyperion*. It recombines in one figure—that of the dreamer-narrator—the functions that in the first *Hyperion* were distributed between the weakening Hyperion and the newly deified Apollo.[20] The dreamer-narrator experiences the same agony that Hyperion felt creep through his frame, "Like a lithe serpent vast and muscular" (*Hyperion*, 1.261; *KP*, 337):

> suddenly a palsied chill
> Struck from the paved level up my limbs,
> And was ascending quick to put cold grasp
> Upon those streams that pulse beside the throat:
> I shriek'd.   (1.122–26; *KP*, 481)

This shriek, unwilled yet powerful, is the speaker's eleventh-hour claim to the role of prophet, like the shriek that Shelley records in

18. Vendler, *The Odes of John Keats*, 133.
19. Friedman, "Erotics of Interpretation," 238, 239. There is a parallel here with Wordsworth's "Three Years She Grew." See above, Chapter 3.
20. Nancy M. Goslee, in "Phidian Lore: Sculpture and Personification in Keats's Odes," 78, interestingly proposes that the Titans in the first *Hyperion* move from the repose suggested by sculptural images to an anguished (though still static) "modern" consciousness.

"Hymn to Intellectual Beauty." It marks his transition from fearful mortal to privileged initiate: "What am I that another death come not / To choak my utterance sacrilegious here?" (lines 139–40). The dreamer-narrator's speech is thus a permitted sacrilege: like the "Was it for this?" trope in the first book of *The Prelude*, this anomalous granting of permission is both the cue and the justification for poetic utterance in a situation and on a subject where one has been led to expect silence. A further maneuver must take place, however, to circumvent what Wordsworth calls the "sad incompetence of human speech" (*WPrelude* [1850], 6.593): what is about to be narrated must be brought to the narrator's consciousness not as discovered but as "remembered" knowledge. The dreamer questions the "Shade of Memory" (line 282), a figure who transcends the distinction between mortal and immortal, since she evidently embodies a power of knowing compared to which human sorrows are as nothing, and yet she is "deathwards progressing / To no death" (lines 260–61; *KP*, 484). For his description of the ivory face of the goddess, Anne Mellor has suggested, Keats probably drew on the image of Phidias' statue of Athena Parthenos. This image—in its context as the focus of the Panathenaic cult for which the Parthenon was built, as well as in the context Keats gives it in *The Fall of Hyperion*—signifies the reconciliation of humankind with suffering, through the transformation of suffering into "soul-making" or the progressive deification of man.[21] As Moneta's power of seeing "as a God sees" passes to the dreamer-narrator, the mere "image huge" of Saturn is recognized and "remembered" as part of an unfolding *mythos*, a story in process, by the dreamer-narrator's now prophetic consciousness.

> Onward I look'd beneath the gloomy boughs,
> And saw, what first I thought an image huge,
> Like to the image pedestal'd so high
> In Saturn's temple. Then Moneta's voice
> Came brief upon mine ear,—"So Saturn sat
> When he had lost his realms."—Whereon there grew
> A power within me of enormous ken,
> To see as a God sees, and take the depth
> Of things as nimbly as the outward eye

21. Anne K. Mellor, "Keats's Face of Moneta: Source and Meaning," 66–69, 77.

Can size and shape pervade. The lofty theme
At those few words hung vast before my mind,
With half unravel'd web. I set myself
Upon an eagle's watch, that I might see,
And seeing ne'er forget.
                    (lines 297–310; *KP*, 485–86)

Moneta, putative origin of the narrative, is silent now; but her presence still presides over the re-creation of the myth, since she is after all the surviving Titaness, "Shade of Memory," giving form to the poet's desire to reenact the story of the sower-father, the oak-mother, their quarrel, and their overthrow by the shining race of their children, the Gods. Such a universal myth can only present itself as a remembered not a newly invented tale, but the poet who breaks silence on this theme without knowing his or her humanity fully is rash indeed.

In choosing the myth of the Titans' fall as the subject for his projected epic, Keats was in no sense evading his particular historical situation, as Stuart Sperry has astutely pointed out. Writing of the first *Hyperion*, Sperry says

> The sense of loss, endemic to the times, was one that could be described or elaborated in a variety of ways. . . . It was the loss of control over the great, simple forms and modes of belief—those of mythology, for example—for an understanding fractured by reason, science, and the growth of historical awareness. . . .
>
> The change was partly cultural and historic. Nevertheless, coming back to the permanent aspects of the myth, [Keats] had come to conclude that the state it described was also individual and universal. (157–58)

The first canto of *The Fall of Hyperion*, in its account of the dreamer-narrator's struggle to climb the temple steps and interrogate Moneta, delineates the complex processes through which the aspiring poet recalls, recognizes, and begins to re-create the myth. Even though unfinished, the two versions of *Hyperion* constitute a major account of the activity of interpretation as the post-Enlightenment writer must approach it, keeping in balance two seemingly opposed and irreconcilable needs: to remain conscious of his limited, human perspective and powers, as though silent before an object of overwhelming magnitude, and to assert his own power to reimagine and rearticulate the myth for his own time. The meeting between the self-doubting dreamer-interpreter and the mysterious figure of Moneta in *The Fall of Hyperion* is, however, the culmination of a series of similar confrontations in Keats's poetry, from "On Seeing the Elgin Marbles" and *Endymion* to "Ode on a Grecian Urn." In tracing the development of this topos in Keats's poetry, we have seen how the sense of belatedness or of "loss," dramatized in such confrontations, was not always or inevitably paralyzing for Keats, and how he discovered in poetic tradition itself the metaphors through which the powers of poetic utterance could be invoked and poetic creation achieved. But the poetic tradition, in *The Fall of Hyperion*, is no longer an avenue of escape from history, nor even a merely personal resource in which the poet seeks personal therapy or individual salvation. In this fragment, Keats finds a way for the poet to confront history. Like *Paradise Lost*, the poem offers an explanatory prelude to human history, drawing on reinterpreted myth that, had it been completed, would have opened *into* history. Moneta and the vatic poet who is of her mind are Promethean participants in history, bound to it, like Shelley's Prometheus, by their admission of a shared humanity.

Nine

Myth and the War of Ideas

Coleridge and Shelley on
the *Prometheus* of Æschylus

Most readers of *Biographia Literaria* remember the story of Coleridge's schoolmaster James Boyer and his fierce hatred of the mythological trappings with which his pupils too often adorned their verses. *"Harp? Harp? Lyre? Pen and ink, boy, you mean! Muse, boy, Muse? your Nurse's daughter, you mean! Pierian spring? Oh 'aye! the cloister-pump, I suppose!"* (*BL*, 1:10). The anecdotal vigor of this passage has helped to make it an exemplary instance of how Coleridge's generation was taught to reject the poetic conventions of its predecessors, the conventions that Coleridge describes elsewhere as "arbitrary and illogical phrases, at once hackneyed and fantastic" (*BL*, 1:79). Yet it would be wrong to assume on the basis of this anecdote that Coleridge simply derived from Boyer a lifelong dislike of the standard trappings of Greek mythology. We cannot be sure what the real effect of Boyer's injunctions was. Coleridge quite possibly exaggerated their importance, in order to emphasize the difference between the kind of mythology he preferred and the poetic conventions of an earlier age. The poet of "Kubla Khan," "Christabel," and "The Rime of the Ancient Mariner" was not someone for whom myth itself was an outmoded form.

Indeed, he even defended Gray's use of Greek mythology against the severe criticisms Wordsworth had brought to bear in the Preface to *Lyrical Ballads*. Commenting on Gray's use of "Phoebus" for "sun,"

which Wordsworth had ridiculed, Coleridge conceded that Phoebus
was part of an exploded mythology.

> [Yet] when the torch of ancient learning was re-kindled, so cheering were
> its beams, that our eldest poets, cut off by christianity from all *accredited*
> machinery, and deprived of all *acknowledged* guardians and symbols of
> the great objects of nature, were naturally induced to adopt, as a *poetic*
> language, those fabulous personages, those forms of the supernatural
> in nature, which had given them such dear delight in the poems of their
> great masters. (*BL*, 2:75–76)

The tone here is that of the judicious commentator on past con-
troversy—almost that of the genial lecturer, inviting his audience's
easy assent ("our eldest poets . . . were naturally induced to adopt . . .
fabulous personages," and so on). Yet Coleridge's innocent-sounding
assertions are truly astonishing. Would Spenser, Sidney, Milton, and
Dryden have described themselves as "cut off by christianity from
all *accredited* machinery, and deprived of all *acknowledged* guardians
and symbols of the great objects of nature"? (Would they even have
accepted the term "fabulous personages" as descriptive of Phoebus and other classical deities?)[1] It takes some effort to realize that
Coleridge is boldly rewriting the history of seventeenth- and early-
eighteenth-century English poetry from the standpoint of a nineteenth-century Christian poet-critic who is now engaged in a war
against what he would describe as "infidelity" and "atheism." The
real importance of this passage for the development of Romanticism
in England, especially the split into a "hebraizing," religious, and
largely conservative older generation and a "hellenizing," skeptical,
politically progressive second generation, is that it is part of an attack on Greek polytheism, amounting to a sustained campaign, that
Coleridge incorporated into his major works.

   This was not an attack on myth as such, for Coleridge had too
much understanding of the significance of myth, both poetic and
cultural, to wish it eradicated from literature. Like A. W. Schlegel,
Coleridge had attended the lectures of C. G. Heyne, professor of
Greek at the University of Göttingen, and it was from Heyne's
lectures on Greek art and poetry that he derived much of his

---

1. Milton saw classical myths as distorted versions of Bible narratives,
but he adopted them in his poetry, invoking the "meanings" rather than the
"names" of pagan deities. See Allen, *Mysteriously Meant*, 290–91.

understanding of the ways myth can be an expression of religious or social structures, a window through which the historian can peer into the organizing centers, the thought forms, of ancient societies. Heyne provided both classical and biblical scholars with a method by which to analyze the "web of national and local traditions" that made up the mythological part of ancient literature, and Heyne's way of interpreting myth was the foundation of the "mythological school" in biblical as well as classical scholarship.[2] Nor did Coleridge dismiss all myths emanating from the Greek tradition as inferior to those of the Jewish world, even though in general he found Jewish mythmaking to be the more profound. Coleridge distinguished between myth that expresses or mysteriously gestates an otherwise inexpressible metaphysical truth, and myth that merely celebrates sensuous pleasure, human passions, or the visible wonders of nature.

If this preference of Coleridge's were merely aesthetic, it would still be of interest to critics, since it has a bearing on Coleridge's own poetry, philosophy, and literary criticism. What gives it even wider importance, however, is that—as I shall try to demonstrate—the preference for myth that expresses metaphysical truth over myth that "merely" celebrates nature took on an enormous ideological weight during the decade following the Battle of Waterloo. The "higher" kind of myth became a clear analogue to Coleridge's own politically conservative though often doctrinally unorthodox Christianity. And the nature-worshiping polytheism with which he contrasted it became an analogue to the belief systems Coleridge feared, principally the "Mechanical Philosophy" that, Coleridge held, was ever an adjunct and a cause of democratic sentiments and "jacobinism" (*Friend*, 1:447). As Coleridge clarifies and consolidates his position in *The Friend* (1818), the *Philosophical Lectures* (1818–1819), and the essay on Æschylus (1821–1825), it becomes more and more evident that Coleridge's reading of Greek myth is closely related to his reading of the contemporary political climate in England.

2. The phrase "a web of national and local traditions" is quoted from Schlegel by A. C. Dunstan, "The German Influence on Coleridge. II," 195. On the importance of Heyne, see also E. S. Shaffer, *'Kubla Khan' and* The Fall of Jerusalem: *The Mythological School in Biblical Criticism and Secular Literature 1770–1880*, 29, 34, 122.

In the lectures, delivered between December 1818 and March 1819, Plato is the supreme example of a philosopher possessed by a profound new truth of which even he himself is but dimly aware, and who must use symbolic and mythic utterance to express it. This new truth, which Plato saw by glimpses and outlined in his "myths," was the idea that the mind is superior to all external appearances, the mind's sense that it is "greater than aught it has done."

> [Plato] taught the idea, namely the possibility, and the duty of all who would arrive at the greatest perfection of the human mind, of striving to contemplate things not in the phenomenon, not in their accidents or in their superficies, but in their essential powers, first as they exist in relation to other powers co-existing with them, but lastly and chiefly as they exist in the Supreme Mind. . . .
>
> How the grand Idea of the Universe worked in him before it found utterance! In how many obscure, and as it were oracular, sentences, in what strange symbols did it place itself! All great and bold ideas in their first conception, in their < very > nature are TOO GREAT FOR utterANCE [*sic*]. (*P Lects*, 166)

Coleridge here views Plato as a distinctly Coleridgean thinker, resorting to the language of myth in order to convey the immensity of the idea that has taken hold of him. This view of Plato is as much a literary as a philosophical one. It is literary, or rhetorical, in the sense that Coleridge views Plato's use of myth and symbol as an appropriate choice of medium for the audience he sought. The most sublime new ideas cannot be given direct utterance, because language is a shared medium of communication, so the philosopher has to begin a reshaping of the language before truly new things can be said. "Veracity does not consist in *saying*, but in the intention of *communicating* truth; and the philosopher who can not utter the whole truth without conveying falsehood . . . is constrained to express himself either *mythically* or equivocally" (*BL*, 1:157). This is quite different from the common notion that the poor and the illiterate must be instructed through pictures ("Picturae Pauperum Libri")—an idea Coleridge consistently and vehemently rejected (*CN*, 2480; see also *P Lects*, 90). The difference is that the "Plotino-platonic Philosophy" inspired those who learned it to become aware of the powers of their own minds. It never permitted its disciples to forget their own nature and themselves, never allowed them to become "lost and scattered in sensible Objects disjoined or *as* disjoined from themselves" (*CN*,

3935). The Platonist is always aware of a consciousness interpreting the "Objects," and of the "Objects" only as bearing a meaning beyond their isolated existence as objects. Such "philosophical or allegorical" use of myth must be carefully distinguished from the "sacerdotal," or official, state religion, and the "poetical" mythology (*CN*, 3656). For Coleridge, these inferior mythologies were actually inconsistent with the nature and world-historical role of the Greek people, as he saw it; they were an anomaly, an "alien Life," which, but for the "Antidote" of the Mysteries and the similarly healthy effect of Æschylean drama, conveying higher philosophic truth in mythic form, would have ruined the moral character of Greece far sooner than they actually did.[3]

There is, then, a philosophically respectable use of myth which Coleridge thought should be carefully distinguished from the "popular theology" of the Homeric poets, often judged immoral by later philosophers, and from the demoralizing tendencies of the officially sanctioned state religions. In an extended comparison of the Jewish to the Greek culture, Coleridge argues that the Jewish people attended more to their inward, moral feelings, and for them, "to know that a thing was right and congruous to their moral nature they held as the evidence of its truth." Greek thought, on the other hand, drew its conceptions of divine power and the just order of things from external objects. The Greeks, seeing living things moving around in the natural world, concluded that this revealed "a vital or motive power," and called it "soul" when it was manifested in one separate being; but "when they raised their sensuous imagination to the utmost and conceived the indefinite idea of an All, they carried on the same analogy, and the All was God" (*P Lects*, 91–92). The same "sensuous imagination," that is, gives rise to both polytheism and pantheism; in both cases, the mind acts on sense impressions received from without, endowing things in nature (either individually or in the aggregate) with divine energy and purposiveness.

A notebook entry, dated 1820–1821 by the editors of Coleridge's notebooks, develops this genealogy of ancient religious beliefs by

---

3. See Notebook 36, fol. 55ᵛ: "The Greek Mythology with all its ingrafted Beauties an anomaly, and or false and alien Life, in an *historic* Race—and but for the express contranitence and herculean Antidote of the Mysteries . . . would have worked still more rapidly and deleteriously than it did."

suggesting that the polytheistic Greek pantheon may have originated in pantheism; or alternatively, "did it begin in Monotheism
(World – God = 0. God – World = God + World) but by soon
degenerated into Pantheism, & thence . . . into Polytheism?" This is,
Coleridge adds, "the opinion to which my own belief inclines." The
note continues: "—Was it not the subordination of *moral* grounds to
Physiology, & the *magical* study of Nature joined with astronomical
& meteorological Observations as the grounds of Prediction, the
cause & occasion of this degeneracy into Pantheism?" (*CN*, 4794).
Pantheism and polytheism are for Coleridge but the higher and
the lower forms of the same "sensual" doctrine, and their results he
characterizes as "cruelty and brutality . . . selfishness and sensuality"
(*P Lects*, 127). Cruelty and sensuality are bound to follow, Coleridge
argues, when human beings subjugate their conscience and moral
judgment to the pattern of amoral nature.

A similar point occurs in the "Opus Maximum." In vain do human
beings look for moral authority to the idea of an absolute One or to
the visible world in its diversity and proliferation. Either procedure
leaves a dark void, amoral and godless, which only conscience, or the
"moral being" of humankind itself, can fill:

> From whichever of the two points the Reason may start, from the Things
> that are seen to the One Invisible, or from the idea of the absolute One
> to the Things that are seen, it will find a Chasm, which the *Moral* Being
> only, which the Spirit and Religion of Man alone can fill up or over-
> bridge. . . . To deduce a Deity wholly from Nature is in the result to
> substitute an Apotheosis of Nature for Deity.[4]

Coleridge's hostility to Greek polytheism, then, is the obverse of
his preference for a poetry and philosophy that draw their authority
from an invisible, transcendent source. Myth that puts itself forward
as a symbolic code for what cannot be expressed directly, for the
moral nature of humankind in relation to what is infinite and mysterious, is beneficent. Myth that confines the hearer's imagination
to the world of phenomena, and celebrates the life of individual
beings in nature, is harmful and demoralizing, even when, as in the

---

4. "Opus Maximum," Victoria University Library, Toronto, S MS 29,
fols. 38ᵛ–39, 61. On Coleridge's view of Spinoza's "absolute," see Thomas
McFarland, *Coleridge and the Pantheist Tradition*, 188. See also *BL*, 1:202–
3; and *CN*, 3981, 4005.

Greek city-states, it forms part of a state religion. Such philosophers as Pythagoras and Plato are praised for couching difficult and novel metaphysical ideas in mythic language that allows their full meaning to remain concealed from all but a few awakened minds.

As is often the case with Coleridge, a later doctrine turns out to be an adaptation of an earlier one, but with important ideological differences. In the lectures and sermons delivered to an audience of radicals and dissenters at Bristol in 1795, Coleridge had shown himself sympathetic to the idea that God is revealed in the language or script of nature, an idea that in some respects anticipates his later theory of the philosophical or esoteric use of myth. "The Omnipotent has unfolded to us the Volume of the World, that there we may read the Transcript of himself." Similarly, in a fragment that may be a draft of a lecture or sermon: "We see our God everywhere— the Universe in the most literal Sense is his written Language" (*Lects 1795*, 94, 339). In the 1795 Lectures, however, Coleridge's enthusiastic, proselytizing tone strongly suggests that the presence of the Infinite in our world is there for *all* to see. Human knowledge, in these lectures on revealed religion, may be imperfect compared to the divine plenitude, but it is still claimed as in a true sense "divine" in that it is "an imparted ray of divine omniscience," or of the "divine Foreknowledge" (*Lects 1795*, 110, 150). In 1795, then, Coleridge did not envisage the need for difficult philosophical truth to be couched in equivocal terms or in mythical narratives, because there are no truths that are beyond the grasp of the human intellect in its steady progress toward maturity, and there are no classes of human beings who are excluded from this progressive development.

The Priestleian progressivism of the 1790s also gave Coleridge a rather more tolerant view of polytheistic mythology than that expressed in the 1818–1819 *Philosophical Lectures*. Unlike the eighteenth-century libertarian thinkers who ridiculed ancient myths for picturing the gods as cruel, arbitrary, and irrational, and slyly hinted at certain similarities between Greek and Judeo-Christian mythology, Coleridge at this period in his life accepted pagan myths as a necessary first stage in the progressive historical development of human reason. Just as even the Israelites themselves in the early years of the Mosaic dispensation were, comparatively, children, still freeing themselves from Egyptian idolatry, so the Gentile nations had to be prepared for the revelation of man's divine nature in Jesus

Christ by learning the discipline of the "superstitious" worship of awe-inspiring goddesses and gods.

There is even in the early Coleridge a certain nostalgia for what he called "the old names" of the gods who lived in forest and stream, a feeling that, while mature faith rejects such ways of naming the divine, some residual instinctual fondness for them lives on. German classicizing being more to his taste than French, he translates from Schiller, in rather limping meter, the "Dithyrambe," "Nimmer, das glaubt mir, / Erscheinen die götter, / Nimmer allein," which pictures the poet elevated to Olympian heights by a vision of the return of the classical deities Bacchus, Eros, Apollo, and Zeus. This is a classicizing deeply imbued with nostalgia, however. As he puts it in a passage inserted in his translation of Schiller's *Wallenstein,*

> The Power, the Beauty, and the Majesty,
> That had their haunts in dale, or piny mountain,
> Or forest by slow stream, or pebbly spring,
> Or chasms and wat'ry depths; all these have vanished.
> They live no longer in the faith of reason!
>
> (*CPW,* 2:649)[5]

What is remarkable about Coleridge's treatment of myth in the mid–1790s is the way he actually accepts the Enlightenment view that the inculcation of obedience to the gods is a primitive way to control human behavior, but attempts to rehabilitate it by seeing it as a necessary stage in human development, analogous to the discipline that eighteeth-century parents would impose on their children. He is sympathetic to the Platonist Henry More's argument that without a belief in spirit, there can be no belief in God, so that to ridicule pagan stories of the supernatural may eventually lead a person to atheism (*CN,* 1000G).

"The Destiny of Nations," written in conjunction with Robert Southey's epic *Joan of Arc* (1796), and partly incorporated in Southey's poem, illustrates very well this reinterpretation of the place of myth.

---

5. John Beer, in his edition of Coleridge's *Poems* (London: Dent; New York: Dutton, 1974), says that this and some other passages owed little or nothing to Schiller (212).

> For Fancy is the power
> That first unsensualizes the dark mind,
> Giving it new delights; and bids it swell
> With wild activity; and peopling air,
> By obscure fears of Beings invisible,
> Emancipates it from the grosser thrall
> Of the present impulse, teaching Self-control,
> Till Superstition with unconscious hand
> Seat Reason on her throne. Wherefore not vain,
> Nor yet without permitted power impressed,
> I deem those legends terrible, with which
> The polar ancient thrills his uncouth throng.
>   (*CPW*, 1:134)

The fragment not included in the Southey poem was variously named, among other things, "The Progress of Liberty" and "The Vision of the Maid of Orleans," so that Joan of Arc is presented to us as one of the apostles of a progressive, libertarian Christianity, a prophet foreseeing the liberation of the race from its state of superstitious servitude. Even the polytheistic mythology of ancient times takes a permitted place in this scheme, however, since it tended to "unsensualize" the mind and so prepare it for the advent of Reason. This view of mythology tries to neutralize the Enlightenment critique of religion as an atavistic hangover from an irrational age, and co-opt religion into a libertarian philosophy, as Joseph Priestley did in his *Essay on the First Principles of Government* (see *Lects 1795*, lxii).

Although the later writings retain the notion that natural objects may symbolize the infinite, they differ in one important respect. Coleridge now considers the perfection of human nature as a much more remote future event, and therefore the truth of Reason that this perfected nature is fitted to contemplate is treated as much more in need of mediation and interpretation. Coleridge's hermeneutic, in other words, becomes increasingly a hermeneutic of the mysterious, the oracular. Yet the distinction drawn in the *Philosophical Lectures*, between a popular mythology that is vivid and sensuous, tending to debase and sensualize its hearers, and an esoteric mythology that conveys profound spiritual doctrine only to those spiritually prepared to interpret it, helps us to see how well Coleridge understood the ways in which myth and ideology are interconnected. The vision of society implied by this view of myth (the one put forward in *Biographia Literaria* and *Philosophical Lectures*) differs a great deal from that suggested in the 1795 Bristol lectures. In the later treatment, the esoteric kind of myth seems to be used not to make difficult truths available to an audience unprepared to receive them, but precisely to *limit* the audience and protect the sacredness of philosophical truth.

The key to this analysis of the relation between myth and ideology is in Coleridge's contrast between Jewish and Greek religious thought, which can be traced back to a well-known passage in a letter of September 1802.[6] In distinguishing Greek from Jewish mythology, Coleridge not only sets out the distinction between the two kinds of culture that is to play such a large part in the *Philosophical Lectures*, but also proposes that the two faculties responsible for these two mythologies be named "Fancy" and "Imagination."

> The Greeks in their religious poems address always the Numina Loci, the Genii, the Dryads, the Naiads, &c &c—All natural Objects were *dead*—mere hollow Statues—but there was a Godkin or Goddessling *included* in each—In the Hebrew Poetry you find nothing of this poor Stuff—as poor in genuine Imagination, as it is mean in Intellect— / At best, it is but Fancy, or the aggregating Faculty of the mind— not *Imagination*, or the *modifying*, and *co-adunating* Faculty. This the Hebrew Poets appear to me to have possessed beyond all others—& next to them the English. In the Hebrew Poets each Thing has a Life of its own, & yet they are all one Life. In God they move & live, & *have* their Being. (*CL*, 2:865–66)

The distinction between two kinds of culture—and two mythologies, each quite different in its moral and social impact—is here revealed to be essentially between two powers or faculties of mind, one of which Coleridge regards as superior aesthetically and morally. One mental faculty is associative, not changing the mental images drawn from sense perception but playing with them as if they were so many wood blocks or coins. Coleridge gives this mental faculty the name "Fancy," and in a famous passage in the *Biographia* he emphasizes its inferiority because it is confined to the realm of sensuous

---

6. Piper points out that in translating Gessner's *Der Erste Schiffer* that year, Coleridge had been forced to reconsider the use of mythological references in poetry, as he found Gessner's mythological machinery silly and commonplace (*The Active Universe*, 137).

appearances: "FANCY . . . has no other counters to play with, but fixities and definites. The Fancy is indeed no other than a mode of Memory emancipated from the order of time and space" (*BL*, 1:305). The higher faculty draws on an inner living power in human beings to see or reshape the world as a unity; not the pantheist's "unity," which Coleridge represents or misrepresents as a mere aggregate of dead objects, but the living unity that the Hebrew poets gave utterance to, as manifesting the omnipresent spirit of God. This power is the Imagination, later subdivided (in another well-known passage of the *Biographia*) into "primary" and "secondary." Coleridge there emphasizes that the secondary Imagination is "essentially *vital*, even as all objects (*as* objects) are essentially fixed and dead" (*BL*, 1:304). Imagination, though grounded in the supernatural, is not supposed to be in any way hostile to nature. Coleridge's point in the 1802 letter had been, in fact, that Hebrew poetry evoked nature so much better than Greek poetry precisely because of its "vital" quality: in Hebrew poetry "each Thing has a Life of its own, & yet they are all one Life." One does not become a poet of Imagination, a Wordsworth, by ignoring or despising nature. This becomes clearer still in Coleridge's condemnation of Fichte, who—though right to start by challenging Spinoza—fell into "boastful and hyperstoic hostility to NATURE, as lifeless, godless, and altogether unholy" (*BL*, 1:159). Imagination, as shaping spirit, answers to the living spirit in nature without which nature is merely empty forms, fixed and dead. "To become all things and yet remain the same, to make the changeful God be felt in the river, the lion and the flame—this is, that is true Imagination."[7] It seems that Coleridge associated this superior mental power, which is "essentially *vital*" and therefore creates its poetic images of the world as a living unity, with the monotheistic Jewish mind, and the inferior power, Fancy, was characteristic of the polytheistic Greek mind.[8] At times, however, Coleridge apparently regards some elements of the Greek mythology as approximating the religious perceptions of the Hebrew poets, even though the Greeks tended to reduce the Infinite to finite forms: "In the elder world the Infinite was hidden in the Finite—Every Stream had its Naiad—the Earth its Cybele,

7. Coleridge's *Literary Remains*, 2:59, quoted by René Wellek, *A History of Modern Criticism: 1750–1950*, 2:163.
8. See McFarland, *Originality and Imagination*, 93–94, and chap. 6.

the Ocean its Neptune/the upper Air was Jupiter, the lower Juno—
Fire was Vesta, as the fixive, preservative Power—and the artificial
technical Fire Neptune—all was reduced to the Finite" (*CN*, 4378).
It is possible to argue, too, that Coleridge is not so much discovering
a real difference between the Greek and Jewish mythologies as using
his own interpretation of each to bolster an already determined
religious and philosophical preference. In a sense, the preference
for the poetry of the "imagination" may be said to reach back to
his childhood, when, as he told Tom Poole, his mind "had been
habituated *to the Vast*—& I never regarded *my senses* in any way
as the criteria of my belief" (*CL*, 1:354).

Clearly by the period of *Biographia Literaria* and *Philosophical
Lectures* the distinction between a polytheistic mythology and a
monotheistic faith has acquired important ideological dimensions.
Coleridge is aware that the mythic personages and events our ancestors believed in may be given new meaning by later reinterpretations.
His own "Ancient Mariner," much glossed and much revised, is a
microcosm of the process. Coleridge says in the *Biographia* that he
did not expect his readers to believe in the supernatural appearances
the Mariner narrates, though he does ask us to believe that the
Mariner believed in them. What we supposedly have in "The Rime
of the Ancient Mariner," as in the reinterpreted mythologies, is not a
belief system as such but a model of the human mind, at one stage of
its development, in its relation with the world. The particular event,
the immediate human impact of the experience, is dissolved in (or,
as Jerome McGann puts it, "contained by") the larger concern of
the interpreter, whose business is to ask "what advance in the development of human reasoning powers does this event symbolically
denote?" This strategy of surrounding and containing the poem in
a universalizing hermeneutic, as McGann has argued, derives from
Coleridge's reading of Eichhorn and other "Higher Critics."[9]

In his public lectures, Coleridge applies this hermeneutic to the
Bible, but usually with great circumspection. *The Statesman's Manual* (1816) is itself addressed to a defined, limited audience, namely,
"the higher classes of society," or in Coleridge's revised version
"the Learned and Reflecting of all Ranks and Professions, especially
among the Higher Class." In this "lay sermon," Coleridge explains the

9. McGann, *Beauty of Inflections*, 143.

"signs and wonders" narrated in the Bible as necessary preliminaries, or devices, the purpose of which was "to startle and break down that superstition, idolatrous in itself and the source of all other idolatry, which tempts the natural man to seek the true cause and origin of public calamities in outward circumstances, persons and incidents." These signs and wonders were mere vehicles, however: "With each miracle worked there was a truth revealed, which thence forward was to act as its substitute." Thus Coleridge can argue that the Jewish prophets and poets conveyed not superstitious beliefs but "universal principles . . . principles and ideas that are not properly said to be confirmed by reason as to be reason itself!" (LS, 9, 17). In order to defend the Scriptures against the accusation that no one could take all the events as the literal truth, Coleridge makes the principles revealed in the Bible superior to the narratives themselves, in the sense that—from a world-historical perspective—the narratives exist only to convey to future generations these supremely important principles. The founding of the city of Jerusalem and the crossing of the Red Sea are not so much events to celebrate and be thankful for in their own right, as symbolic harbingers of eternally valid religious (and philosophical) truths. This is the way that "the higher classes of society" are encouraged to understand the Bible. The prerogative of the interpreter—whose business is the development of doctrine, and whose real loyalty is to certain principles and ideas that are "reason itself"—has displaced the credo of the literalist.

Coleridge recognizes that religious narratives can serve the interests of good government, and that the way the governing class reads those narratives necessarily differs from that of the simple believer. Where the latter is impressed by the evidences of divine goodness and power proclaimed in the myths, the "learned and reflecting" admire them because they body forth certain necessary principles of human reason in a form that is fully accessible only to the learned themselves. Myths are a means of communicating moral principles to those in any given generation who are not equipped to deal with abstract ideas.

This kind of argument—explaining an ancient and to us incomprehensible event or belief by appealing to some later institution the event or belief is held providentially to have produced—has disconcerting similarities to Rousseau's strategy in Du contrat social. Rousseau's position and Coleridge's are not that far apart, in one respect: they both see myth as a means of social control. Faced with an apparent logical impossibility when he has to explain how a people, not yet formed into a sovereign body (which they can become only by assent to a binding constitutional law), can nevertheless meaningfully impose such a law on themselves, Rousseau argues that the ancient legislators, those all-powerful beings who must renounce all personal power if they are to be effective as legislators, had to have recourse to something other than either force or reason. Force carries no moral weight, and reason cannot be communicated in the language of the common people. The necessary validation for the authority of early legislators, then, was religious belief. The common people remained "free," in the sense that they obeyed the state's laws from motives of religious piety, not from fear of actual physical violence.[10] In this series of paradoxes (legislators who are men but more than men; a people not yet so constituted agreeing to abide by laws that alone can make them a people; and a nonviolent "sublime reason" [*raison sublime*] that enforces obedience to reason) not the least of Rousseau's ironies is his explaining religion as a necessary condition for the creation of the civil state at the same time as its *raison d'être* is removed from theology and placed in the realm of Realpolitik. Yet Rousseau, thought of as the implacable enemy of organized religion, parallels Coleridge: both writers dissolve the intrinsic value of the original religious belief or experience and reconstitute it as the logical precondition of a later system that thereby validates it. It is as if the original belief or experience were

10. See J.-J. Rousseau, *Du contrat social,* 262–63:

Les sages qui veulent parler au vulgaire leur langage au lieu du sien n'en sauroient être entendus. Or, il y a mille sortes d'idées qu'il est impossible de traduire dans la langue du peuple. . . . Ainsi donc le législateur ne pouvant employer ni la force ni le raisonnement, c'est une nécessité qu'il recoure à une autorité d'un autre ordre, qui puisse entraîner sans violence et persuader sans convaincre.

Voilà ce qui força de tout temps les pères des nations de recourir à l'intervention du ciel et d'honorer les dieux de leur propre sagesse, afin que les peuples soumis aux lois de l'État comme à celles de la nature, et reconnoissant le même pouvoir dans la formation de l'homme et dans celle de la cité, obéissent avec liberté, et portassent docilement le joug de la félicité publique.

only of value insofar as it lent credence to the ideology built on it. Rousseau and Coleridge both confirm indirectly the inaccessibility of the original religious experience to the later civilization that it inaugurates.

Coleridge's way of interpreting the past according to this Christian-philosophical perspective has some remarkable consequences for his view of Greek literature and history, as well as for his reading of the Bible. Of considerable importance here, as Nigel Leask has shown, is F. W. J. Schelling's reevaluation of the Greek Mysteries, in the lectures published in 1803 as *Vorlesungen über die Methode des akademischen Studiums*. Schelling, attempting like Coleridge to rescue religion from the rationalist assumption that it is a relic of a merely superstitious, unenlightened age and people, "found in the Mysteries a new relevance as providential guardians of the evolving religious experience of humanity." The public or civic religion of the Greek state raised the "real"—the natural world—to predominance: it worshiped the "natural gods of polytheism." The providentially inspired function of the mystery cults was to preserve, among a few initiates, the polar opposite to the real, namely, "ideality or infinity," in order that the eventual synthesis of these poles may occur in a future "organism in the form of the state." Such a synthesis of real and ideal Schelling puts forward as the "goal of the Absolute in history": "Schelling regarded the domain of history as the dialectical self-revelation of the Absolute, the new basis for a 'higher' mythology of Christianity freed from the limits of revealed religion."[11]

Adapting this argument of Schelling's to his own purposes in the 1818 edition of *The Friend*, Coleridge explains how one may see divine providence at work in "pagan" Greece. His evidence for this claim is the alleged beneficial effect of the Mysteries in protecting that nation from the worst effects of its own officially polytheistic religion.

> As the representative of the youth and approaching manhood of the human intellect, we have ancient Greece, from Orpheus, Linus, Musaeus,

11. Nigel Leask, *The Politics of Imagination in Coleridge's Critical Thought*, 178–79. Leask notes that Coleridge's providential history remained more orthodox than Schelling's in including "an 'original' creation and a primordial revealed patriarchal monotheism," doctrines Schelling rejected (179).

and the other mythological bards, or perhaps the brotherhoods impersonated under those names, to the time when the republics lost their
independence. . . . That we include these as educated under a distinct
providential, though not miraculous, dispensation, will surprise no one,
who reflects that in whatever has a permanent operation on the destinies
and intellectual condition of mankind at large—that in all which has
been manifestly employed as a co-agent in the mightiest revolution of
the moral world, the propagation of the Gospel; and in the intellectual
progress of mankind, the restoration of Philosophy, Science, and the in-
genuous Arts—it were irreligion not to acknowledge the hand of divine
Providence. The periods, too, join on to each other. The earliest Greeks
took up the religious and lyrical poetry of the Hebrews; and the schools
of the Prophets were, however partially and imperfectly, represented by
the mysteries, derived through the corrupt channel of the Phoenicians.
With these secret schools of physiological theology the mythical poets
were doubtless in connection: and it was these schools, which prevented
Polytheism from producing all its natural barbarizing effects.   (*Friend*,
1:503–4)[12]

The importance of this passage and the method it advances for
reading the history of non-Jewish peoples is indicated by Coleridge's
recurring to it in his 1825 essay "On the Prometheus of Æschylus."
Nowhere in Coleridge's work is the connection between myth and
ideology clearer than in this essay. First written in 1821, and delivered
as a lecture to the Royal Society of Literature on May 18, 1825, the
essay is an interpretation of the "mythic import" of Æschylus' play
that strikingly reveals the range and depth of Coleridge's conservative reading of myth.[13] The essay is the culmination of Coleridge's
sustained effort during the latter part of his life to present polytheism as a morally harmful doctrine that leads to false philosophy,

12. John Beer argues that such a theory of myth—"the possibility of
law handed down from the patriarchs having been preserved in the Temple
of Isis," and the belief that "the Greek mysteries derived ultimately from
patriarchal traditions"—may have been in Coleridge's mind from the 1790s
on. See *Coleridge the Visionary*, 66–67.

13. Evidence for the date of composition is presented by S. W. Reid, "The
Composition and Revision of Coleridge's Essay on Aeschylus' *Prometheus*,"
178. Two MS fragments of the essay are in existence: one, a transcript by
John Watson with notes by Coleridge, is in Duke University Library, and
one is in the Berg Collection, New York Public Library (Reid, 176). For
corrections to Reid's account, see *CN*, 4843n; and John Beer's Excursus
Note 14 in S. T. Coleridge, *Aids to Reflection*, 561–62.

to materialism, sensuality, and brutality, while the theism of Genesis and Exodus gives humankind true philosophy, dignity, justice, and morality. It is an essential part of his argument that Æschylus' *Prometheus Bound* was the most important of a series of works intended to reveal to the Greek people enough of the secret doctrines of the Mysteries to counteract the bad influence of polytheistic religions. Æschylus' play, according to Coleridge's reading of it, belongs to the "beneficial" category of myths, as it encodes in mythic form the philosophical doctrine of Mind revealed in the Book of Genesis, preserved in Greece through the Samothracian Mysteries.

As William K. Pfeiler first pointed out in 1937, some of the main points of the essay, especially those based on various etymological theories, are taken from F. W. J. Schelling's *Ueber die Gottheiten von Samothrace*, written to show that the Cabiric Mysteries were the first to introduce into Greece the belief in an afterlife.[14] Coleridge annotated a copy of the 1815 edition of this work. The comparison between the philosophical ideas encoded in the Samothracian Mysteries and those enshrined in the Old Testament originates with Schelling, as does the suggestion that "Cabiri" means "companions" or "comrades" and that Ceres derives from a Hebrew word meaning "emptiness, lack, hunger."[15] However, in advancing the theory that the Mysteries establish a connection between Eastern (specifically, Jewish) religion and the cultural and political life of Greece, Coleridge has his own purposes very much in mind. He believes that Greek political and cultural life was secretly controlled by what he calls a kind of "internal theocracy." This theocracy derived its

14. William K. Pfeiler, "Coleridge and Schelling's Treatise on the Samothracian Deities," 162. Among other likely sources for Coleridge's ideas about Æschylus' play are George Stanley Faber, *Dissertation on the Mysteries of the Cabiri* (Oxford, 1803), which he annotated; Bryant, *A New System*; and Creuzer, *Symbolik und Mythologie*. For Faber, see S. T. Coleridge, *Marginalia*, 2:575. For a summary of Coleridge's use of Creuzer, both the 1810–1812 four-volume edition and the 1819–1823 six-volume edition (which I cite), see *CN*, 4831n.

15. Creuzer offers an alternative etymology for "Cabiri," that it derives from a Hebrew word meaning "powerful" (*Symbolik und Mythologie*, 2:315). Creuzer mentions Schelling's definition but argues that the Cabiri were known as "strong ones" because they were the first among the Pelasgians to manufacture metal weapons (2:309, 313).

justification and its doctrines from ancient Hebrew wisdom and poetry, transmitted to Greece through the spreading of Phoenician mythology and esoteric doctrine along Phoenician trade routes. It was maintained by the Mysteries, forms of religious observance open only to initiates, and its immediate achievement was that it prevented the officially polytheistic state religion from causing the degeneration of the Greek people, at least for a few centuries ("On the Prometheus of Æschylus," *CW*, 4 [1853]: 349).[16] The function of Æschylus' play is to present a "philosopheme" (a term Coleridge could have found in Creuzer, 2:488–89), a philosophic myth or fundamental philosophical truth embodied in poetic form: the proposition

16. See also *Friend*, 1:504 and n. The theory that the Phoenicians, a Semitic people learned in the esoteric theology of the Chaldeans and Egyptians (and who perfected the ancestor of modern Western alphabets), would have transmitted this wisdom and that of the earliest Hebrews to pre-Hellenic Greece through the priestly brotherhood known as the Cabiri, is expounded at length by Creuzer (*Symbolik und Mythologie*, 2:12–16, 302–3), who as always is eager to discover signs of the emergence of a primitive idealist philosophy:

Schon in dem alten Gedichte Phoronis war der Idäischen Dactylen gedacht worden (Scholiast. Apollon. I.129). Gewiss waren es dergleichen Poeme hauptsächlich, die jenes Sagengewirre geknüpft hatten, das dem Strabo so viele, zum Theil fruchtlose Mühe machte. Ist es wahr, was doch nicht zu läugnen steht, dass darin Erinnerungen aufbehalten sind an die Verpflanzung Phönicischer und Aegyptischer Religionen und Cultur unter die rohen Stämme der Pelasgischen Griechen, so ist wohl, beim Untergange der Phönicischen Literatur, eine Erkenntniss des Einzelnen dieser Mythen und Gebräuche kaum jemals zu hoffen, wenn auch von Aegyptens Denkmalen und aus Oberasiatischen Urkunden noch manche Aufklärung dafür gewonnen werden könnte. (2:303)

(The ancient poem Phoronis already was reminiscent of the Idaean Dactyls [Scholiast. Apollon. I.129]. Certainly, this was the kind of poetry that created such a tangle of legends and that caused Strabo so much and such unnecessary pain. If it is true, what cannot be denied, that within it there are reminiscences of the spreading of Phoenician and Egyptian religions and cultures among the rough tribes of the Pelasgic Greeks, it might well be the case that through the decadence of the Phoenician literature a recognition by the individual of these myths and customs can hardly ever be expected, even if we could obtain many additional explanations from Egyptian monuments and Upper Asia documents.)

that the human reason, the Nous, differs in origin and in kind from all other human faculties, which indeed it "ennobles"; that it did not evolve from, or develop along with, the lower faculties or animal creation; and that it is timeless, transcendent, and spiritual, rather than historical, material, and sensual. In a notebook entry of 1821, Coleridge distinguishes the philosopheme or philosophic myth from the popular myth on the basis that "the signs [of the philosophic myth] are conventional < only > within the pale of some particular guild, or societas in societate, as the Priesthood, the Mysteries, &c" (CN, 4832).

Not far from Coleridge's thoughts in all this, we may be certain, is the principle he enunciated in *The Friend* and repeated in his later polemic *On the Constitution of the Church and State*, that "religion . . . is and ever has been the moral centre of gravity in Christendom, to which all other things must and will accommodate themselves" (*Friend*, 1:447).[17] And since Greece was to be instrumental in delivering the Christian gospel to the world, a significant part of Coleridge's purpose is to show that Greece was under the guidance of divine providence even while apparently dominated by a thoroughly pagan form of religion.

The modern reader, too, may well see more than a casual similarity between the internal theocracy Coleridge describes as guiding Greek political life, and Coleridge's own notion of a "clerisy," that class of cultivated individuals whose function is to influence the moral quality of national life not by direct involvement in politics but simply by representing, and when appropriate propagating, higher, more permanent values, derived from religious faith and

---

However, whatever his dependence on Creuzer and on Schelling's *Ueber die Gottheiten von Samothrace*, Coleridge was convinced that his view of the role of the Mysteries and of Æschylean drama in preserving Greece from the evils of polytheism originated with himself: "I do not recollect to have met with a Hint of the such a Position except in my own Friend" (Notebook 36, fol. 55ᵛ). Despite this disclaimer (and Coleridge's critical comments on Creuzer's overly sympathetic view of pantheism), it is clear from the notebook entries based on his reading of Creuzer (CN 4831, 4832, 4839, 4856) that Creuzer's account must have helped him elaborate his views in the Prometheus lecture.

17. See also S. T. Coleridge, *On the Constitution of the Church and State*, 70.

from a transcendent system of ethics not unlike Plato's. As Ben Knights shows, those nineteenth-century writers—beginning with Coleridge—who espoused some form of the clerisy as a way of correcting the narrow expediency characteristic of actual governments, wanted the clerisy to constitute "a group in society which sees more clearly, describes the permanent and truly important behind the ever-shifting, untrustworthy phenomena, and consequently knows society's needs better than its ostensible rulers."[18] Coleridge's clerisy was not meant to be a secret or Masonic society, but in other respects the parallels are instructive.

It is also appropriate to point out that Coleridge specifically addresses the members of the Royal Society of Literature, a group very representative of that "remarkably unalienated intellectual class" from which the clerisy was to be drawn. Like *Biographia Literaria,* which Donald Reiman has rightly compared to *The Statesman's Manual* in this respect, Coleridge's lecture is "designed . . . to win the sympathy of his upper-class audience," identified as "the Learned and Reflecting of all Ranks and Professions, especially among the Higher Class."[19] Coleridge's lecture is not just an afternoon's amusement for a group of dilettantes. It has a definite social purpose, clearly signaled by Coleridge's beginning the lecture with a sneer at French "Infidelity" and, by extension, the supposed incompetence or untrustworthiness of French archaeologists. (Coleridge was probably thinking of Jean François Champollion, whose study of the Rosetta Stone led to the deciphering of Egyptian hieroglyphics, and his brother Jacques Joseph Champollion-Figeac, who provided Jean François with an outline chronology of the Egyptian pharaohs [see CN, 5219n].) Coleridge follows this anti-Gallic gibe with the claim

18. Ben Knights, *The Idea of the Clerisy in the Nineteenth Century,* 6. See also Leask, *Politics of Imagination,* 165, 188.
19. Donald Reiman, "Coleridge and the Art of Equivocation," 328, 334. In *Aids to Reflection,* which is intended for a wider audience (not only for the higher ranks), Coleridge refers to the Prometheus story only twice. The first is the historical judgment that, because Prometheus combines the characters of redeemer and satanic rebel, the myth illustrates "the forced amalgamation of the Patriarchal Tradition with the incongruous Scheme of Pantheism." Later in the work, he uses Prometheus nailed to the barren rock as a figure of *"Law"* (in the natural world) "without an Agent to realize it" (*Aids to Reflection,* 284, 402).

that those who have deduced the "demonstrable laws of the human mind" will necessarily find the biblical account of the progress of civilization infinitely superior to any fashionable theories emanating from France (*CW,* 4:344). Far from being a casual or peripheral matter, this comment about the inadequacy of French archaeology is intimately related to the interpretation of Æschylus that Coleridge has to offer. It reveals that his wider purpose is to invite the assistance of "the Learned and Reflecting" in building an English ideology.

Coleridge's immediate aim, though, is to clarify the nexus that he believes exists between the political secret governing body, or "theocracy," of ancient Greece, and the analysis of mind presented, according to his interpretation, in Æschylus' play. It is a favorite claim with Coleridge—one repeated in chapter 5 of the *Biographia*—that historically "in Egypt, Palestine, Greece, and India, the analysis of the mind had reached its noon and manhood, while experimental research was still in its dawn and infancy" (*BL,* 1:90–91). As we have seen, Coleridge thought that polytheism ran counter to the profoundest understanding of the mind's laws, and that pantheism was at best a more intellectually respectable way-station on the road to the inevitable degeneration into polytheism. At the time of the Exodus, Coleridge argues, Egypt was declining from a tolerably philosophical pantheism into one of the grossest forms of polytheism, which it shared, in many essentials, with Greece. But Greece was providentially preserved from the worst demoralizing effects of its polytheistic, state-approved religion by an infusion of monotheistic lore and philosophy, derived from Hebrew sources by way of Phoenician migrations, kept alive through the secret societies that practiced the ritual worship known as the Cabiric Mysteries, and selectively communicated to Greek society at large through the medium of the drama. Naturally the form this philosophy takes in the *Prometheus* of Æschylus—that is, mythic form—differs from the form it takes in the Book of Genesis, where it is historically conceived: "For the patriarchal religion, as the antithesis of pantheism, was necessarily personal; and the doctrines of a faith, the first ground of which, and the primary enunciation, is the eternal I AM, must be in part historic, and must assume the historic form" (*CW,* 4:351). But even though the *Prometheus* takes mythic form and Genesis locates the creation of humankind at the beginning of a historical epoch, they both—

according to Coleridge—affirm the timelessness and superiority of Nous, or Reason.[20]

The starting point of Coleridge's analysis (although he does not quote a specific passage in the lecture) appears to be Prometheus' references to the miseries humankind had to suffer before he gave them Mind. His first soliloquy establishes the connection between that gift and its symbolic equivalent, fire:

> This yoke of suffering is mine
> Because I granted mortal men prerogative:
> I sought the source of fire by stealth and carried it

20. Creuzer traces to Persia the notion that the first of gods embodies two principles, the One (Monas) and the Good, or Nous:

Thales und Anaxagoras waren die Ersten, welche Rechenschaft forderten über ihren Gott, und so entstand denn die älteste philosophische Schule in Jonien, obschon noch ganz priesterlich, in Versen und Bildern sich aussprechend. In Prosa sprachen zuerst Pherecydes und Pythagoras. Ersterer hatte unter Zeus (Ζην) den Aether verstanden, d.h. den äussersten, höchsten, Alles umschliessenden Feuerhimmel, oder das Licht, als das potenzirte Urelement; eine Idee, welche Persischen Religionsideen, die ich oben im ersten Theile zum öftern . . . berührt habe, ganz ähnlich ist, und uns an den Ursprung dieser Philosopheme aus dem Magiersystem erinnert. Eben daher stammt auch die Pythagorische Ansicht . . . von zwei Principien, das eine, Gott, Zeus, oder die Monas (ἡ μονὰ) und das Gute (τό ἀγαθόν)—der νους. Ihm steht die δυὰς, die Zweiheit, als Grund der Materie und auch des Bösen, gegenüber (vergl. Stobaei Eclogg. I. p. 59). (*Symbolik und Mythologie* 2:488–89).

(Thales and Anaxagoras were the first to demand a just account of their god and henceforth the oldest Ionian school of philosophy came into being. Although still quite priestly, they expressed themselves through verses and images. Pherecydes and Pythagoras were the first to speak in prose. Pherecydes understood Zeus [Ζην] to be the ether, in other words, the all-encompassing, ultimate, all-inclusive sky of fire, or Light as the all-powerful original element; an idea that closely resembles Persian religious ideas . . . and in its origin this philosopheme reminds us of the system of the Magi. And that is also exactly the origin of the Pythagorean view . . . of two principles, the one, God, Zeus, or the Monas [ἡ μονὰ] and the Good—[τό ἀγαθόν]—the νους. This is contrasted to the δυὰς, duality as the basis of matter and also of evil [see Stobaei Eclogg. (the "Eklogia" of Johannes Stobaeus) I. p. 59].)

Within a hollow fennel reed. My gift to man
Has taught him every skill and been his great resource.[21]

Later in Æschylus' play, Prometheus tells the Daughters of Ocean, who form the chorus, how he pitied humankind, "the griefs / Of mortal men, their helpless state before I placed / Intelligence within them and the use of mind." Prometheus then reviews the various skills and abilities the human race developed as a result of his gift, such as astronomy, arithmetic, and language itself, as well as the ability to distinguish the seasons; woodworking; the management of the horse and ox; medicine; the reading of omens; the preparation of fit sacrifices for the gods; and the use of metals. "In brief," he concludes, "All arts that men possess are from Prometheus' hand" (lines 442–44, 505–6; 22–24). The connection between the possession of fire and these specific skills—all of them, it should be said, combining practical expertise with what would now be considered a more spiritual kind of knowledge—is established when the Chorus questions Prometheus about the reasons for his being condemned to endless torture:

PROMETHEUS: Through me, the race of mortals turned their eyes from
              death. . . .
CHORUS: A great and profitable service done to men.
PROMETHEUS: But I bestowed on them still more: the gift of fire!
CHORUS: Is flashing fire now theirs, these creatures of a day?
PROMETHEUS: —And with its aid they shall search out a hundred skills.
                                        (lines 248, 251–54; 13–14)

The myth from which Æschylus takes the substance of his play, then, shows Prometheus the Titan stealing fire from heaven to give to humankind, as a means of alleviating the miseries to which Zeus' rule has subjected them. Æschylus, in the lines just quoted, develops the symbolic implications of Prometheus' name ("Forethought"): the gift of fire suggests the ability to sacrifice to the gods and to live on cooked rather than raw meat, but also, and of no less importance for the growth of civilization, the "use of mind," which brings with it a variety of skills. Prometheus' gift comprises not only what we designate as "intelligence," "intellect," and "science" but also practical

21. Æschylus, *Prometheus Bound*, trans. Warren D. Anderson, lines 107–11 (8).

skills (or *technai*) and certain no longer prized abilities, like being able to read omens and sacrifice to the gods.

Coleridge explicates the myth as a philosopheme or philosophical statement about the nature of mind. Reason, he says,

> was superadded or infused, *a supra* to mark that it was no mere evolution of the animal basis . . . "stolen,"—to mark its *hetero-* or rather its *allo*-geneity, that is, its diversity, its difference in kind, from the faculties which are common to man with the nobler animals . . . stolen "from Heaven,"—to mark its superiority in kind, as well as its essential diversity . . . a "spark,"—to mark that it is not subject to any modifying reaction from that on which it immediately acts . . . stolen by a "god," and a god of the race before the dynasty of Jove . . . to mark the pre-existence, in order of thought, of the *nous*, as spiritual, both to the objects of sense, and to their products. (*CW*, 4:351–52)

What the Prometheus myth affirms, then, is the priority and superiority of Reason to any manifestation of nature, any material forms. In the midst of a predominantly polytheistic culture, one that worships the forms of nature in the guise of anthropomorphic figures, Æschylus' version of the myth upholds a theory of mind that in philosophical content (though not in its theological rationale or its place in a religious cult) is very close to the Pentateuch. It both explains and justifies the existence of an internal theocracy in Greek society, since it demonstrates that only those who recognize the priority and superiority of intellect are qualified to see beyond the calculating materialism of pragmatic rulers, and guide the state by higher principles.

This theory of mind is therefore at once a philosophy, a method of self-discipline, and a rationale for the establishment of a cohesive, influential, and yet apolitical or suprapolitical intelligentsia, an "unalienated intellectual class," that will be the conscience of the state.[22]

22. This nexus between a model of the state, or "Law" as it applies to the political order, and a model of Mind, or "Law" as it applies to moral and spiritual self-discipline, is also in *BL*. Jerome C. Christensen points out that Coleridge's phrase "the constitution of the mind" (*BL*, 1:200) echoes Edmund Burke's "Letter to a Noble Lord": "In the *Biographia* the equivalent of Burke's ancient constitution, that which grounds and entails all our reflections, is the mind itself" ("'Like a Guilty Thing Surprised': Deconstruction, Coleridge, and the Apostasy of Criticism," 777).

It is instructive to look at Coleridge's interpretation of Prometheus and Jupiter, with its emphasis on the correlation between Idea, the divine bringer of Reason to humankind, and Law, the embodiment of Idea in nature and in the state, in conjunction with Shelley's revolutionary reading of the same relationship. In Shelley's version, as is well known, Jupiter is the creation of Prometheus himself and despite this has become Prometheus' persecutor: "I gave all / He has," Shelley's Prometheus laments, "and in return he chains me here / Years, ages, night and day" (*SP&P*, 147). Jupiter is a usurper, a Urizenic tyrant limiting the free play of spirits to gross, material forms and condemning not only humankind but all creatures on earth to the misery of his rule. He is not a true originator of things, a First Cause—that role is given to Demogorgon—but he is (as Edward Duffy says) "a false and man-made god, a power-mad rapist who, as such, may indeed be the very breath of our noxious social being, but nothing more than that."[23] From a philosophical perspective, Jupiter is the personification of the materialistic Necessitarianism Shelley once embraced, but later repudiated as inadequate to a truly regenerative, Orphic vision of the world. From a political perspective, he is that monarchical rule in which the poets and other creative persons once mistakenly vested power, having no desire to govern humankind themselves. In other words, the special pain of Prometheus' situation as Shelley presents it is that Prometheus set Jupiter on his throne in the first place.[24] Shelley does everything he can to show this Jupiter as tyrannical. In the curse Prometheus hurls against him Jupiter is addressed as

> the God and Lord . . .
>   Who fillest with thy soul this world of woe,
> To whom all things of Earth and Heaven do bow
>   In fear and worship—all-prevailing foe!   (*SP&P*, 144)

23. Edward Duffy, "Where Shelley Wrote and What He Wrote For: The Example of 'The Ode to the West Wind,'" 363.
24. On Jupiter as symbolic of Necessitarianism, see Woodman, *Apocalyptic Vision*, 113; for the political symbolism of the relationship with Jupiter, see especially Lewis, *Promethean Politics*: "[Prometheus'] serious misjudgment in vesting power in Jupiter makes him guilty as an accessory before the fact in Jupiter's rebellion" (167). Lewis usefully stresses the ambivalence of Prometheus—that he is both betrayer and emancipator.

Strongly identifying his own agonistic stance as political and prophetic poet with the struggle of Prometheus, Shelley takes a Promethean view of Jupiter, responding to such lines in Æschylus' play as
the following, which Prometheus speaks:

> No sooner was Zeus seated on his father's throne
> Than straightway he allotted privilege among
> The several gods, to each his duly ordered share
> Of power. But to mortals in their misery
> He paid no heed: his wish was to annihilate
> Their race and then beget another in their stead.
> To this design none made resistance—none but I:
> I dared oppose it.   (lines 228–35; 13)

As Shelley reads Æschylus' play, Prometheus himself, though subjected by his own hatred of Jupiter to an eon of painful suffering,
is compassionate, wise, defiant—in a word, humane: as his mother
the Earth tells him, he is "more than God, / Being wise and kind"
(*SP&P*, 140). "Law," for Shelley, is the negation of "Idea" in the true
Platonic and spiritual sense. The lines Prometheus speaks to Io, near
the end of the play—"There is laid down for me no end / To troubles
until Zeus is stripped of sovereignty" (lines 755–56; 35)—indicate to
Shelley that what Prometheus represents in humankind cannot be
free until the patriarchal order of Zeus/Jupiter is overthrown. Shelley
reads the conflict as at least partly about the status of the liberator's
poetic language, and, as one recent critic proposes, he anticipates the
modern sense among feminists and some others of the difficulty of
escaping the oppressive effect of the patriarchal discourse: "Jupiter's
speech [in act 3] to his assembled cohorts in heaven summarizes
nicely the indebtedness of mortals to a preordained language and
the polluting effects of that Law."[25]

25. Claridge, *Romantic Potency*, 136. Claridge finds Shelley given to characterizing poetic language in terms of maleness or metaphors of maleness
(fire, for instance). She stresses his "investment in the linguistic analogues
or enactments of phallic power" even while it perpetuates his debt "to the
contexts he would undo" (150). This specifically anticipates, for Claridge,
the perception in Lacan and more especially his feminist reinterpreters
that finding authentic speech outside the domain of phallic signification
is difficult.

In Coleridge's interpretation of the Jupiter-Prometheus relationship, there is more of a complementarity between the Titan and his successor-opponent. Coleridge follows the lead of a number of early-nineteenth-century syncretic mythographers who—as Stuart Curran points out—saw, behind the apparent conflicts and enmities among Greek divinities, a "super-divinity," combining not only Zeus and Prometheus but other deities as well.[26] In his emphasis on the philosophical notions of the One and the Good encoded in the figure of Zeus, however, Coleridge is closer to Creuzer, who observes that the earliest philosophical accounts of the gods interpreted Zeus as the One and therefore at enmity with duality (2:489). Coleridge argues for such inner complementarity between Jupiter and Prometheus in this way: the spark of divine fire that Prometheus stole and gave to humankind is indeed the spiritual in us, or Reason—but the spiritual as *viceroy* of the authority that in a different manifestation, as Zeus/Jupiter, gives shape to the world. The embodiment of Nous in the forms of the material world, of "nature," is not for Coleridge an unfortunate error, an enslavement, but a holy act parallel to the creation story in Genesis 1. Thus Jupiter is in Coleridge's interpretation the mythic author, symbol, and embodiment of Law in all its forms: of law in the intellectual realm, law as the counterpart to Idea; of law in nature, as governing the behavior of the elements; and of law in the *polis*, or the realm of earthly governments. The relationship between Law conceived in this way and Idea or the transcendent, purely spiritual source of Reason, Coleridge describes as follows: "The groundwork of the Æschylean *mythus* is laid in the definition of idea and law, as correlatives that mutually interpret each the other,—an idea, with the adequate power of realizing itself being a law, and a law considered abstractedly from, or in the absence of, the power of manifesting itself in its appropriate product being an idea" (CW, 4:358).

Both Shelley and Coleridge draw on a Platonic definition of the term "idea," but unlike Shelley, whose reception of Plato was

26. The mythographer George Stanley Faber even saw one divinity in figures as diverse as Zeus, Prometheus, Pan, Cronos, Apollo, and Adonis. See Curran, "Political Prometheus," 432. Curran gives a useful account of the sudden upsurge of interest in Æschylus' play in England after Thomas Morrell's translation appeared in 1773.

strongly colored by a hatred of the confining forms of "law" both in the political sense and in the sphere of nature, Coleridge sees the correlation of idea and law as a simple condition of existence. Shelley sees in Prometheus a revolutionary, a defender of humankind, but Coleridge sees a god who participates in due and fit manner in the divine process of creation. Plato, Coleridge argues, held that ideas are "one in essence with the power and life of nature" (*CW*, 4:359), and this (according to Coleridge) was the philosophy of Æschylus and the mythic poets of Greece. The order of nature reflects the order of intellect. Prometheus, as symbol of Idea, though forced by the very circumstances he has created (the actual existence of the material world) to withhold from Jupiter for an eon the secret of Jupiter's ultimate demise, is still of the same lineage as he: "a god of the same race and essence with Jove, and linked of yore in closest and friendliest intimacy with him" (*CW*, 4:352). As in Shelley's reading, Prometheus is the older and superior power; but whereas Shelley stresses the tyranny and arbitrariness of Jupiter's rule over earth, humankind, and his fellow deities, Coleridge chooses to emphasize his understanding that Law is the sanctioned expression of Idea (at least for as long as this world lasts), and that only in eternity will the spiritual in man, the Reason, be reunited with its author, Idea, which in turn he identifies with the divine Logos of Christian tradition.

Coleridge's emphasis on the patriarchal aspect of the Jupiter-Prometheus relationship is perhaps sufficiently clear from the above discussion, but it is worth pointing out that in his reading of Æschylus' drama Coleridge does not completely ignore the female part of the Greek pantheon. Those readers who think of nature in Greek myth as symbolized by female deities—Demeter, Korè/Persephone, Aphrodite, Hera, Themis, and others—may well be puzzled to find nature in Coleridge's scheme so exclusively portrayed as the domain of Zeus. What has become of the Triple Goddess, the maternal power, the exuberant fertile power of nature, represented in other Greek mythologies as Demeter or Aphrodite?

In the scheme that Coleridge adopts from Schelling, She is identified with the Greek and Asian concept of chaos. The philosophical or mental meaning of "chaos," Coleridge argues, is "a striving of the mind to distinguish being from existence." This striving, or yearning ("Sehnsucht" is the word Schelling uses, equating it with the Greek "Pothos"), is in Schelling's interpretation a characteristic of the whole company of the original Cabiric deities.[27] In nature, it is darkness, emptiness, hunger, and in the Greek Mysteries this idea was symbolized as Ceres, "the ever-seeking maternal goddess," manifesting herself as "esurience," or desire, or lack (*CW*, 4:353). Ceres' name, Coleridge goes so far as to suggest, may derive from a Hebrew word meaning "hunger, and thence capacity."[28] Her "fertility" therefore lies (paradoxically) in her emptiness, or *capacity*, her being a con-

27. See F. W. J. Schelling, *Ueber die Gottheiten von Samothrace*, 15–16:

Als aber der Geist von der Liebe gegen die eigenen Anfänge entbrannte und eine Zusammenziehung entstand, wurde dieses Band Sehnsucht genannt, und dieß war der Beginn der Erschaffung aller Dinge. Hier wird der Anfang in ein Entbrennen gegen sich selbst, ein sich selber Suchen gesetzt, das hieraus entstehende Band ist wieder, nur die gleichsam verkörperte, Sehnsucht und der erste Anlaß zur Erschaffung aller Dinge. Einheimisch phönischen Kosmogonieen war also die Vorstellung der Sehnsucht als Anfangs, als ersten Grundes zur Schöpfung. Aber war sie darum auch samothracisch? Hierauf antwortet eine Stelle des Plinius, der unter den Werken des Skopas die Venus, den Pothos, d.h. die Sehnsucht und die Phaëton nennt, Gottheiten (setzt er hinzu), die in Samothrace mit den heiligsten Gebräuchen verehrt werden. Gewiß also ist, daß unter den samothracischen Gottheiten eine war, mit den Begriff: Sehnsucht, verbunden wurde.

(But when the spirit of love became aroused against its own beginnings, the resultant drawing-together was then called Longing; this was the beginning of the creation of all things. This beginning becomes an arousal against itself, a search for itself. The resulting bond is again none other than the equally embodied Longing, and the initial event in the creation of all things. To native Phoenician cosmogonies the concept of Longing as the beginning was the first reason for the creation. But was it also Samothracian? Relevant to that question is a passage by Pliny who, among the works of Skopas, names Venus, Pothos, that is, Longing, and Phaëthon, deities [he adds] who in Samothrace are worshiped with the holiest of rituals. It is certain that among the Samothracian deities there existed one who was associated with the concept of Longing.)

Creuzer says that "Pothos" (or "das Verlangen") was one of the three original principles in the Phoenician cosmogony—Cronos, or Time; Pothos, or Want; and "der Nebel," or Mist (2:18–19).

28. The derivation of "Ceres" from Hebrew *cheresh* is suggested by Schelling, *Ueber die Gottheiten von Samothrace*, 63. See also Coleridge, *Marginalia*, 1:653, 665.

tainer or withholder waiting to be fulfilled with the formative, all-creating power of Jupiter, "the coercer and entrancer of free spirits under the fetters of shape, and mass" (*CW*, 4:352). Thus, with an eye to reconciling Greek myth with the Genesis account, Coleridge develops a highly specialized and certainly patriarchal interpretation of the oldest female divinity associated with the Mysteries. This is in distinct contrast to Shelley, who shows his chief female deities as in some ways limited in their perspectives just as the male figures are (for instance, Earth misinterprets Prometheus' revoking of his curse as an admission of defeat, and Asia has to learn that Demogorgon cannot give her the answers she seeks), nevertheless also makes the relationship between Earth and her son, and that between Prometheus and Asia, one of sympathy, and participation in the common cause—determined opposition to Jupiter's tyranny.

Coleridge's lecture on the *Prometheus* of Æschylus is an excellent instance of the way in which myth operates as a vehicle of ideology and cannot be considered beyond ideological analysis. Indeed, it demonstrates that the ideological dimension of myth was fully apparent to the Romantics themselves. This recognition is of more than merely historical interest because it shows how much in the understanding of myth depends upon the interpreter's stance. It warns the student of myth, if he or she needed such a warning, that myth contains, not simplistic "universal truths," but patterns of relationships, sequences of actions, that may be read from widely different political or religious standpoints. Finally, to those who have tended to confuse an interest in "myth criticism" with a conservative resistance to the more innovative kinds of literary analysis, it may suggest a way of uniting the study of myth with a deconstructive, or ideologically alert, approach to the use of myth in Romantic writing. Myth criticism will have lost ground if it bypasses the more challenging questions criticism has to deal with, and especially if it ignores those ways in which ideology and myth intertwine.

Selected Works Cited

Note: For primary texts not included here, see Abbreviations.

Abbey, Lloyd. *Destroyer and Preserver: Shelley's Poetic Skepticism.* Lincoln: University of Nebraska Press, 1979.

Abrams, M. H. *Natural Supernaturalism: Tradition and Revolution in Romantic Literature.* New York: Norton, 1973.

Æschylus. *Prometheus Bound.* Trans. Warren D. Anderson. Indianapolis: Bobbs-Merrill, 1963.

Allen, Don Cameron. *Mysteriously Meant: The Rediscovery of Pagan Symbolism and Allegorical Interpretation in the Renaissance.* Baltimore: Johns Hopkins University Press, 1970.

Archer, John. "Authority in Shelley." *Studies in Romanticism* 26 (1987): 259–73.

Aske, Martin. *Keats and Hellenism.* New York: Cambridge University Press, 1985.

Baker, Carlos. *Shelley's Major Poetry: The Fabric of a Vision.* Princeton: Princeton University Press, 1948.

Baker, Jeffrey. *Time and Mind in Wordsworth's Poetry.* Detroit: Wayne State University Press, 1980.

Bayle, Pierre. *Dictionnaire historique et critique.* 4th ed. 4 vols. Amsterdam, 1730.

Beatty, Arthur. *William Wordsworth: His Doctrine and Art in Their Historical Relations.* University of Wisconsin Studies in Language and Literature, 17. Madison: University of Wisconsin Press, 1922.

Beer, J. B. *Coleridge's Poetic Intelligence.* London: Macmillan, 1977.
———. *Coleridge the Visionary.* London: Chatto and Windus, 1959.

————. "The Languages of *Kubla Khan*." In *Coleridge's Imagination: Essays in Memory of Pete Laver,* ed. Richard Gravil, Lucy Newlyn, and Nicholas Roe, 220–62. Cambridge: Cambridge University Press, 1985.

————. *Wordsworth and the Human Heart.* New York: Columbia University Press, 1978.

Behrendt, Stephen. "Introduction." In *History and Myth: Essays on English Romantic Literature,* ed. Stephen Behrendt, 13–32. Detroit: Wayne State University Press, 1990.

Belmonte, Thomas. "The Trickster and the Sacred Clown: Revealing the Logic of the Unspeakable." In *C. G. Jung and the Humanities,* ed. Karin Barnaby and Pellegrino D'Acierno, 45–66. Princeton: Princeton University Press, 1990.

Beyer, Werner W. "Coleridge, Wieland's *Oberon,* and *The Ancient Mariner.*" *Review of English Studies* 15 (1939): 401–11.

Blake, William. *The Complete Poetry and Prose.* Ed. David V. Erdman, commentary by Harold Bloom. Rev. ed. Berkeley: University of California Press, 1982.

Bloom, Harold. *A Map of Misreading.* New York: Oxford University Press, 1975.

Blumenberg, Hans. *Work on Myth.* Trans. Robert M. Wallace. Cambridge: MIT Press, 1985.

Bohm, Arnd. "Georg Forster's *A Voyage Round the World* as a Source for *The Rime of the Ancient Mariner*: A Reconsideration." *ELH* 50 (1983): 363–77.

Bostetter, E. E. "The Nightmare World of *The Ancient Mariner.*" *Studies in Romanticism* 1 (1961–1962): 241–54.

Brown, Nathaniel. *Sexuality and Feminism in Shelley.* Cambridge: Harvard University Press, 1979.

Bryant, Jacob. *A New System, or, an Analysis of Ancient Mythology.* 3 vols. London, 1774–1776.

Butler, Marilyn. "Myth and Mythmaking in the Shelley Circle." *ELH* 49 (1982): 50–72.

Cameron, Kenneth Neill, et al., eds. *Shelley and His Circle.* 6 vols. Cambridge: Harvard University Press, 1961–1973.

Cantor, Paul. *Creature and Creator: Myth-making and English Romanticism.* Cambridge: Cambridge University Press, 1984.

Chase, Richard. "Notes on the Study of Myth." In *Myth and Literature: Contemporary Theory and Practice,* ed. John B. Vickery, 67–73. Lincoln: University of Nebraska Press, 1966.

Chayes, Irene H. "Little Girls Lost: Problems of a Romantic Archetype." *Bulletin of the New York Public Library* 67 (1963): 579–92.

Chernaik, Judith. *The Lyrics of Shelley.* Cleveland: Press of Case Western Reserve University, 1972.

Christensen, Jerome C. *Coleridge's Blessed Machine of Language.* Ithaca: Cornell University Press, 1981.

———. " 'Like a Guilty Thing Surprised': Deconstruction, Coleridge, and the Apostasy of Criticism." *Critical Inquiry* 12 (1986): 769–87.

Claridge, Laura. *Romantic Potency: The Paradox of Desire.* Ithaca: Cornell University Press, 1992.

Clarke, C. C. *Romantic Paradox: An Essay on the Poetry of Wordsworth.* London: Routledge and Kegan Paul, 1962.

Coleridge, S. T. *Aids to Reflection.* Ed. John Beer. *Collected Works,* Bollingen Series 75, vol. 9. London and Princeton: Routledge and Kegan Paul and Princeton University Press, 1993.

———. *Literary Remains.* 4 vols. London, 1836–1839.

———. *Marginalia.* Ed. George Whalley and H. J. Jackson. *Collected Works,* Bollingen Series 75, vol. 12. London and Princeton: Routledge and Kegan Paul and Princeton University Press, 1980.

———. *On the Constitution of the Church and State.* Ed. John Colmer. *Collected Works,* Bollingen Series 75, vol. 10. London and Princeton: Routledge and Kegan Paul and Princeton University Press, 1976.

Collins, William. *See* Gray, Thomas.

Condorcet, marquis de (Marie Jean Antoine Nicolas Caritat). *Esquisse d'un tableau historique des progrès de l'esprit humain.* Ed. O. H. Prior, rev. Y. Belaval. Paris: J. Vrin, 1970.

Cook, Albert. *Myth and Language.* Bloomington: Indiana University Press, 1980.

Cottom, Daniel. *The Civilized Imagination: A Study of Ann Radcliffe, Jane Austen, and Sir Walter Scott.* Cambridge: Cambridge University Press, 1985.

Cranz, David. *The History of Greenland.* 2 vols. London, 1767.

Creuzer, [Georg] Friedrich. *Symbolik und Mythologie der alten Völker.* 2d ed. 6 vols. Leipzig and Darmstadt, 1819–1823.

Crisman, William. "A Dramatic Voice in Keats's Elgin Marbles Sonnet." *Studies in Romanticism* 26 (1987): 49–58.

Curran, Stuart. "The Political Prometheus." *Studies in Romanticism* 25 (1986): 429–55.

————. *Shelley's Annus Mirabilis: The Maturing of an Epic Vision.* San Marino: Huntington Library, 1975.

————. "Shelley's Emendations to the *Hymn to Intellectual Beauty.*" *English Language Notes* 7 (1970): 270–73.

De Man, Paul. *The Rhetoric of Romanticism.* New York: Columbia University Press, 1984.

Dryden, John. *Works.* Gen. ed., H. T. Swedenberg. Vol. 3, *Poems 1685–1692,* ed. Earl Miner. Berkeley: University of California Press, 1969. Vol. 5, *The Works of Virgil in English,* ed. William Frost. Berkeley: University of California Press, 1987.

Duerksen, Roland A. "The Critical Mode in British Romanticism." *Romanticism Past and Present* 7:1 (1983): 1–21.

Duffy, Edward. "Where Shelley Wrote and What He Wrote For: The Example of 'The Ode to the West Wind.'" *Studies in Romanticism* 23 (1984): 351–77.

Dunstan, A. C. "The German Influence on Coleridge. II." *Modern Language Review* 18 (1923): 183–201.

Dupuis, Charles François. *Origine de tous les cultes ou religion universelle.* 7 vols. Paris, 1795.

Eliade, Mircea. *Shamanism: Archaic Techniques of Ecstasy.* Trans. Willard B. Trask. Bollingen Series 76. Princeton: Princeton University Press, 1964.

Eliot, T. S. *Collected Poems 1909–1962.* London: Faber and Faber, 1963.

Ellis, David. *Wordsworth, Freud and the Spots of Time: Interpretation in* The Prelude. Cambridge: Cambridge University Press, 1985.

Ellison, Julie. *Delicate Subjects: Romanticism, Gender, and the Ethics of Understanding.* Ithaca: Cornell University Press, 1990.

Emerson, Ralph Waldo. *Representative Men.* Vol. 4 of *Works,* Riverside Edition, 11 vols. London: George Routledge, 1893.

Estlin, John Prior. *The Nature and the Causes of Atheism . . . To which are added, Remarks on a Work, entitled Origine de tous les cultes, ou Religion universelle.* Bristol, 1797.

Evert, Walter H. *Aesthetic and Myth in the Poetry of Keats.* Princeton: Princeton University Press, 1965.

————. "Coadjutors of Oppression: A Romantic and Modern Theory of Evil." In *Romantic and Modern: Revaluations of Literary Tradition,* ed. George Bornstein, 29–52. Pittsburgh: University of Pittsburgh Press, 1977.

Fackenheim, Emil. *The Jewish Return into History: Reflections in the Age of Auschwitz and a New Jerusalem*. New York: Schocken, 1978.

Feldman, Burton, and Robert D. Richardson, eds. *The Rise of Modern Mythology 1680–1860*. Bloomington: Indiana University Press, 1972.

Ferguson, Frances. "The Lucy Poems: Wordsworth's Quest for a Poetic Object." *ELH* 40 (1973): 532–48.

———. *Wordsworth: Language as Counter-Spirit*. New Haven: Yale University Press, 1977.

Fields, Beverly. "Keats and the Tongueless Nightingale: Some Unheard Melodies in 'The Eve of St. Agnes.'" *The Wordsworth Circle* 14 (1983): 246–50.

Fink, Z. S. *The Early Wordsworthian Milieu*. Oxford: Clarendon Press, 1958.

Fogle, Richard Harter. *The Idea of Coleridge's Criticism*. Berkeley: University of California Press, 1962.

Frankiel, Tamar. "New Age Mythology: A Jewish Response to Joseph Campbell." *Tikkun* 4, no. 3 (May–June 1989): 23–26, 118–20.

Frazer, James. *The Golden Bough*. Abr. ed. New York: Macmillan, 1945.

Friedman, Geraldine. "The Erotics of Interpretation in Keats's 'Ode on a Grecian Urn': Pursuing the Feminine." *Studies in Romanticism* 32 (1993): 225–43.

Fry, Paul H. *The Poet's Calling in the English Ode*. New Haven: Yale University Press, 1980.

Frye, Northrop. *Anatomy of Criticism*. Princeton: Princeton University Press, 1957.

———. *Fables of Identity: Studies in Poetic Mythology*. New York: Harcourt, Brace and World, 1963.

———. *A Study of English Romanticism*. New York: Random House, 1968.

———. "Towards Defining an Age of Sensibility." *ELH* 23 (1956): 144–52.

Gill, Stephen. "Wordsworth's Poems: The Question of Text." *Review of English Studies*, n.s., 34 (1983): 172–90.

Gombrich, E. H. "Representation and Misrepresentation." *Critical Inquiry* 11 (1984): 195–201.

Goslee, Nancy M. "Phidian Lore: Sculpture and Personification in Keats's Odes." *Studies in Romanticism* 21 (1982): 73–85.

Gould, Eric. *Mythical Intentions in Modern Literature*. Princeton: Princeton University Press, 1981.

Grady, Kelley, and Martha Michael. "A New Manuscript of Wordsworth's 'To M. H.'" *The Wordsworth Circle* 16 (1985): 38–40.

Gray, Thomas; William Collins; and Oliver Goldsmith. *The Poems of Thomas Gray, William Collins, Oliver Goldsmith*. Ed. Roger Lonsdale. London: Longmans, 1969.

Greene, Donald. "Latitudinarianism and Sensibility: The Genealogy of the 'Man of Feeling' Reconsidered." *Modern Philology* 75 (1977): 159–83.

Hall, Jean. "The Socialized Imagination: Shelley's *The Cenci* and *Prometheus Unbound*." *Studies in Romanticism* 23 (1984): 339–50.

———. *The Transforming Image: A Study of Shelley's Major Poetry*. Urbana: University of Illinois Press, 1980.

Hall, Spencer. "Power and the Poet: Religious Mythmaking in Shelley's 'Hymn to Intellectual Beauty.'" *Keats-Shelley Journal* 32 (1983): 123–49.

———. "Shelley, Skepticism(s), and Critical Discourse—A Review Essay." *Southern Humanities Review* 18 (1984): 65–74.

———. "Shelley's 'Mont Blanc.'" *Studies in Philology* 70 (1973): 199–221.

Hamilton, Paul. "Romantic Irony and English Literary History." In *The Romantic Heritage*, ed. Karsten Engelberg, 11–32. Publications of the Department of English, University of Copenhagen, no. 12. Copenhagen: University of Copenhagen, 1983.

Haney, David P. "The Emergence of the Autobiographical Figure in *The Prelude*, Book I." *Studies in Romanticism* 20 (1981): 33–63.

Harding, Anthony John. *Coleridge and the Idea of Love*. Cambridge: Cambridge University Press, 1974.

Hartman, Geoffrey H. *Beyond Formalism: Literary Essays 1958–1970*. New Haven: Yale University Press, 1970.

———. *The Fate of Reading*. Chicago: University of Chicago Press, 1975.

———. *Wordsworth's Poetry 1787–1814*. New Haven: Yale University Press, 1971.

Hayter, Alethea. *A Voyage in Vain*. London: Faber and Faber, 1973.

Heinzelman, Kurt. "Self-interest and the Politics of Composition in Keats's *Isabella*." *ELH* 55 (1988): 159–93.

Hertz, Neil. *The End of the Line: Essays on Psychoanalysis and the Sublime.* New York: Columbia University Press, 1985.

Hinchliffe, Keith. "Wordsworth and the Kinds of Metaphor." *Studies in Romanticism* 23 (1984): 81–100.

Hoagwood, Terence Allan. *Skepticism and Ideology: Shelley's Political Prose and Its Philosophical Context from Bacon to Marx.* Iowa City: University of Iowa Press, 1988.

Hodgart, Patricia. *A Preface to Shelley.* London: Longman, 1985.

Holbach, Paul Henri Thiry, baron d'. *Système de la nature, ou Des loix du monde physique et du monde moral.* New ed. 2 vols. London, 1770–1775.

Homans, Margaret. "Eliot, Wordsworth, and the Scenes of the Sisters' Instruction." *Writing and Sexual Difference,* ed. Elizabeth Abel, 53–71. Chicago: University of Chicago Press, 1982.

House, Humphry. *Coleridge: The Clark Lectures 1951–52.* London: Rupert Hart-Davis, 1953. Reprint, 1969.

Jackson, J. R. de J., ed. *Coleridge: The Critical Heritage.* London: Routledge and Kegan Paul, 1970.

Jacobus, Mary. *Tradition and Experiment in Wordsworth's Lyrical Ballads (1798).* Oxford: Clarendon Press, 1976.

Johnston, Kenneth. "'Home at Grasmere': Reclusive Song." *Studies in Romanticism* 14 (1975): 1–28.

———. "The Idiom of Vision." In *New Perspectives on Coleridge and Wordsworth,* ed. Geoffrey H. Hartman, 1–39. New York: Columbia University Press, 1972.

———. *Wordsworth and* The Recluse. New Haven: Yale University Press, 1984.

———. "Wordsworth and *The Recluse*: The University of Imagination." *PMLA* 97 (1982): 60–82.

Jortin, John. *Tracts, philological, critical, and miscellaneous.* 2 vols. London, 1790.

Kaczvinsky, Donald P. "Coleridge's Polar Spirit: A Source." *English Language Notes* 24 (1987): 25–28.

Keats, John. *Letters.* Ed. Hyder Edward Rollins. 2 vols. Cambridge: Harvard University Press, 1958.

Kelley, Theresa M. "Proteus and Romantic Allegory." *ELH* 49 (1982): 623–52.

Klossowski, Pierre. "Nietzsche's Experience of the Eternal Return."

In *Friedrich Nietzsche: Modern Critical Views*, ed. Harold Bloom, 43–57. New York: Chelsea House, 1987.

Kneale, J. Douglas. *Monumental Writing: Aspects of Rhetoric in Wordsworth's Poetry*. Lincoln: University of Nebraska Press, 1988.

———. "Wordsworth's Images of Language: Voice and Letter in *The Prelude*." PMLA 101 (1986): 351–61.

Knight, Richard Payne. *An Account of the Remains of the Worship of Priapus*. London, 1786.

Knights, Ben. *The Idea of the Clerisy in the Nineteenth Century*. Cambridge: Cambridge University Press, 1978.

Kramer, Lawrence. "The Return of the Gods: Keats to Rilke." *Studies in Romanticism* 17 (1978): 483–500.

Kuhn, Albert J. "English Deism and the Development of Romantic Mythological Syncretism." PMLA 71 (1956): 1094–116.

Leask, Nigel. *The Politics of Imagination in Coleridge's Critical Thought*. New York: St. Martin's Press, 1988.

Leighton, Angela. *Shelley and the Sublime: An Interpretation of the Major Poems*. Cambridge: Cambridge University Press, 1984.

Lewis, Linda M. *The Promethean Politics of Milton, Blake, and Shelley*. Columbia: University of Missouri Press, 1992.

Lowes, John Livingston. *The Road to Xanadu*. 2d rev. ed. London: Constable, 1951.

Magnuson, Paul. *Coleridge and Wordsworth: A Lyrical Dialogue*. Princeton: Princeton University Press, 1988.

Mahmoud, Fatma Moussa. *Sir William Jones and the Romantics*. Cairo: Anglo-Egyptian Bookshop, 1962.

Matlak, Richard. "The Men in Wordsworth's Life." *The Wordsworth Circle* 9 (1978): 391–97.

Matthews, G. M. "A Volcano's Voice in Shelley." In *Shelley: Modern Judgements*, ed. R. B. Woodings, 162–95. 1969. Reprint, Nashville: Aurora Publishers, 1970.

Maurice, Thomas. *The History of Hindostan: Its Arts, and Its Sciences*. 2 vols. London, 1795–1798.

McFarland, Thomas. *Coleridge and the Pantheist Tradition*. Oxford: Clarendon Press, 1969.

———. *Originality and Imagination*. Baltimore: Johns Hopkins University Press, 1985.

———. "Romantic Imagination, Nature, and the Pastoral Ideal." In *Coleridge's Imagination: Essays in Memory of Pete Laver*, ed.

Richard Gravil, Lucy Newlyn, and Nicholas Roe, 5–21. Cambridge: Cambridge University Press, 1985.

———. *Romanticism and the Forms of Ruin : Wordsworth, Coleridge, and Modalities of Fragmentation*. Princeton: Princeton University Press, 1981.

McGann, Jerome J. *The Beauty of Inflections*. Oxford: Clarendon Press, 1988.

———. *The Romantic Ideology*. Chicago: University of Chicago Press, 1983.

Mellor, Anne K. *English Romantic Irony*. Cambridge: Harvard University Press, 1980.

———. "Keats's Face of Moneta: Source and Meaning." *Keats-Shelley Journal* 25 (1976): 65–80.

———. *Mary Shelley: Her Life, Her Fiction, Her Monsters*. New York: Routledge, 1989.

———. *Romanticism and Gender*. New York: Routledge, 1993.

Merivale, Patricia. *Pan the Goat-God: His Myth in Modern Times*. Cambridge: Harvard University Press, 1969.

Miall, David S. "Guilt and Death: The Predicament of *The Ancient Mariner*." *Studies in English Literature 1500–1900* 24 (1984): 633–53.

———. "The Meaning of Dreams: Coleridge's Ambivalence." *Studies in Romanticism* 21 (1982): 57–71.

Mileur, Jean-Pierre. *Vision and Revision: Coleridge's Art of Immanence*. Berkeley: University of California Press, 1982.

Milton, John. *Works*. Ed. Frank Patterson. 18 vols. New York: Columbia University Press, 1931–1938.

Modiano, Raimonda. "Blood Sacrifice, Gift Economy and the Edenic World: Wordsworth's 'Home at Grasmere.'" *Studies in Romanticism* 32 (1993): 481–521.

———. "Words and 'Languageless' Meanings: Limits of Expression in *The Rime of the Ancient Mariner*." *Modern Language Quarterly* 38 (1977): 40–61.

Moore, Marianne. *Complete Poems*. New York: Macmillan/Viking Press, 1967.

Morland, Kjell. "The Disturbing 'Presence': A Central Problem in Wordsworth's 'Tintern Abbey.'" In *The Romantic Heritage*, ed. Karsten Engelberg, 33–52. Publications of the Department of

English, University of Copenhagen, no. 12. Copenhagen: University of Copenhagen, 1983.

Mudge, Bradford K. "Song of Himself: Crisis and Selection in *The Prelude*, Books 1 and 7." *Texas Studies in Literature and Language* 27 (1985): 1–24.

Nelson, Jane A. "Entelechy and Structure in 'Christabel.'" *Studies in Romanticism* 19 (1980): 375–93.

Nietzsche, Friedrich. *The Birth of Tragedy and The Genealogy of Morals*. Trans. Francis Golffing. Garden City, N.Y.: Doubleday Anchor, 1956.

——. *Thoughts Out of Season*. Vols. 4 and 5 of *Complete Works*, ed. Oscar Levy. 18 vols. 1909–1911. Reprint, New York: Russell and Russell, 1964.

Ochshorn, Judith. *The Female Experience and the Nature of the Divine*. Bloomington: Indiana University Press, 1981.

Ong, Walter J., S.J. "Evolution, Myth, and Poetic Vision." *Comparative Literature Studies* 3 (1966): 1–20.

——. *The Presence of the Word*. 2d. ed. Minneapolis: University of Minnesota Press, 1981.

Onorato, Richard J. *The Character of the Poet: Wordsworth in* The Prelude. Princeton: Princeton University Press, 1971.

Ostendorf, Bernhard. *Der Mythos in der Neuen Welt: Eine Untersuchung zum amerikanischen Myth Criticism*. Frankfurt am Main: Thesen Verlag, 1971.

Panofsky, Erwin. "*Et in Arcadia ego*: Poussin and the Elegiac Tradition." In his *Meaning in the Visual Arts: Papers in and on Art History*, 295–320. Garden City, N.Y.: Doubleday Anchor, 1955.

Peterfreund, Stuart. "*The Prelude*: Wordsworth's Metamorphic Epic." *Genre* 14 (1981): 441–72.

——. "The Way of Immanence, Coleridge, and the Problem of Evil." *ELH* 55 (1988): 125–58.

Pfau, Thomas. "Rhetoric and the Existential: Romantic Studies and the Question of the Subject." *Studies in Romanticism* 26 (1987): 487–512.

Pfeiler, William K. "Coleridge and Schelling's Treatise on the Samothracian Deities." *Modern Language Notes* 52 (1937): 162–65.

Philo Judæus. *Works*. Trans. C. D. Yonge. 4 vols. London: Bohn, 1854.

Phinney, A. W. "Keats in the Museum: Between Aesthetics and

History." *Journal of English and Germanic Philology* 90 (1991): 208–29.

Pierce, John B. " 'Mont Blanc' and *Prometheus Unbound*: Shelley's Use of the Rhetoric of Silence," *Keats-Shelley Journal* 38 (1989): 108–26.

Piper, H. W. *The Active Universe: Pantheism and the Concept of Imagination in the English Romantic Poets*. London: Athlone Press, 1962.

———. "The Disunity of *Christabel* and the Fall of Nature." *Essays in Criticism* 28 (1978): 216–27.

Plotinus. *The Enneads*. Trans. Stephen MacKenna. 3d ed., rev. B. S. Page. London: Faber and Faber, 1962.

Pope, Alexander. *Poems*. Ed. John Butt. London: Methuen, 1965.

Priestley, Joseph. *A Comparison of the Institutions of Moses with those of the Hindoos and Other Ancient Nations; with Remarks on Mr. Dupuis' Origin of all Religions*. Northumberland, 1799.

———. *A Course of Lectures on the Theory of Language, and Universal Grammar*. 1762. Reprint, Menston: Scolar Press, 1970.

———. *The Doctrines of Heathen Philosophy, compared with those of Revelation*. 1804. Reprint, Delmar, N.Y.: Scholars' Facsimiles and Reprints, 1987.

———. *An History of the Corruptions of Christianity*. 2 vols. 1782. Reprint, New York: Garland, 1974.

Pulos, C. E. *The Deep Truth: A Study of Shelley's Skepticism*. Lincoln: University of Nebraska Press, 1954.

Quinn, Mary A. "The *Daemon of the World*: Shelley's Antidote to the Skepticism of *Alastor*." *Studies in English Literature 1500–1900* 25 (1985): 755–74.

Rajan, Tilottama. *Dark Interpreter: The Discourse of Romanticism*. Ithaca: Cornell University Press, 1980.

Ramsey, Jonathan. "Wordsworth's Silent Poet." *Modern Language Quarterly* 37 (1976): 260–80.

Ray, Rhonda Johnson. "Geraldine as Usurper of Christ: An Unmystical Union." *Philological Quarterly* 63 (1984): 511–23.

Reid, S. W. "The Composition and Revision of Coleridge's Essay on Aeschylus' *Prometheus*." *Studies in Bibliography* 24 (1971): 176–83.

Reiman, Donald. "Coleridge and the Art of Equivocation." *Studies in Romanticism* 25 (1986): 325–50.

———. "Wordsworth, Shelley, and the Romantic Inheritance." *Romanticism Past and Present* 5:2 (1981): 1–22.

Rieder, John. "Shelley's 'Mont Blanc': Landscape and the Ideology of the Sacred Text." *ELH* 48 (1981): 778–98.

Rist, Anna. *The Poems of Theocritus*. Chapel Hill: University of North Carolina Press, 1978.

Rogers, Neville. *Shelley at Work: A Critical Inquiry*. Oxford: Clarendon Press, 1956.

Ross, Marlon B. "Naturalizing Gender: Woman's Place in Wordsworth's Ideological Landscape." *ELH* 53 (1986): 391–410.

Rousseau, Jean-Jacques. *Du contrat social*. Paris: Garnier, 1962.

Ryan, Robert M. *Keats: The Religious Sense*. Princeton: Princeton University Press, 1976.

Schelling, F. W. J. *Ueber die Gottheiten von Samothrace*. Stuttgart and Tübingen, 1815.

Schlegel, Friedrich. *Dialogue on Poetry and Literary Aphorisms*. Trans. Ernst Behler and Roman Struc. University Park: Pennsylvania State University Press, 1968.

Schwartz, Kathleen M. "Prayer in the Poetry of S.T.C." Ph.D. diss., Princeton University, 1975.

Schwartz, Robert. "Speaking the Unspeakable: The Meaning of Form in *Christabel*." *University of South Florida Language Quarterly* 19:1–2 (1980): 31–34.

Scott, Grant F. "Beautiful Ruins: The Elgin Marbles Sonnet in Its Historical and Generic Contexts." *Keats-Shelley Journal* 39 (1990): 123–50.

[Sept-Chênes, Leclerc de]. *Essai sur la religion des anciens Grecs*. 2 vols. Geneva, 1787.

Shaffer, E. S. *'Kubla Khan' and* The Fall of Jerusalem: *The Mythological School in Biblical Criticism and Secular Literature 1770–1880*. Cambridge: Cambridge University Press, 1975.

Shakespeare, William. *Complete Works*. Ed. Peter Alexander. London: Collins, 1951.

Shelley, Mary. *Proserpine and Midas: Two Unpublished Mythological Dramas*. Ed. A. Koszul. London: Humphrey Milford, 1922.

Shelley, Percy Bysshe. *The Letters of Percy Bysshe Shelley*. Ed. Frederick L. Jones. 2 vols. Oxford: Clarendon Press, 1964.

———. *The Poems of Shelley*. Ed. Geoffrey Matthews and Kelvin Everest. Vol. 1, *1804–1817*. London: Longman, 1989.

Spatz, Jonas. "The Mystery of Eros: Sexual Initiation in Coleridge's *Christabel.*" *PMLA* 90 (1975): 107–16.

Sperry, Stuart. *Keats the Poet.* Princeton: Princeton University Press, 1973.

Spivey, Ted R. *Beyond Modernism: Toward a New Myth Criticism.* Lanham: University Press of America, 1988.

Stevenson, Warren. *Nimbus of Glory: A Study of Coleridge's Three Great Poems.* Salzburg Studies in English Literature, Romantic Reassessment no. 109:2. Salzburg: Universität Salzburg, 1983.

Stillinger, Jack. *The Hoodwinking of Madeline and Other Essays on Keats's Poems.* Urbana: University of Illinois Press, 1971.

———. "Textual Primitivism and the Editing of Wordsworth." *Studies in Romanticism* 28 (1989): 3–28.

Swann, Karen. " 'Christabel': The Wandering Mother and the Enigma of Form." *Studies in Romanticism* 23 (1984): 533–53.

Tetreault, Ronald. *The Poetry of Life: Shelley and Literary Form.* Toronto: University of Toronto Press, 1987.

Tooke, Andrew, ed. and trans. *The Pantheon, Representing the Fabulous Histories of the Heathen Gods and Most Illustrious Heroes in a Short, Plain and Familiar Method . . . for the Use of Schools.* 1713. Reprint, New York: Garland, 1976.

Vendler, Helen. *The Odes of John Keats.* Cambridge: The Belknap Press of Harvard University Press, 1983.

Vernant, Jean-Pierre. *Myth and Society in Ancient Greece.* Trans. Janet Lloyd. Brighton: Harvester, 1980.

Vogler, Thomas. " 'A Spirit, Yet a Woman Too!': Dorothy and William Wordsworth." In *Mothering the Mind: Twelve Studies of Writers and Their Silent Partners,* ed. Ruth Perry and Martine Watson Brownley, 238–58. New York: Holmes and Meier, 1984.

Volney, comte de (Constantin François Chasseboeuf). *Les Ruines, ou méditation sur les révolutions des empires.* Paris, 1791.

———. *Ruins; or meditations on the revolution of empires.* Trans. Thomas Jefferson and Joel Barrow. 2 vols. Paris, 1802.

Warren, Robert Penn. "A Poem of Pure Imagination." *Kenyon Review* 8 (1946): 391–427.

Warton, Joseph. *Odes on Various Subjects (1746).* Augustan Reprint Society publication no. 197. Los Angeles: William Andrews Clark Memorial Library, 1979.

Wasserman, Earl R. *The Finer Tone.* Baltimore: Johns Hopkins University Press, 1963.

Watkins, Daniel P. "History as Demon in Coleridge's *The Rime of the Ancient Mariner.*" *Papers on Language and Literature* 24 (1988): 23–33.

Watson, J. R. "Lucy and the Earth-Mother." *Essays in Criticism* 27 (1977): 187–202.

Webb, Timothy. "Romantic Hellenism." In *The Cambridge Companion to British Romanticism,* ed. Stuart Curran, 148–76. Cambridge: Cambridge University Press, 1993.

Weisinger, Herbert. *The Agony and the Triumph: Papers on the Use and Abuse of Myth.* East Lansing: Michigan State University Press, 1964.

Wellek, René. A *History of Modern Criticism: 1750–1950.* 8 vols. New Haven: Yale University Press, 1955–1992.

Westbrook, Sue Weaver. "The Influence of David Hartley's *Observations on Man* on Wordsworth's Post–1802 Poetry and Aesthetics." Ph.D. diss., Vanderbilt University, 1977.

Wheeler, Kathleen. *The Creative Mind in Coleridge's Poetry.* Cambridge: Harvard University Press, 1981.

Wheelwright, Philip. "Myth." In *The Princeton Encyclopedia of Poetry and Poetics,* ed. Alex Preminger. Enl. ed. Princeton: Princeton University Press, 1974.

Williams, Raymond. *The Country and the City.* St. Albans: Paladin, 1975.

Wilson, Milton. *Shelley's Later Poetry: A Study of His Prophetic Imagination.* New York: Columbia University Press, 1959.

Wimsatt, W. K. "Northrop Frye: Criticism as Myth." In *Northrop Frye in Modern Criticism: Selected Papers from the English Institute,* ed. Murray Krieger, 75–107. New York: Columbia University Press, 1966.

Wolfson, Susan J. "Individual in Community: Dorothy Wordsworth in Conversation with William." In *Romanticism and Feminism,* ed. Anne K. Mellor, 139–66. Bloomington: Indiana University Press, 1988.

Woodman, Ross G. "The Androgyne in *Prometheus Unbound.*" *Studies in Romanticism* 20 (1981): 225–47.

———. *The Apocalyptic Vision in the Poetry of Shelley.* Toronto: University of Toronto Press, 1964.

Wordsworth, Dorothy. *Grasmere Journals*. Ed. Helen Darbishire, rev. Mary Moorman. Oxford: Oxford University Press, 1971.

Wordsworth, Jonathan. "On Man, on Nature, and on Human Life." *Review of English Studies*, n.s., 31 (1980): 17–29.

———. *William Wordsworth: The Borders of Vision*. Oxford: Clarendon Press, 1984.

Wordsworth, Jonathan, and Stephen Gill. "The Two-Part Prelude of 1798–99." *Journal of English and Germanic Philology* 72 (1973): 503–25.

Wordsworth, William. *The Borderers*. Ed. Robert Osborn. Ithaca: Cornell University Press, 1982.

———. *The Fourteen-Book* Prelude. Ed. W. J. B. Owen. Ithaca: Cornell University Press, 1985.

———. *The Letters of William and Dorothy Wordsworth*. Ed. E. de Selincourt. 2d ed. Vol. 1, *The Early Years 1787–1805*, rev. Chester L. Shaver. Oxford: Clarendon Press, 1967.

———. *The Ruined Cottage and The Pedlar*. Ed. James Butler. Ithaca: Cornell University Press, 1979.

Wright, John W. *Shelley's Myth of Metaphor*. Athens: University of Georgia Press, 1970.

Index